The Chief Minister and the Spy

An Unlikely Friendship

A.S. Dulat

JUGGERNAUT BOOKS
C-I-128, First Floor, Sangam Vihar, Near Holi Chowk,
New Delhi 110080, India

First published by Juggernaut Books 2025

Copyright © Amarjit Singh Dulat 2025

10 9 8 7 6 5 4 3 2 1

P-ISBN: 9789353454746
E-ISBN: 9789353457020

The views and opinions expressed in this book are the author's own. The facts contained herein were reported to be true as on the date of publication by the author to the publishers of the book, and the publishers are not in any way liable for their accuracy or veracity.

All rights reserved. No part of this publication may be reproduced, transmitted, or stored in a retrieval system in any form or by any means without the written permission of the publisher.

Typeset in Adobe Caslon Pro by Mukul Chand

Printed at Replika Press Pvt. Ltd.

*To Kashmir and Kashmiris, whose debt
I can never repay*

'Sands are running out. Time is on nobody's side. We need to move on.'

– Y.D. Gundevia

Contents

Foreword by M.K. Narayanan   ix
Preface   xi

1. Getting to Know the Chief Minister   1
2. The Making of Farooq Abdullah   53
3. 1984: The Coup   79
4. Conversations and Confidences   101
5. 1996: A Pivotal Election   135
6. Power Plays and Betrayal   165
7. Father and Son   185
8. Abrogation and Its Aftermath   203
9. The Importance of Being Farooq Abdullah   227
10. The Lion in Winter   257

Acknowledgements   279
Notes   281

Foreword

This is a fascinating account of Kashmir, written by one who is not merely an expert but, more importantly, whose emotional attachment to Kashmir and with the mercurial Dr Farooq Abdullah is, perhaps, unrivalled. On one level, this is an honest and unvarnished account of the events that have taken place in Kashmir since the 1980s to the present, but what is more fascinating is that it is an insider's account, unrivalled in terms of understanding the forces at work during a very turbulent period.

The author's sympathetic portrayal of Dr Farooq Abdullah as a 'colossus' who dominated the course of many, if not most, events in Kashmir is closest to the truth and reality than most other portrayals. The true merit of the work, though, lies in recognizing the centrality of Dr Abdullah as far as contemporary Kashmir is concerned, and also how critical Dr Abdullah's role was in ensuring that Kashmir did not drift away from India.

Foreword

The author's reference to Dr Abdullah as the tallest of modern-day Kashmiri leaders may again attract criticism from many, but it is the unvarnished truth and is acknowledged by a person who is among the very few in the world who can be considered an expert on Kashmir. The true worth of this book, written in conversational style, is how the narrative brings out a fundamental truth – that notwithstanding several other problems that India has had to face since independence, Kashmir is probably the most complex and enduring.

Written with empathy and sympathy, but 'seeing with the mind's eye', the author, who had a distinguished career in intelligence over several decades, has provided an insightful account of a chaotic phase in Kashmir's modern history. Few accounts of similar situations across the world quite compare with this eponymous work.

– **M.K. Narayanan**, former National Security Advisor to the Government of India

Preface

Main bhi mooh mein zubaan rakhta hun,
Koi poochhe ki mudda kya hai.

(I too have a voice,
If only someone would ask me what I have to say.)

– Ghalib

This is not a biography, but a memoir of my times with Doctor Sahib.

A biography requires detailed research, and many books have been written on Farooq Abdullah. Real answers, in my view, come from conversation: speaking, listening, watching. This is my story of my knowledge of Farooq Abdullah.

Now, I have never ventured an interview with Doctor Sahib. I have listened instead, to him and those around him, for close to 37 years, without ever attempting to pry into his privacy or peep into his bedroom. A few years ago, during a dinner at K.M. Singh's house, inevitably, the discussion centred on Kashmir. I was telling KM, 'Narayanan was responsible for sending me to Kashmir.' Just at that moment, Narayanan himself walked in. Having overheard my remark, he looked at me and asked, 'Are you complaining?'

I said, 'Not at all. How can I complain? Kashmir has made me all that I am.' There would never have been a book on Kashmir, least of all this one.

Even thinking of writing this story has been far from easy. Kashmiris are myriad-minded, and yet, if it were not for this quality, this book would be meaningless.

When I began thinking of writing this book, I talked it over with Doctor Sahib. In fact, we spoke about it umpteen times. He never said no, but there was never a clear *yes* – until the summer of 2024, when I told him that I had finally begun writing it.

'*Karo na,*' he said. (Go ahead.)

It was a response typical of the man. Doctor Sahib could be both reticent and forthcoming, depending on the time, place and his mood. That is why, rather than a biography, I like to think of this as a story, one that has been waiting to be told ever since I first met Doctor Sahib in the winter of 1987.

In October that year, I received a call from my friend and former colleague, M.K. Rathindran, who was at the Intelligence Bureau (IB) headquarters in New Delhi.

Preface

I was posted in Bhopal at the time, and wasn't particularly expecting that call.

'How would you react to a posting to Srinagar?' Rathindran asked without preamble. I was considerably taken aback – not to mention slightly nervous – at the prospect.

The very first time I heard of Farooq Abdullah was when he entered into a political accord with Rajiv Gandhi in December 1986. At the time, I was on an assignment as the security officer for a presidential visit to Belgrade, the capital of erstwhile Yugoslavia. One morning, Romesh Bhandari – the secretary travelling with us – excitedly brought Giani Zail Singh, who was then the president of India, a copy of *The Times of India*. He exclaimed, '*Dekho, Gianiji, ki khabar aayi hai!*' (Look, Gianiji, see what news has come!)

The great news was, of course, the signing of the accord between Farooq and Rajiv. In the corridors of power in New Delhi, this was an idea that had been floating around for a while. Rajiv had long wanted his own man in Kashmir – a man who shared his vision of politics. Farooq was ideal for the task, given how close the Abdullahs and the Gandhis had always been.

Gianiji responded to news of this accord with typical fatalism. 'This is the beginning of the end of Farooq Abdullah,' he observed. But like many others who have tried to estimate where Farooq stands on the great political chessboard that is Kashmir, he was wrong.

Nobody can ever predict the end of Farooq Abdullah – except for the man himself.

1

Getting to Know the Chief Minister

'For there is only one thing in the world worse than being talked about, and that is not being talked about.'

– Oscar Wilde, *The Picture of Dorian Gray*

As a chapter title, this is an ambitious one, I'll confess.

The subtitle of this book refers to 'an unlikely friendship' – but a friendship, in its truest sense of the word, implies that you are on intimate terms with another person. Now, in the three decades that I have known Farooq, I can't say with any real confidence that I truly know him. You see, that is the enigma of Doctor Sahib. It is not easy to *know* him. It requires patience and dedication, and even then, he has never made the going easy.

I made that discovery upon my very first meeting with the big man. It all began at my predecessor K.P. Singh's farewell tea party, hosted by the chief minister of Jammu

The Chief Minister and the Spy

and Kashmir. I had been newly transferred to Srinagar as the IB station chief from Bhopal. It was October 1987, and India was still simmering over the breaking of the locks of the Babri Masjid in Ayodhya. In November 1986, Rajiv and Farooq had signed an accord that reinstated Farooq as chief minister, and proposed a roadmap for stabilizing the state, with the Centre's cooperation. After the rioting in early 1987, Kashmir was walking a delicate political tightrope. In March the previous year, Rajiv had had the then chief minister of Jammu and Kashmir, Gul Shah, sacked. Governor's Rule had been imposed. The whisper was that Mufti Mohammad Sayeed, the seniormost Congress leader in Kashmir – and, some said, Delhi's man in the state – had been shifted out to make way for Farooq.

The events that followed seemed to lend credence to those whispers.[1] When Farooq was asked at the time why he needed the Congress's support at all when he had won a comfortable majority in the state, he replied, 'The Congress commands the Centre. In a state like Kashmir, if I want to implement programmes to fight poverty and disease, and run a government, I have to stay on the right side of the Centre. That is a hard political reality that I have come to accept.'[2]

Ironically, this became the first moment when Farooq began to be referred to snidely as Delhi's 'stooge'.

On 23 March 1987, elections were held in the state, which would come to be considered a watershed moment. Conducted only four months after Farooq had been sworn in, they had reportedly been rigged in order to prevent Delhi from losing control of Kashmir. Contesting the elections were Abdullah's Jammu and Kashmir National Conference (NC), the Indian National Congress (INC) and the Muslim United Front (MUF), a coalition of Islamic parties that had come together in 1987. By all accounts, the MUF leader, Muhammad Yusuf Shah, had won that election. Disillusioned, he would take on the name Sayeed Salahuddin, and rise to head the Hizbul Mujahideen. His election manager, Yasin Malik, would go on to head the Jammu and Kashmir Liberation Front (JKLF). But that's another story.

In the spring of 1987, the turnout in the Valley was massive. As the counting progressed, it became apparent that the conservative Sayeed Salahuddin was way ahead of his opponent, Ghulam Mohiuddin Shah of the NC. With Salahuddin's lead growing bigger by the hour, Mohiuddin Shah left the counting centre thoroughly disappointed. However, he was soon summoned back as the winner of the Amira Kadal assembly seat by 4,289 votes.[3] The backlash was immediate and vicious. Supporters of the MUF and Salahuddin clashed with security personnel, crying foul. Immediately, parts of the Valley – Anantnag, Sopore, Handwara and Baramulla – were put under a virtual curfew. Top MUF leaders – Salahuddin and Yasin Malik to begin with – were promptly jailed.

With the shadow of these stormy elections still looming over Kashmir, the IB headquarters advised me to visit Srinagar on a recce in November 1987, before KP left to join the National Defence College. On my way to Srinagar, I passed through Delhi. The director of the IB, M.K. Narayanan, called me in and said: 'Please make sure that Dr Farooq is kept in good humour, that our relationship with him is okay and that he's on our side. Please see to that.'

I was puzzled at this insistence on keeping Farooq on Delhi's side. Not only had I heard this from the IB director, but when I had gone to say goodbye to him in Bhopal, Chief Minister Arjun Singh had said much the same thing: 'Doctor Sahib is a nationalist and our best bet, so stay close to him.'

With these words echoing in my head, I came out of the director's room and went to his special assistant, Ratan Sehgal, who also happened to be my friend. 'Ratan,' I said, 'I thought Farooq was a good guy from whatever I've heard. Is there a problem?'

'No, I don't think so,' said Ratan. 'But Rajiv [Gandhi] is very keen that we have a good relationship with Farooq.'

That, then, was basically my brief. In view of the accord he had signed with Farooq, this was the way that Prime Minister Rajiv Gandhi looked at it. For Rajiv, Farooq was the key to Kashmir. Clearly, this was going to be a posting that would keep me on my toes.

That was the backdrop against which, in November 1987, I found myself sitting on the balcony of K.P. Singh's residence on Gupkar Road, sipping pink gin and discussing the future of my proposed posting to Kashmir. Singh told me that only 'hand-picked officers' made it to Srinagar. This was flattering, but it just put my guard up even further; I needed to find out as much as I could about Kashmir, its political intricacies – and Farooq Abdullah. As it turned out, staying close to Farooq would be one of the more pleasant pursuits of my career.

I didn't know it then, of course. When KP introduced me to Farooq at the tea party, I shook hands with Doctor Sahib and then sat quietly in a corner, wondering how I would manage this towering personality. He was a tall man, in his traditional achkan and Kashmiri cap, with a compelling face characterized by the typical Abdullah charisma. I could see that the rumours I had heard contained a kernel of truth. Farooq had the air of one born to command, yet another legacy of the Abdullah heritage – and though he was perfectly pleasant during the gathering, I could see that he held a part of himself very politely aloof. He appeared to take absolutely no notice of me – and to be fair, why should he have noticed a young fellow on his first posting to Kashmir?

It was only later that I would realize that even though Doctor Sahib appeared not to notice anything, in reality, he noticed everything. It was a quality that kept even the laziest among us alert. You never knew what Doctor Sahib was observing, or how he would bring it to your notice at a time of his choosing.

At the end of the party, Farooq said a few flattering words about KP and presented him with a carpet. I remember wondering if this was a signal that I, too, in my time, might get a carpet at my farewell – if I managed to come up to the chief minister's expectations. That was the only exciting prospect of that tea party then!

My three-day recce with visits to Gulmarg and Pahalgam was exhilarating, to say the least. In winter, snow-laden Kashmir seemed as though it would be a wonderful holiday destination rather than the volatile state the newspapers reported. It was a beautiful land, with green vales and snow-capped misty mountains. Of course, I had heard of the state's legendary and serene beauty, but to experience it first-hand fairly took my breath away. This was right before the Valley became mired in bloodshed and bullets. It was easy to love Kashmir – easier, still, to imagine myself living there, amid all this tranquil beauty. I knew Paran, my wife, would love it as much as I already did.

My early days in Srinagar passed mostly in briefings from KP, and entertainment provided by our younger colleague Praveen Mahindroo and his charming wife, Nisha, who fed me the most delicious Kashmiri food and cakes from the best bakeries. KP briefed me on the Kashmir that he had lived in, while describing the who's who in the state and telling me anecdotes of who really mattered in Srinagar. He was full of praise for Farooq, and Mahindroo was even more taken by him. Mahindroo's wife was a great golfer, and during a game, she had been hit over her eye by an errant ball. Almost as soon as he heard of the incident, Farooq visited her to find out how she was – a mark of his solicitude for those whom he knew. Nisha was fine, but she was touched by the chief minister's visit.

Remarkably, neither KP nor Mahindroo uttered one word on the so-called rigging of the 1987 elections. I use the word 'remarkably' because those polls – and what had come before and after – would become the main focus once the bloodbath began in Kashmir. Farooq himself was furious when he heard the charges of rigging. He screamed at the seasoned political journalist Harinder Baweja: 'Who are you calling corrupt? Rigged election, my foot. I don't believe it. Why did they not go to the Election Commission and complain? ... You accept all other elections as unrigged. All of you make the '87 election out to be the turning point. It is India that is responsible for what has happened in Kashmir and not Farooq Abdullah. They betrayed my father in 1953. They betrayed my father in 1975. They betrayed me in 1984. They are responsible, not Farooq Abdullah.'[4]

Doctor Sahib has never stopped being blamed for everything that went wrong in Kashmir thereafter. Even today, his adversaries never miss an opportunity to rake up the thorny question of 1987. For himself, he has always maintained that if indeed any rigging did occur, it was done at the behest of the Centre.

Clearly, though, Farooq was carrying a lot of rage and bitterness even then. It would take some reading of the history of the Abdullah family and its relationship with Delhi before I could begin to understand why. But given his reputation and the kind of remarks he was so unafraid to utter, small wonder that not only was Delhi worried about keeping Farooq close, but that everyone was silent on tricky subjects during my early days in Kashmir. Even when I finally joined my post in May 1988, after a short course abroad, our officers had nothing to say about the rigging. Instead, all of them – and this included some deputationists from the Jammu and Kashmir Police – were full of praise for Doctor Sahib.

Now, all of this is a matter for which I still have no definite answers. After all, it happened almost a year before I joined. When I finally got Francis T.R. Colaso, the director general of police (DGP) of Jammu and Kashmir in 1986–87, to discuss the subject with me, he was absolutely clear that the whole issue of rigging was hugely exaggerated. If at all there had been rigging, he said, it had occurred only in a few constituencies. For that, he held Kashmiri bureaucrats, who were more loyal than the king, wholly responsible. Colaso made it a point to say that this period in Kashmir was the happiest in his career, both for him and his family.

Lucky people, I thought ironically to myself.

I, on the other hand, was feeling a distinct flutter of nerves. I was a young officer, newly arrived in a state that was important for India but of which I had little to no knowledge. Farooq was a rising political star in the Valley, known to be imperious in his manner, a man who rarely allowed anyone to get to him or the better of him. He was capable of impressing prime ministers as easily as he was capable of exasperating the citizens of his state. Highly intelligent and quick-tempered, he was rumoured to be someone who could, should he wish to, cut you down to size immediately. The moods of Farooq Abdullah were already as legendary as his career trajectory so far. His first spell in government (1982–84) had been almost dazzlingly energetic, buoyed by the enthusiastic goodwill of the Kashmiri people. As a chief minister, bureaucrats described Farooq as a good man-manager and motivator, though he possessed some eccentric paradoxes. He was decisive but he could be fickle. He was restless and mercurial, his critics said, pointing to what they saw as a lack of seriousness. But his admirers were of the opinion that there was nobody who understood the state quite like Farooq. It wasn't surprising that I was a little unsure of what to expect.

My first task was to gain a meeting with Farooq, but he had been playing hard to get for a few weeks since my arrival. In time, I was to learn that this was part of his style of dealing with people. Since I didn't know it at the time, you can imagine my anxiety! Finally, a call came, summoning me to his official residence. Even more apprehensively, I asked my colleagues what I should address him as when I did meet him. Should I call him Farooq Sahib or Dr Abdullah? The then home secretary and security advisor to the chief minister, O.P. Bhutani, told me: 'He's known as Doctor Sahib. That should be good enough.' So, off I went to meet Farooq, armed with just his colloquial nickname and scraps of information about the man himself. He was on the move that day, brusque and quick. When I arrived at his home on Gupkar Road, he was already out of the house, heading towards his car, with an impatient air. I was taken aback.

Didn't we have an appointment?

'Come on,' he said, barely registering my question. 'Hop in the car with me. We'll talk on the way.'

Puzzled but willing, I did so.

Where were we going?

To the airport, as it turned out. Farooq had a flight to Delhi.

I have forgotten what we talked about that day. But I discovered on that scenic drive that Farooq loved to be behind the wheel of a car. He was at his most comfortable there. It was a pleasant way to start my acquaintance with him, albeit a trifle unusual. As we neared the airport, Farooq glanced at me and said, 'I'm coming back in a few days and we'll meet again.'

I went back to the office, wondering what sort of unconventional fellow this was. Chief ministers, from what I had seen of them, did not frequently command the resident IB head to hop into a car on the way to the airport. Nor did they choose to drive themselves!

Farooq's style was inimitable, and I had to admit, despite his undoubted quirks, this was a likeable man, with no airs or graces and a lot of freshness, to which I was unaccustomed. There was an openness about him that appealed to me.

But those were still early days and I wasn't quite used to flinging protocol out of the window in my interactions with Farooq. So, a few days later, when I received word that the chief minister was back in Kashmir, I decided to try to meet him again, in a more formal manner.

I telephoned him and requested a convenient time when Paran and I could come to call on him. Farooq immediately disarmed me, 'What is this "call on me" business?' he demanded. 'Come and have a meal with us at home.'

Getting to Know the Chief Minister

My wife and I readily accepted. Dinner at the Abdullah home would soon become almost a part of our lives. The food was always superb, and I was soon introduced to the wonderful Mollie, Farooq's wife. I could immediately see that she was the anchor that Farooq needed. Here was a woman who was intelligent, attractive and restful. Mollie came from a working-class family of Suffolk; her father worked in a transport company, her brother had joined the Royal Air Force, while her sister taught at a school. They were traditional English folk, with the quiet, steady characteristics that define them. From the start, I liked Mollie very much. She was English to her fingertips, though she wore her salwar kameez beautifully, merging perfectly not only with the Abdullah family, but with Kashmir itself.

There's this impression in public life that Farooq can do what he likes, but his wife is very much the anchor in his domestic life. As I would discover during my time in Kashmir, there was a quiet serenity to their relationship, an understanding of each other that is both rare and incomparable.

'Would you like a drink?' Farooq asked as soon as we had arrived, and the inevitable pleasantries were over. I must be honest: I was a bit startled at the prospect of a chief minister offering me, the local head of the IB, a drink, but I decided to go with the flow. 'If you're having a drink, I don't mind one.'

'Yes, of course, I'll have a drink,' he said briskly, beginning to pour us both one.

And so it was that Farooq and I had drinks and dinner, and talked of many different things. It was the first of many meetings, and it opened the doors for a friendship that has lasted three decades.

As an intelligence officer, my life – and by default, the relationships I have – has been defined by IB protocols. But despite that, I am a laid-back guy – at least I like giving that impression – and I also enjoy talking to people. It is an aspect of intelligence-gathering that I really enjoy, because it is through talking with people that you learn that people look at life very differently from you. Spooks provide politicians not only with crucial information but also with a cover for accountability. Quite possibly, that is why Farooq, with his characteristic instinct, told me, 'This is a very important job that you've come to. Always tell the truth [to Delhi]. Never lie.'

He knew that I was his conduit to Delhi, and that whatever happened in Srinagar would always be relayed back to the corridors of power. I respected his recognition of that fact. In Kashmir, the IB plays a much greater role than in any other state, out of necessity. The IB's presence is almost all-pervading, and every Kashmiri citizen and leader knows that they have 29 Gupkar Road (the station chief's office plus residence) to contend with in all spheres of life. The IB headquarters in New Delhi should have taken advantage of this fact. But over the years, we have had chiefs who have been too strait-laced. As a result, Delhi has seen things only in black and white. Now, this approach doesn't work in difficult areas, like the Northeast, Punjab or Kashmir. Kashmir, in particular, is mostly a grey area, a state constantly in need of empathy, compassion and compromise. It took Delhi a very long time to understand Sheikh Abdullah, and even today, we do not understand why Kashmiri leaders talk a different language in Kashmir and a different language in Delhi.

As frustrating as that might be, none of this means that you need to stop engaging. To be a spook is to understand humanity in all its shades and nuances. In my view, the simplest and most effective way of doing that is to talk. It sounds easy enough, but in politics, talking requires preparation and a strategy. Don't get me wrong: talking does not necessarily mean negotiating or bargaining. It simply refers to building relationships with important people. I was, behind the scenes, building relationships with people who had lost faith in India, and it was a long, slow process that required a lot of patience. You had to talk if you wanted the separatists in the Hurriyat to enter formal talks with the government. You had to talk to Farooq himself, in order to keep the Abdullahs relevant to India's political process. For us in the IB, it has ever been the nature of the beast.

In Farooq Abdullah, though, perhaps Delhi and the IB had met its match. Here was a chief minister who was never afraid of living life precisely as he desired to live it; he was not afraid to give as good as he got; he was unconventional, theatrical and often impetuous, but he was also brilliant. At no point during my entire association with him has Farooq ever been anything but two steps ahead of Delhi's best games.

This is not to say that he is underhanded or manipulative. If anything, Farooq's integrity and honesty have been his defining characteristics. He was fully aware of Kashmir's politics, its volatility and the state's importance to Delhi. Over time, the more I watched him, the more I realized that Farooq Abdullah is afraid of nobody and nothing. He was always keen to work with Delhi; to be on, as he called it, 'the right side of Delhi'. For him, it was important that Delhi understand the mind of the Kashmiri. Slowly, through our conversations, I began to discover why Delhi found it so difficult to deal with Farooq. He may have been what Rajiv wanted, but as the days passed, it became clear that he was not what *Delhi* wanted. By the time I had met him, he had run the gauntlet of first being exactly what Delhi was looking for, and then turning into its exact opposite. It was a pattern of Farooq's political life, though in his personal life – I can attest – he rarely had a pattern to speak of!

As for myself, I think my advantage was that I was never a traditional suited-booted *Dilliwala*. Farooq seemed to enjoy my laid-back attitude to life, and the fact that I honestly did enjoy having a good time myself. I was never averse to having a drink or dinner, or even, as he sometimes asked me to, impulsively hop on board a helicopter into rural Kashmir to accompany him on the campaign trail.

All of these are checklist-type qualities, but as I say, it all comes down to rapport. It's not really easy to have a friendship with the chief minister if you are the head of the IB desk in a state like Kashmir.

Indeed, Kashmir's relationship with Delhi is best defined by the presence of the IB in the state. The Sheikh had raged against its presence, futilely insisting that the bureau pack its bags and close down its desk. But Farooq was cut from a different cloth. From the beginning, he chose to work with the IB – just in his own unique way. The IB had its share of Kashmir experts. Foremost among them were S.M. Mathur and R.K. Kapoor, both of whom ended up as directors – or chiefs – of the bureau. On the other hand, M.K. Narayanan was not a Kashmir expert by any stretch of the imagination, but for Farooq, he was the only IB director he truly got along with. As my relationship with Farooq grew, so did it with Narayanan, encouraging him to visit the Valley more often than any other director. In fact, he would eventually also take a two-day break in Pahalgam. Ask anyone of our vintage, and they will all tell you that for a workaholic like Narayanan to even dream of taking a break anywhere – two days or any other amount – is nothing short of unthinkable! But in those days, Narayanan's influence with Farooq was at its height. On a visit to Srinagar, Farooq insisted that the IB director travel in a four-star car, surprising Kashmiris who wondered who the Field Marshal in town was!

Yet another incident that comes to mind, illustrative of Narayanan and Farooq's growing relationship, is from the winter of 1988. I received a message from the IB headquarters in New Delhi: 'Your chief minister hasn't been to Delhi for a while and the home minister [Buta Singh] wants to know why the chief minister is avoiding him.'

I went off to meet Farooq, and in the course of conversation, I said, 'Buta Singh was remembering you.'

It was a match to gunpowder.

'Who the hell is Buta Singh?' he snapped. 'Why would I want to meet him?'

Trying to keep the tenor of our conversation reasonable, I asked, 'What's the big deal? What happened?'

'When I go to Delhi and when I want to meet the prime minister, I'm kept waiting and I'm told he doesn't have time for me,' Farooq said. 'Why should I have time for your home minister?'

'Well, sir, the IB director would like to see you,' I said tactfully.

'Then tell him I'll be coming tomorrow,' Farooq said immediately.

This was an interesting time for us in the IB. While I was trying to deliver what Delhi wanted in Kashmir, the IB director always delivered what the prime minister wanted. Narayanan's relationship with Rajiv was special. It was a known fact that the young prime minister was greatly inclined towards the advantages that intelligence-gathering could offer. Most of the infrastructure that the IB has today grew during the prime ministership of Rajiv Gandhi. He took a keen interest in intelligence matters, and it helped that he had a cerebral IB director – Narayanan – on hand. Rajiv would often invite Narayanan over late at night, plying him with coffee and chocolates, while discussing the security issues of the day and, obviously, Kashmir.

Getting to Know the Chief Minister

In Kashmir, the protocols governing the IB director somehow never applied to me. Unlike other chief ministers that I have worked with, who required me to formally present my credentials to them every week, Farooq didn't expect a thing. All that was tacitly understood was that I would go and see him every two weeks or so. Mind you, he never said a word nor did he instruct me to do that. It was just something I was expected to do. But God help me if I turned up any later than that! That's when Farooq would put me very firmly in my place. 'So,' he'd say coolly, 'you've finally found time to come and see me, have you? What is it you want?'

Despite his imperiousness, this was a man who had mastered the art of being liked. He went out of his way to meet people and to be good to the people he encountered. He was rarely in his office, only because he was out in the state, travelling across towns and villages to meet his people. This culminated in Farooq building himself a wide web of friends and connections.

The dental surgeon, Siddharth Mehta, who attends to the who's who of Delhi, once said to me that no one bigger than Doctor Sahib had visited his clinic. He laughingly added, *'Yahan jo aata hai, sab Doctor Sahib ko jaante hain.'* (Everyone who comes here knows Doctor Sahib.) O.P. Bhutani, once Doctor Sahib's security advisor, now in his 97th year, refuses to comment on politics but has no hesitation in saying that Farooq is one of the nicest people he is privileged to have known. That is Farooq's unique quality – he makes himself entirely accessible, while keeping one part of himself aloof from the public. I have never yet met another man who can combine the curiously distinct qualities of empathy and enigma quite so well. He lives for life, and he lives for love – and I have never known him to be malicious to anyone.

Though he might be pleasant and open, Farooq also doesn't like his authority being undercut in any way. He might not impose his power on you, but he certainly never lets you forget who he is. The fact was – and still is – that Farooq is not easy to handle. He never has been. His attitude has always been 'Who the hell are you?' He hates being taken for granted, and he despises anyone trying to tell him what to do.

Did the Sheikh recognize that his son was of a different cut? I like to think so. The story goes that in the days when the Sheikh was grooming Farooq to take over in Kashmir, he told his son: 'Remember one thing – politics is like jumping into the Jhelum and swimming against the tide.'

It was a fair warning.

Even in the early days, Farooq had no desire to metaphorically jump into any river, much less swim against a tide. He had watched his father go through all kinds of hell in his growing-up years, and he had determined that he would never live the way that his father had. To paraphrase the great Frank Sinatra, Farooq has always done it his way. He has chosen to swim *with* the tide, rather than against it. He said exactly this to party workers during a meeting at Lal Chowk on 28 June 1989: '... if you have in mind someone who ends up in jail, you can count me out. I am the last person to like being jailed. I like to play golf. What am I going to do in jail? You may suggest that I read books to while away the time, but I would not like to do that because reading puts pressure on my eyes!'[5]

It was typically insouciant, but it was also typically Farooq. He was very clear about the fact that he didn't want to be anything like the Sheikh. He respected and adored his father, but he wanted – quite naturally – to be his own person. Perhaps it was a difficult task that he set himself: after all, the Abdullah legacy is not an easy one to step away from. But his force of will and strength of character had been more than evident from the start.

Not for him the constant swimming against the political currents. He would do what it took to succeed in his political goals, even if it meant indulging in some harmless theatrics in order to play to Kashmir's delighted galleries. I recall a moment in 1989, on 15 August, when he gave a brilliant speech at the Bakshi Stadium in Srinagar. Kashmir was going through some of its worst phases of violence and bloodshed at the time. Most cities resembled ghost towns. It was the same on that day too. Ordinarily, hundreds would have turned up to hear Farooq giving one of his eloquent speeches, but I remember that that day only a hundred or so were present, including myself. Outside the stadium, we could hear the dull thuds of bombs exploding on the streets. Farooq's speech was a stirring one: nationalist, strongly pro-India, and punctuated by the sounds of falling debris outside.

I watched him declaiming to his audience, unruffled and focused. He had chosen to refuse the speech that had been carefully scripted for him. That day, he spoke straight from the heart. As I listened, my admiration grew. His speech made you proud to be an Indian. Later, he went to inspect the guard of honour. It was only a question of walking some 60 or 70 yards. But because of the high security threat at the time, the Jammu and Kashmir Police had lined up a special jeep, under the escort of the DGP. Farooq went along as far as the line-up. Then, with his customary sangfroid, he jumped out of the jeep and did the slow march better than the DGP himself. Like I said, it was a bit of excellent theatre, a memorable moment for those of his followers who saw it in real time.[6]

Typical of Farooq, he had once earlier said at a public meeting in Anantnag that there were a hundred militants in Kashmir when we were still looking for the first few. This agitated Delhi, and I was asked what the chief minister had said.

Puzzled, I went off to see Moosa Raza, Farooq's Tamilian chief secretary. Moosa was Delhi's man in Kashmir – much more so than I was – and he wasn't particularly liked either. But in this case, he was as confused as I was, so I decided to find out the truth from the horse's mouth. I went to Farooq himself.

'Sir,' I said, 'in your speech in Anantnag, did you mention a hundred militants?'

'Did I?' Farooq enquired airily.

'Well, sir, that's what Delhi is saying.'

'Tell Delhi not to get so excited,' retorted Farooq, brushing it aside with an impatient wave of his hand. 'If there are a hundred militants in Kashmir, we'll deal with them.'

It was emblematic of the man he was. He couldn't have given a damn about toeing a line. That made my job in Srinagar that much harder to do. Not that I was capable of making Farooq do anything that he didn't want to do, of course – but my brief was to stay close to him. Delhi wanted to know what he was thinking at all times. That was, I was discovering, much easier said than done.

Talking to Farooq is not – and never has been – easy. He doesn't make it easy. He holds his cards very close to his chest – an instinctive quality, born from the kind of intrigues he has had to navigate in his political career. If he doesn't want to talk to you about something, you have to give up perforce, for you would never get a peep out of him. If you don't know him, he makes you feel uncomfortable because he takes a while to work the chemistry. Unfortunately, that's why the chemistry never worked with Ajit Doval, though Doval's successor, friend and batchmate K.M. Singh had no problem with the chief minister and got along famously with him. You see, Farooq's a pretty good judge of people, with a peculiar skill at seeing through the façade everyone usually maintains. Even after so many years of knowing Farooq Abdullah, I never take him for granted. If anyone does so, God help them.

But he *does* understand politics – the intricacies of it and the things you have to do sometimes to keep the ball rolling. This meant that not everything worked to Farooq's liking. He was very aware of Delhi's puppeteering and he never lost a chance to let Delhi know that he knew all its games and he wasn't having it. Even today, Farooq remains the man best informed about Kashmir thanks to his network of contacts, which includes separatists, political people and administrators. His maxim even then was to keep all doors open to everyone. There was nobody to whom Farooq did not talk. In fact, during my time in Kashmir with him, I would watch as children and old ladies milled around Farooq when he was out among the people. He never thought twice about pausing to listen, to sit down and share a meal from a traditional Kashmiri *trami* (platter) if he was asked to. If you asked me what his method was, I'd have summed it up as spontaneity. Farooq was not a man who did anything in a practised, measured way. By nature, I would learn that he was an impulsive man, ruled equally by his heart as much as by his head. As an administrator, however, Farooq was a man in a hurry, someone who did not appreciate bureaucratic delays.

It was just as well that I arrived in Srinagar with an open mind, however apprehensive it might have been. My initial encounters with Farooq eased a lot of my apprehensions. He was certainly everything that they said he was – but he was also so much more that I did not yet know. How would Farooq Abdullah treat me? I knew what Delhi expected of me in Kashmir, but what did the chief minister expect? As it turned out, ours would be a relationship that went beyond the purely professional. It was an unlikely friendship. How

Getting to Know the Chief Minister

much Doctor Sahib has trusted me, I will never know – and how much I knew of him, he will never understand.

Separatist militant violence began in the Valley two months after I took over in the summer of 1988. In July, the JKLF began a separatist insurgency for Kashmir's independence from India. The JKLF was founded in 1977 by Pakistan-based Amanullah Khan and Maqbool Bhat, who was hanged in 1984 following the kidnapping and murder of Indian diplomat Ravindra Mhatre in England, and whose execution was mourned annually by Kashmiris to defiantly show their anger with India. This, then, was the dominant 'nationalist' separatist group in my early days in Kashmir, and they fought for *azaadi* – independence. Most of the boys who first crossed over into Pakistan for terrorist training under the Inter-Services Intelligence (ISI) were involved as poll agents for the new opposition party, the MUF (most of whose leaders would six years later form the separatist All Parties Hurriyat Conference).

Before the JKLF exploded – literally and metaphorically – on to the political and public scene, there were, of course, whispers. But we could never pin it down to anyone. Nobody, it seemed, had any clue of what was happening. When I first heard of the JKLF boys, I met with one of our better informed deputy SPs on deputation from the Jammu and Kashmir Police, a man called Sapru, and I asked, '*Sapru Sahib, yeh sab kya ho raha hai?*' (Sapru Sahib, what is happening?).

Even he was clueless. He said, '*Sir, yeh kuch nahin hai. Yeh sab aana jaana chalta rehta hai Kashmir mein. Aap mat ghabraiye.*' (This is nothing really. All this going and coming is routine in Kashmir. Nothing for you to worry about.)

Once the insurgency really took off, though, whatever intelligence we had dried up. The situation changed yet again on the ground. Where nobody had a clue before, now nobody was willing to talk to us. Our officers were being openly targeted by the JKLF boys – in the space of three weeks, we lost four of our men. It was a terrible time. Kidnappings, at the time, were happening so fast and furiously that it was no use trying to keep up.

As far as Rubaiya Sayeed's case was concerned, it emanated from a long-held plan from within the JKLF. Their first target was Farooq's eldest daughter, Safia. But, naturally, they were finding it hard to get her – Gupkar Road was ringed around with security and protection, and Mollie and Farooq were protective of her. After a while, the JKLF gave up on the plan to kidnap Safia. Their next target was the daughter of the senior superintendent of police, Allah Baksh, a straightforward man who only spoke the language of the '*danda*' and followed strictly whatever orders he got. While they were planning this kidnapping, on 2 December 1989, Vishwanath Pratap Singh was sworn in as the new prime minister of India, and having decided to give the Kashmir issue priority, he gave India its first Muslim home minister, who was also a Kashmiri: Mufti Mohammad Sayeed. At any other time, V.P. Singh's decision could have been momentous.

But at this particular moment in the state's politics, the Valley was unimpressed. Mufti was seen as Delhi's man, with no real connection to the Valley.

One of the JKLF fellows had a brainwave: Why not pick up Rubaiya? We had no idea that this was coming. To make matters worse, Farooq – struck by one of his occasional spells of despondency – had gone off to England.

Anyway, that winter, the winter of 1989–90, is one that is bleakly remembered for the kidnapping of Rubaiya Sayeed, the daughter of Mufti Mohammad Sayeed (then home minister in V.P. Singh's government). At 3.45 p.m., on the cold, grey afternoon of 8 December 1989, Rubaiya was forced out of the local minivan in which she was travelling home from the Lal Ded Memorial Women's Hospital. She was bundled, at gunpoint, into a waiting Maruti car. Two hours later, Mohammad Sofi, the editor of the local newspaper *Kashmir Times* received a phone call from the representatives of the JKLF. They had kidnapped Rubaiya, they said tersely. She would remain their hostage until the government released Abdul Hamid Sheikh, Noor Mohammed Kalwal; Javed Mohammed Zargar; Mohammed Altas Bhat, the brother of Maqbool Bhat, and Sher Mohammed Khan Azad.[7]

Hastily, Sofi telephoned Delhi to break the news. It was the worst possible thing that could have happened. In my memoir, *A Life in the Shadows*,[8] I've written about the loneliness of that winter in Kashmir, of the troubles that had erupted months after I joined the IB. It was my first test in the field, and I was out of my depth, alone in a situation

The Chief Minister and the Spy

that was rarely the same for a week at a stretch. The optics for the bureau were not the best either in 1989. Militancy was increasing by the day in the Valley, and we were clueless about how to stem the tide.

Fear spread its tentacles through the IB, and perhaps inevitably things got so terrible on the ground that people began fleeing the state. The word was that it simply was not safe to be on the ground in Kashmir anymore, unless it was absolutely necessary to be there. As head of the IB, it soon came to my ears that two or three of our guys had put in requests to be transferred out. Nobody wanted to be in Srinagar that winter. A lot of questions were being asked of me – by my own staff, by Delhi. They were right to question me. People were being killed everywhere. How many people had to die?

Outside, in the city, blood was flowing freely. In 1989, Neelkanth Ganjoo, the judge who had sentenced Maqbool Bhat to death, was killed in a market near the Srinagar High Court in broad daylight. Journalist-lawyer Prem Nath Bhat was shot dead near his house in Anantnag shortly after. Hit lists of Kashmiri Pandit leaders were believed to be in circulation. Fear began to set in, in the homes and hearts of the Kashmiri Pandit community in the Valley. The Abdullah distrust of the Kashmiri Pandit goes back to the days of Sheikh Abdullah, on the suspicion that it was the Kashmiri Pandit who filled the ears of Jawaharlal Nehru against the Kashmiri Muslim. The mistrust cut both ways in the history of modern Kashmir. Now, in 1989–90, we were seeing the fruits of that mistrust. A number of Kashmiri Muslims, NC leaders, and Indian government officials were also terrorized. Bombs exploding on the streets were a daily occurrence. Panic was running high. It was stress like I had never known.

For Farooq, it was an abrupt reality check. He was away from the state at the time, in London. Was he under stress as well? Knowing Farooq as I do, I'd say the answer to that is yes. Farooq had a way of responding to stress that was frustrating to the outside world, or to those who did not know him. He would withdraw into a shell, seemingly cut off from facing his actual problems. There was no way that he was blind to the deterioration in Kashmir. In fact, he went into a state of deep depression, staying inside as much as he could before he left for London – and refusing to see any files connected to administrative work. He knew that he was being blamed for signing the accord with Rajiv. He was angry at the circumstances that, he felt, had let him down. Farooq was also worried about the Congress losing in the upcoming elections, '*Woh doobengey, aur humein bhi le doobengey,*' as he put it. (They'll sink and take us with them.)

India was fighting a war in Sri Lanka at the time, and so, instead of assisting in the clampdown on rising violence in Kashmir, troops had been sent overseas, to Jaffna. Punjab was also seeing a rise in violence. There was trouble in Ladakh as well. In August 1989, Union Deputy Minister P. Namgyal, of Ladakh, started the Buddhist Action Committee's agitation for granting Scheduled Tribe (ST) status to Buddhists. Now, Farooq had long since requested ST status for the people of Doda, Rajouri, Poonch, Uri, Kangan and other backward hilly areas in Kashmir – but that had fallen on seemingly deaf ears. In the meantime, Delhi was refusing to help Srinagar suppress the agitation in Ladakh.

Farooq went to Rajiv. 'It is strange,' he told him severely, 'that, on one hand, we have to fight elements who want to destabilize the state and the region, while on the other hand, I have to fight my own people, who are being instigated by the people in your government.'[9]

As the 1989 elections drew closer, Farooq realized that the Congress was losing. That could mean the end of his government in Kashmir as well. So he stopped meeting people. I was told that he was suffering from high blood pressure. But when I did meet him a few weeks later, he told me, 'The Congress is going to lose the elections.'

From Delhi, he asked for 29 companies of the Central Reserve Police Force (CRPF), but was fobbed off: the Centre, he was told, had no forces to spare. As a result, Farooq had to send extra state police forces to Ladakh to quell the agitation, at a time when they were most needed in the Valley. The winter of 1989–90 was, for him, a lonely and difficult time – as much as it was for me. He cut short his visit to London and returned promptly, on 11 December.

In retrospect, Kashmir has defined so much of my relationship with Farooq. It is perhaps Kashmir that has made our friendship both so unlikely and so strong. The Valley has never been a stable place, and certainly during my early years there, it was ruled by immense strife. As violence escalated, Kashmir's equation with Delhi – always volatile – dipped as well. Given the circumstances, I should have been the last person that Farooq turned to. For the Valley, as I say, the IB has not exactly been a trustworthy institution, after all. There is immense mistrust attached to any institution vaguely associated with Delhi. The Kashmiri is immediately on his guard. But at the end of the day, a spook's work is based largely on rapport. If you can build that with your subject, then you can actively work together fruitfully. That's how Farooq and I began our time together, professionally speaking. It was only over time, as we passed from adversity to adversity, that we began to understand each other better. A lot of this, of course, had to do with the amount of time we spent with each other. Farooq was a busy man, even when he wasn't in the chief minister's chair. He was perennially travelling across his state, if he wasn't travelling elsewhere – but the meetings we had, the rounds of golf we began to play together and the occasional dinners we had, laid a nice foundation from which to observe him closely. With other chief ministers, there was always a thin film of protocol and distance. With Farooq, there was nothing of the sort. He was not the kind of man who stood on his high horse simply because of the position he held in public life.

Slowly, I began to understand how he thinks, and to gauge his reactions to certain situations. Delhi noticed the rapport, and that was how, as the months passed, I began to work more closely not just on the subject of Kashmir but on Farooq himself.

The Chief Minister and the Spy

In the winter of 1989, as I was dealing with unrest at the IB station in Srinagar, so, too, was Farooq dealing with unrest in his own administration and state. He became paranoid about what his own friends and colleagues were saying about him. It was a terrible time for both of us, and our experiences at this time drew us closer almost insensibly.

Farooq knew when to let people in and when to push them out. He never suffered fools. During my posting in Srinagar, I found that the DGP – the last Kashmiri to be in the post – Ghulam Jeelani Pandit, was not one of his favourites. I guess when things started going wrong, Farooq felt that it was unfair for the chief minister to get all the blame. He referred to his DGP as 'General' and gave him utmost respect, as he did with all officers. But he told me, 'This fellow only comes to me with problems and not solutions. My former DG, Peer Ghulam Hussain Shah, did not meet me so often, but always came to me with solutions.'

At some point, the pressure got to Farooq. An unstable blood pressure problem took him to Houston, to Denton Cooley's famous centre, for an angiography. He was told that a slight spasm of the coronary artery might have caused slight changes in the ECG patterns. While he was away, Rajiv Gandhi lost the elections. Farooq – who rarely took his finger off his state's political pulse – told journalists in Washington that whether or not Rajiv was prime minister, his loyalties would always be with him. That was another sign of the greatness of the man. With his prime minister, Farooq had brangled and argued. Rajiv had not tried to understand –

at least not yet – how important Farooq was, and yet Farooq was ready to let bygones be bygones.

That would be the pattern of his political life, as I would discover, and as you will see as my story continues.

As soon as he landed, it was clear to Farooq that I was in a soup, along with the rest of the state.

It was a time when already fissured ties between men and politicians alike were close to breaking point. Mufti and Farooq, as you can imagine, had always had a strained relationship. I remember once asking Sajad Lone what he thought of both Farooq and Mufti. His answer was that Mufti was his father's friend, but he was unreliable, and like a scorpion, could sting anytime. Farooq, he said, was ten times more reliable. Mufti had been the PCC (Pradesh Congress Committee) chief for a long time, and he knew that it was what had ultimately led to the People's Democratic Party (PDP). As long as he was in the Congress, he knew that his chances of becoming the chief minister himself were slim.

But it remained a frustrated ambition of his.

As for Farooq, he was hugely criticized for being away from Srinagar at a time of crisis. It fanned the story that he wasn't a serious man, that he was never there when the people needed him, that he was perennially holidaying or philandering. In what I would come to recognize as true Farooq style, he withdrew into an imperious shell in the face of a barrage of criticism. That particular trait, given the pressure that was building on all of us, was not going to be helpful.

The Chief Minister and the Spy

As head of the station in Kashmir, I was getting repeated calls from Mufti Sahib. It was only natural, since he was terribly worried about his daughter. Perhaps it was that worry that made him say the things he did about Farooq. I'll give you an example. One day, he had a half-an-hour conversation with me on the telephone. He began by asking pleasantly how I found the chief minister. I replied, equally pleasantly, that there was nobody better to be chief minister of Kashmir. Mufti Sahib's conversation then went down the suggestive line that Farooq was essentially useless. I should endorse this view, he hinted, as the IB chief in Kashmir. That was the main thrust of his conversation. But I maintained throughout that there was no one better suited to handle Kashmir and Kashmiri politics than Farooq. At the time, I can tell you, it felt good. I was standing up for my chief minister.

You see, that winter had taught me one of the most vital lessons I would learn as a spook: the gun is not a solution. Seeing the violence around me, I had come to the conclusion that if we all were going to die by the gun, why didn't we speak to each other first? That was the most obvious question on my mind as I watched the violence of the winter of 1989–90 come to a head. Since then, I have always felt that engagement is crucial, even if it must be kept secret. It has been the principle of what they call the 'Dulat doctrine', but what I see as just common sense.

But I digress.

To come back to the bloody winter of 1989, I could see where this was going. From the Centre's point of view, here was a chief minister who was not even present during a time of crisis, leaving it to be handled by his chief secretary, the IB and Delhi. It was leading up to the excuse that Farooq, as a leader, was useless and needed to go. Mufti, in his conversations with me, had hinted as much. It was part of yet another facet of Farooq's problematic public image, as far as Delhi was concerned: He was difficult to manage, difficult to understand.

Delhi was getting irritated with him, Mufti hinted.

That, of course, would be a pattern that would settle into difficult grooves as the years passed. But now, in 1989, it was an image that, unsettlingly for Farooq, his people held as well. At an Eid-ul-Fitr gathering at Hazratbal on 7 May 1989, while declaring an 'open war' against militants, Farooq said, 'I don't want to repeat Batmaloo and convert the entire city into a ruin. I don't want that anyone should force entry of the Army into the house of the common man in search of militants, with our women running for shelter ... I warn you beforehand, so that tomorrow you cannot say that Farooq got so many people killed.'[10]

The gathered throng cut his speech off at the knees, shouting that they had come to pray, not to listen to a political rally of sorts. Farooq's friend, Ashok 'Tony' Jaitly, asked him the next day how the speech had gone, observing, 'People are being very critical.'

'I know they're being critical, but I had to say what I had to say,' Farooq replied.

'What was the response?'

'Very hostile.'

'What do you mean?'

'I could see the anger in the eyes of the people there, particularly the youngsters.'

'Why were they angry?' Jaitly asked him.

'They see me as a stooge of Delhi.'[11]

As anecdotes go, this is a revealing one. It highlighted how keenly aware Farooq was about what was happening behind the scenes, not just in Delhi, but in his state as well. It also highlighted his directness. This was another quality that appealed to me about the man. He was not afraid of calling a spade a spade, even when it came to himself.

It was also a fact that Delhi was perennially throwing up obstacles in the path of forging a better understanding between the Centre and the state. I can think of an example. In April 1989, Delhi was seriously upset by Farooq's decision to expand the state cabinet. It had sent him a list of people to be inducted into the government, from among the Congress party. In the meantime, his orders were to set a date and swear in his own people. On 27 April, Farooq and his colleagues went to Raj Bhavan and, with Jagmohan, they waited.

They waited in vain.

Hours earlier, they had had word from Delhi that the flight was just taking off, with the members of the Legislative Assembly (MLAs) on board. But an hour later, there was no sign of any flight. Furious, Farooq decided to swear in four of the NC legislators. At midnight, he got a call from Jagmohan, who reported that Delhi was livid with him for going ahead without waiting for the Congress men. Farooq promptly lost his temper. 'Of course I've sworn them in,' he fumed. 'I'm not your slave; I'm not a Congress Chief Minister whom you can browbeat or push into a corner. I am National Conference and I've taken enough!'[12]

That was just one of the many examples of the times that Delhi threw a rub in Farooq's way. It almost seemed as though the Centre was bent on reminding Farooq that he was nothing without its influence. That was never going to work with him. Right from the start, Farooq had always been aware of who he was. He had his pride and he was aware of what he owed to the Abdullah legacy. He was never going to barter that for a short-term reward.

These dynamics didn't help Farooq's image at this time. Nor did it help that Farooq was being particularly obstinate at this point, a sort of instinctive defence mechanism to the appalling chaos that was reigning in the Valley. He wouldn't hear of the militants being released in exchange for Rubaiya. 'I don't care,' he would huff. 'Even if this was *my* daughter, I'd never agree to the release of those fellows.'

I knew that was nonsense, of course. Farooq could never resist taking a dig at Delhi, even when it was unreasonable. Still, I had some work to do as the spook in charge of the situation. A lot of that, during times like these, was public relations, so to speak. Though he obviously knew better than me, sometimes it was my duty to remind him where his obligations lay. And so, with these conversations playing worryingly at the back of my mind, I went to see Farooq on the evening of 12 December 1989. I knew he was alone. So I dropped in to see him just to cheer him up. He was sitting by himself in his study, and after a few moments of conversation, I asked, 'Sir, have you spoken to Mufti Sahib?'

'*Kyun?*' he said. '*Kaun hai woh?*' (Why? Who is he?)

'Sir,' I said gently, '*Aisa hai. Woh home minister hai, aur aap chief minister ho. Aapko baat karni chahiye.*' (Sir, it's like this. He's the home minister and you're the chief minister. You should talk to him.)

It was all I needed to say.

Farooq's reaction was instantaneous. He rang up Mufti immediately, 'Mufti Sahib, *aap parvaah na karo* [don't worry]. We will do everything to get your daughter. I will do more than I would have done for my own daughter.'

It was Farooq at his best.

This is also the difference between Farooq and his contemporaries and colleagues. I can't think of a better example with which to illustrate just what a leader Farooq was capable of being. Mufti knew it then, Mehbooba knows it now. The whole of Kashmir knows it.

Anyway, the inevitable end of this episode took place on the evening of 13 December.

I'll be brief about this.

We had a small control room set up in the IB offices. Moosa Raza, then the chief secretary of Kashmir, and I were always there. At midnight on 12 December, we got a call from Delhi. On the other end of the line was T.N. Seshan, then the cabinet secretary.

Getting to Know the Chief Minister

'Enough is enough,' Seshan said with his typical brusqueness. 'Let's give these people whatever they want. The prisoners will have to be released and the home minister's daughter will have to be rescued.' He told us that two ministers along with Director of the Intelligence Bureau (DIB) M.K. Narayanan would be landing in Srinagar at five in the morning.

When this new development was taking shape, Farooq told me briskly to bring them straight home. He instructed me, '*Aap batao inko, ki kya hua tha aur kya ho raha hai.*' (You tell them what happened and explain what is happening now.)

And so it was that, apart from being station head for the IB in Srinagar, I had the new and tacit job of being Farooq's mouthpiece, as it were. Unsurprisingly, this would lend credence to nascent rumours that I was Farooq's man. I have never had a problem with being termed that. At a time when the state and the chief minister needed support, I was perfectly happy to supply it. So, when the ministers from Delhi landed at the scheduled time, I was there to receive them and brief them on events, as Farooq had told me to do. It was near five in the morning, and the ministers had barely slept, but all of them were alert. Looking at their faces, I could tell that they had arrived in Srinagar having heard some other narrative of events. As he listened to me, Arif Mohammad Khan, then a cabinet minister, turned to his colleague, the stoic I.K. Gujral, in shock, '*Yeh toh kuch aur kahaani suna rahe hain. Dilli ne toh koi aur kahani batayi.*' (He's telling a completely different story. Delhi told us another story altogether.)

The Chief Minister and the Spy

Gujral being Gujral, whenever he didn't want to hear something, he pretended to be a little more Sphinx-like than he was usually!

Keeping my own counsel for the moment, I drove them to Gupkar Road, as instructed. The chief minister was awake, but the rest of the house, it seemed, was still asleep. As the ministers sat down in the drawing room, rubbing their hands together to warm themselves after the chill of the night air, Farooq went off to the kitchen, saying, '*Chai banaake laata hu.*' (I'll make tea.)

I hastened after him. 'Sir, *main bana leta hoon, aap baith jaiyiye.*' (Sir, I'll make the tea. You sit down.)

'Nonsense,' he said briskly, already getting down the cups and the tea leaves from a cupboard near the stove. '*Tumhe chai banana aata hai?*' (Do you know how to make tea?)

He made the tea – and very good tea it was! – with his own hands and served it himself. It was, to me, an action that underlined the simplicity of the man beneath the veneer of the Abdullah legacy. If you had brought a group of ministers to *my* house in the dead of night, I would have made damn sure that the whole house was awake and on its toes! Anyway, the end of this saga – apart from the obvious political consequences – was that Farooq and I became closer than before. Difficult circumstances don't just define who you are; they define the contours of your relationships with people who work with you and who may be close to you at the time. That's what happened with Farooq and me during these weeks.

Getting to Know the Chief Minister

In the aftermath of Rubaiya's release, I knew that Delhi was gunning for Farooq. Pretty soon, it came to my knowledge that Delhi was gunning for me too. I was told as much by my friend, Vijay Dhar.

Vijay was the son of ambassador D.P. Dhar; his father had been Indira Gandhi's confidant, and he was Rajiv's confidant. Vijay knew I had been preoccupied during the Rubaiya kidnapping. After the saga ended on 13 December at 5.30 p.m., the next day he came to my house and asked to have a cup of coffee. 'I just want to warn you that people in Delhi are gunning for you,' he said. 'You should be careful. You've been branded as a Farooq man.'

'Who are these guys?' I asked.

'Arun Nehru and company,' he said.

It didn't take a rocket scientist to figure out that he meant Mufti Mohammad Sayeed and Arun Nehru. Both men were power centres in their own individual right in Delhi, and both had their reasons to get Farooq – and me – out of Kashmir.

The interesting part of the remainder of this particular story is that Farooq went to Delhi and told Prime Minister V.P. Singh and his friend George Fernandes (whom he was banking on) that he was willing to accept any governor, except Jagmohan. In a way, that suited Mufti and Nehru. It meant that they could kill two birds with one stone: get Jagmohan in and Farooq out.

But what was plied into the system by Mufti was that Farooq himself would never resign. I was questioned about this repeatedly by headquarters, and I had no hesitation about disagreeing.

Will Farooq really resign?

'Hundred per cent he will resign,' was my unwavering reply.

Are you sure?

'I have no doubt about it.'

How do you say that?

'Because,' I would keep repeating, 'Farooq told me. He tells me things and I have no reason to doubt them.'

But for headquarters, it was a conflicted moment. They found it hard to believe Farooq, but they did desperately want to believe him. That dilemma was always at the core of Delhi's misunderstanding of Farooq Abdullah.

Should they? Shouldn't they?

Anyway, at the end of the day, they wanted him out. That, then, is the backstory of how Jagmohan came to Kashmir as governor on 19 January 1990.

I was still in Srinagar that month.

It was a terrible, terrible time.

On the night of 20 January, I was at dinner at the residence of the resident Research and Analysis Wing (R&AW) officer, Duj Nath, who lived in Barzulla, which is quite far from Gupkar Road. During dinner, the loudspeaker of the mosque outside suddenly came on and started broadcasting the sound of wailing at a high volume. A large crowd began to gather. Duj's house was at the rear of a large compound, and at the gate was a lone sentry. There were six of us inside the house, from where we watched the whole tamasha. I was certain that were the crowd to break the gate and storm the house, the six of us would be lynched alive. My assistant director back at headquarters called and asked where I was. When I responded that I was stuck in Barzulla, he told me not to return that night. 'It's not safe,' he said. 'Stay where you are.'

As luck would have it, one of the dinner guests was the Kashmir Valley sub area commander, Brig. Madan Mohan Lakhera, and he called for an army column. A long two hours later, we were back home. In fact, the night of 20 January was one of the most infamous nights in Kashmir. All of Srinagar came out on the roads in protest and there was a lot of wailing and shrieking that rose and fell unnervingly. On 21 January, I was summoned by Jagmohan to meet him at 10.30 a.m. at Raj Bhavan. I was still, despite the circumstances, the first man he would send for in crises like this.

When I arrived at Raj Bhavan, I was told that the governor was with a visitor, but he had given orders that I was to be sent in as soon as I arrived. When I went in, I realized there was a little drama being enacted. Joginder Singh, later the director of the Central Bureau of Investigation, but then the inspector general (IG) of the CRPF and known to us as 'Tiger', was being given hell by Jagmohan.

What had happened was this: When Joginder Singh heard that Jagmohan was returning as governor, he ordered his troops to round up anybody who 'looked' like a terrorist. On the fateful, bloody evening of 20 January, Singh called me, 'We've rounded up 150 people but we don't know who

The Chief Minister and the Spy

they are. Can you send somebody from your office who can identify these people?'

'No,' I said, my tone a bit short. 'I don't have any people and nor will I send them. You rounded them up, sir, now you deal with them whatever way you want.'

That rounding-up led to huge protests in the city. It was a night on which Srinagar did not sleep. The roads were full of people, and the air rang with slogans and chants.

It was for this that Jagmohan was giving Singh hell.

'Why did you do this?' he demanded. 'Now I have to deal with a hostile Srinagar. Why could you not have waited till I arrived for my instruction?'

Singh listened quietly to this tirade. I was embarrassed, and stayed quiet. In fact, I don't think Singh and I exchanged a word during the time we were in Jagmohan's office.

Once he had gone, Jagmohan looked at me, '*Halat kaisi hai?*' (How are things?)

'Sir, *halat bahut kharab hai.*' (Sir, things are very bad.) I wasn't underplaying it.

Kashmir had changed almost unalterably in six months. He couldn't believe it, or he didn't want to believe it.

'*Kya karna chahiye?*' (What should we do?) he asked.

'Sir, *do raaste hain. Ya toh danda laga lijiye, ya baat kar lijiye.*' (There are two ways, sir. Either we use force, or we use dialogue.)

'*Nahi, main baat karna chahta hu,*' Jagmohan said firmly. (No, I want to talk to them.)

Getting to Know the Chief Minister

'*Aapko baat karni chahiye, par log badal gaye, sir. Shayad aaj aapse koi baat na karein,*' I said honestly. (Yes, you *should* talk to them. But people have changed, sir. Maybe today nobody will want to talk to you.)

Jagmohan was, for one of the rare times in his career, speechless.

When I was walking out of Raj Bhavan after that interview, Ved Marwah – one of the only men Jagmohan had brought with him from Delhi – caught up with me. He was outraged.

'What rubbish are you telling the governor?' he demanded. '*Baat-cheet se kya matlab hai. Danda lagane ka waqt hai.*' (What do you mean, talk to them? This is a time to use force!)

'*Main kab keh raha hu ki danda nahi lagao, sir,*' I asked. '*Main toh keh raha hu ki agar baat nahi karni, toh danda lagao.*' (When did I say not to use force, sir? I'm telling you that if you don't want to talk, then use force.)

That afternoon, there was again a protest in the city, and protestors, consisting mainly of youth, were fired upon, leading to a number of deaths at Gow Kadal in the old city. On 21 January, the Indian paramilitary troops of the CRPF opened fire on a group of protesters in what has been described by Victoria Schofield in her book, *Kashmir in Conflict*, as 'the worst massacre in Kashmiri history'.[13]

Such was the atmosphere that Jagmohan was to later claim in his memoir, *My Frozen Turbulence in Kashmir*,[14] that he stopped Kashmir from joining Pakistan on 26 January 1990. Then, a couple of days later, the governor hosted a lunch, to which he invited me. Through the course of that meal, I realized that Jagmohan had been doing some fast thinking. He had, after all, served in Kashmir. He knew the state, even if it was in his own way. Now, he was realizing that he needed a Kashmiri among his advisors, likely a local officer. He had invited a popular DG of the Jammu and Kashmir Police, Pir Ghulam Hussein Shah, for lunch, where he pleaded with the man to join the government as an advisor. But in those days, as a Kashmiri, to be an advisor to Jagmohan was a huge black mark.

When I was seeing Shah off to his car, I said quietly, '*Sir, aapki zarurat hai.*' (Sir, we need you.)

'No,' he said flatly. 'I can't be a party to this mayhem.' He didn't say it to my face – but the implicit subtext was 'Don't forget I'm a Kashmiri.'

So, despite Jagmohan's boast that he knew everybody in Kashmir, his advisors were purely Delhi men.

Our relations – his and mine, that is – began to go downhill rapidly thereafter. I remember one time when a procession was gathering in downtown Srinagar. Things were looking ugly, with the police getting ready to crack down on protestors.

I had a few Kashmiri friends with their ears to the ground and one of them called me right before the violence broke out.

'*Sahib, aaj force istemaal karoge, toh bahut log marenge.*' (Sahib, if you use force today, then many people will die.)

Getting to Know the Chief Minister

Worried, I rang up Jagmohan. But matters between us had reached a point where he no longer liked being told what to do.

The expulsion of Kashmiri Pandits and the violence of the 1990s stands out as the darkest chapter in Kashmir's modern history, but with the appointment of Jagmohan, there was yet another development in progress. On the same day that he arrived in Kashmir, I was informed of an ongoing cabinet meeting during which Farooq had announced that he was going to meet the outgoing governor, Krishna Rao, and offer his resignation.

He did this without thinking further about it.

In her biography of Sheikh Abdullah,[15] Chitralekha Zutshi writes that Farooq was dismissed in January 1990. The truth of the matter – and I say this as someone who was very much in Srinagar at the time – was that Farooq was never dismissed. He resigned on principle.

In a reprise of August 1953, Jagmohan had dismissed Farooq's government in June 1984, hammering it home to Kashmiris that democracy held little meaning in Kashmir. This sentiment was further confirmed when Farooq came back to power a mere two years later through an accord with the Centre to form a government in alliance with the ruling Congress party. To Kashmiris, it was clear that the son was not only no different from the father, but was also most likely far worse, since at least the father had fought the Centre for decades before reaching a compromise.

The Chief Minister and the Spy

The story goes that when Rajiv heard that Farooq was about to resign, he rang him up desperately, 'I'm sending Rajesh [Pilot] to Srinagar,' he told the chief minister. 'Please don't resign. Come and meet me first.'

It's not a confirmed story, of course, but even as an apocryphal anecdote, it underlines how belatedly Delhi had recognized the importance of Farooq Abdullah. Rajesh Pilot *did* come to Kashmir. He did pick up Farooq and take him to Delhi where the prime minister remonstrated with him. But again, the story goes that Farooq heard him out pleasantly, and at the end of it, he said, 'I've heard you and while I thank you for the sentiments, I am still going to resign.'

It was his principles talking – and also the fact that he was annoyed that Rajiv had felt the need to get in an interlocutor when Farooq himself had gone out of his way to show that he was ready for one-on-one dynamics.

'Jagmohan's earlier tenure cannot be forgotten for the way defined powers under Article 370 were encroached upon ... whereby sovereign powers of the legislature of the state were curtailed on vital matters,' Farooq said in a public statement after he had signed his resignation papers. 'He behaved like a colonial ruler. He sought his social base from communal outfits which ultimately resulted in [the] growth and spread of communal politics, unheard of in our state,' he added.[16]

As soon as he resigned, I rang him up – to congratulate him.

'I think you've done the right thing,' I told him. 'We've been proven right. We've been warning Delhi umpteen times.'

Getting to Know the Chief Minister

Now that Farooq had resigned, I knew my time was coming. I had been warned of it by Vijay Dhar. But more to the point, IB headquarters, at that point in time, was at its weakest. It was the triumvirate of Jagmohan, Arun Nehru and Mufti whose decisions were the real orders.

They wanted me out.

I say this with finality, because matters had gone far beyond any shred of doubt. Jagmohan was not an unknown quantity to me. I had worked with him during the summer of 1989, just before he left Srinagar upon completing his first stint as governor. In those days, I had realized that underneath the Congress loyalist lay a rightist streak, similar to Sanjay Gandhi's. That brand of aggressive politics was exactly up Jagmohan's (and Arun Nehru's, if it came to that) alley. Right before he left Srinagar in July 1989, Jagmohan had summoned me for a last meeting, '*Dulat Sahib, main Dilli waapis jaa raha hu, par yeh bataiye* – should I stay with the Congress or not?' (Dulat Sahib, I'm going back to Delhi, but tell me this – should I stay with the Congress or not?)

I was in a mischievous mood. '*Sir, politics ki baat hai. Aap behtar jaante hain. Aap Dilli jaiye aur dekhiye aapko kya suit karega.*' (Sir, that's a question of politics. You know better than I do. Go to Delhi and see what suits you.)

That's exactly what he did then. He went back to Delhi and left the Congress.

So, given what I knew of him, working with Jagmohan now, in the fraught early days of the 1990s, entailed a decent formality. I would call on him as was my duty. He expected certain things from me. For instance, I was expected to call on him on a weekly or fortnightly basis. I was also expected to provide detailed notes for him. Now, I was happy to meet him whenever he called on me. But I refused point-blank to give him any notes.

'Those are notes for the IB, sir,' I told him honestly at one point.

'*KP toh banata tha*,' he retorted, annoyed. (KP used to make notes.)

'*KP se poochhna padega phir, sir, par main toh nahi banata*,' I said quietly. (I'll have to ask him, sir, but I don't make notes.)

Not that there was, in my opinion, any time to make notes, at least any notes that would be of use to a chief minister or governor who actually knew what was happening on the ground. I remember that Farooq certainly had no time for these niceties. I had gone to meet him once. It was yet another week of bloodshed in Kashmir, and when I walked into his office, he was fuming behind a stack of reports on the table. As soon as he saw me, he flung them irritably in my direction, '*Dekho, yeh kya hai?*' (Look, what is this?)

In the IB, we had a system of providing information to the government on a daily basis. In the states, the protocol was that the chief minister would be kept informed by the State Special Branch in what was called a daily diary.

'*Dekho, isme kya likha hai? Roz mujhe bhejte hai par dekho isko. Kuch hai isme?*' Farooq demanded crossly. (Look at what's written in this. They send it to me every day, but look at it. Is there anything in there?)

Farooq, then, never had time for all this. He didn't even have time for briefings!

The fact that Jagmohan was asking me directly for reports meant that he was acting on specific instructions from Delhi. It didn't necessarily mean that Delhi was asking him to demand notes from the IB. There's an important distinction here. You see, Jagmohan thought that he was the lord and master of Kashmir, and that is the attitude he brought to all his interactions with me – and the IB.

It was this attitude that gave him away in the end, as far as his agenda towards my future in Kashmir was concerned. As governor, Jagmohan would send detailed reports to Delhi on the situation in Kashmir. In many of these reports, he stressed on the urgency of getting me out of Kashmir as fast as possible, and suggested that K.P. Singh be brought back as my replacement.

Now, as the IB bureau chief, those reports were routed to Delhi via my desk.

And so it was that I had the unmatched pleasure of knowing exactly what the governor of Kashmir thought about me in my final days in Srinagar in 1990.

This was also the moment that I stopped giving a damn. I stopped going to his meetings. I sent my number two instead.

The mayhem continued around us all. Kashmir was a cauldron of unrest in the early months of 1990. Perhaps that is why, when the axe finally fell three months later, it happened with a subtle swiftness. In fact, I didn't quite understand it for the first few minutes.

The Chief Minister and the Spy

On 6 March 1990, I got a call from Delhi. R.C. Mehta was coming to Srinagar from Ahmedabad, I was told.

Please receive him at the airport.

I agreed politely and put down the phone, wondering (rather naïvely, in retrospect!) who the hell would visit Srinagar of all places at this time.

Then it struck me.

Mehta's arrival meant that *I* was going.

Hastily, I called Delhi back.

'*Mehta Sahib ko main receive kar lunga,*' I said pleasantly. '*Par mere ko kab Dilli aana hai?*' (I'll receive Mehta Sahib, of course – but when do I have to come to Delhi?)

'*Jitni jaldi ho sakey,*' was the response. (As soon as possible.)

So the writing was on the wall.

I called up Farooq as soon as I hung up on Delhi.

'*Humara ek officer aa raha hai* [An officer from the IB is coming out],' I said without preamble. 'I thought I'd bring him across for a cup of tea.'

For a few seconds, there was silence at the other end of the line. Clearly, Farooq was as taken aback as I had been.

'*Kyun aa raha hai?*' he demanded finally. (Why is he coming?)

'*Meri chhutti ho rahi hai,*' I said amiably. (I'm being transferred.)

'Oh boy.'

Farooq agreed to meet with Mehta, though he asked me to meet with him an hour before Mehta arrived at the house. I remember that conversation like it was yesterday. Farooq had never beaten around the bush with me, but during this last conversation, he was particularly frank. I recall something that he told me that evening. 'You know,' he said quietly, 'I'm not my father. Please understand that. I have not joined politics to spend 12 years in jail. I will always be with whoever is in power in Delhi.'

We talked about a lot of things, and I remember thinking that, unlike KP, I would not be getting either a carpet or a farewell party! But in the end, I suppose it was all right. In the bargain, I had learnt a great deal about the great man. I had come to realize, even then, that Doctor Sahib was not just a chief minister.

He was Kashmir.

This is something, as I keep saying, that Delhi has never understood. Why?

Because Delhi does not – or does not *want* to – understand Farooq. At any rate, I was hugely relieved to get out of that mess. I had no attachment with Kashmir at that point in time. I just wanted to get the hell out of there, as fast as possible.

But it was not to be. This is a story almost too improbable to be told – it was not ending, but merely beginning.

2

The Making of Farooq Abdullah

The Valley of Kashmir is but an irregular oval-shaped piece of land, but it is, to my mind, one of the most beautiful places in the world. On a map the Valley appears remote and landlocked, extending for no more than 145 kilometres, isolated by successive ranges of the Himalayan mountains high above the plains of South Asia. But for all that seeming impregnability, the Valley's history has been a turbulent one. Sometimes it formed part of a great empire, at others it comprised a kingdom in its own right. At all times, its peoples have retained a strong attachment to their identity, to their Kashmiriyat, a quality unique to the Valley and one that transcends politics or religion. Even then, Kashmir was a tricky posting, a stage dominated by the Abdullah family.

The Abdullahs were the most important family that I would need to learn about before I got going; though, of course, the best kind of training comes from working on the job. For the most part of the last five decades, the NC, headed by the influential Abdullah family, has been synonymous with Indian politics in Jammu and Kashmir. Yet for years the same family has faced the wrath of Kashmir's local residents, as well as the separatists, for their loyalty to India. At the dawn of the armed rebellion that began three decades ago, an NC leader was the first political leader to be killed by the rebels, who, since my time in Kashmir, have killed several hundred NC party workers.

Indeed, Kashmir was never comfortable with Delhi from the start. In his day, Farooq's father, Sheikh Abdullah, also known as the Sher-e-Kashmir, had led the Kashmiris against Maharaja Hari Singh. At the time of transfer of power, the maharaja wavered tenuously between India and Pakistan. Everyone knows that story, of course, but the important part for Kashmir was that the Instrument of Accession that Hari Singh eventually signed assured him that Kashmir's accession would be conditional on a plebiscite. Now, it suited Sheikh Abdullah to be a part of India. Under the terms of the Instrument of Accession, Kashmir would enjoy special status within India, in charge of its own affairs except defence, foreign affairs and communications, with Sheikh Sahib as Jammu and Kashmir's prime minister.

For Jawaharlal Nehru, however, trouble came immediately. There was pressure from those who came away from Partition with the belief that no one required any special guarantees. From the beginning, there were moves to erode the state's special status and incorporate Jammu and Kashmir into the Indian Union. The Sher-e-Kashmir did his best, but even

The Making of Farooq Abdullah

he could not understand his friend, Nehru. The promised plebiscite, needless to say, was never held. So the fact that this was a troubled state with great trust issues is not surprising at all. Just as Pakistan never forgave the Sher-e-Kashmir for siding with India, it never forgave Farooq either.

Farooq Abdullah grew up in the shadow of that mistrust – and it would define his relations with Delhi permanently.

Farooq was born on 21 October 1937, in a village called Soura, then on the outskirts of Srinagar. He was the second of five children, born to Sheikh Abdullah and Begum Akbar Jahan: Khalida, Farooq, Tariq, Mustafa and Suraiya. The Sheikh had married his Begum in October 1933. He was then already a man of political eminence in Kashmir, the president of the Jammu and Kashmir Muslim Conference.

Though the Begum, when I knew her during my own days in Kashmir, possessed a certain quiet elegance, she was believed to have been a mercurial young woman, both beautiful and impetuous. When her marriage was being arranged to the Sheikh, it is said, the Pir Sahib (the holy man) advised the Sheikh's family that this would be an excellent match. The Sheikh, said the old Pir Sahib, would rise swiftly in his political career. As a result, he would need someone by his side who would be his anchor. This beautiful young woman was the ideal match. And so it was – by his own account, the Begum 'proved a true friend and comrade' to the Sheikh, introducing an element of order and calm in his turbulent life. Farooq had both the Sher-e-Kashmir and Madar-e-Mehrbaan in him as he grew up.

Pandit Nehru's last foreign secretary, Y.D. Gundevia, would later say that no story of Kashmir would be complete without the Sher-e-Kashmir. If I might now add, no story of Kashmir can be complete without Dr Farooq Abdullah.

Of his father, Farooq saw very little. The Lion of Kashmir commanded immediate attention with his 6-foot-4-inch frame, his buck teeth and the receding hairline that was invariably covered with a fur cap in Aligarhi style. The Sheikh was married more to Kashmir than to the Begum – and he was hardly ever at home, forever embroiled in some political imbroglio or the other. He had sacrificed his life to the cause of Kashmir, and he expected his family to understand. As a result, the children clustered around their mother: The Begum was the softer parent, the one who had time for their troubles and qualms. Farooq's childhood was both active and mischievous, punctuated by the typical stunts of all young boys: smoking, climbing trees to steal apples and cherries and (in his case) eating icicles. Nor was he particularly good at his studies, preferring to spend his time outdoors.

As he grew into his teens, he became aware of his father's political exploits. The Sheikh was of the conviction that modern Kashmiri politics needed to reorient itself on a secular and antifeudal axis. Consequently, his party was renamed the National Conference (NC) in 1939 – from the Muslim Conference – when Farooq was two years old. In this guise, the NC formed linkages with both minority leaders within Kashmir and the national-level Congress leadership.

In 1946, the NC started the massive 'Quit Kashmir' movement against the ruling Dogra dynasty. Abdullah also succeeded Nehru as the president of the All India State People's Conference, but was soon arrested by the maharaja on charges of sedition. Nehru protested against this suppression, but was prevented from entering the state. Those were, as history shows, the good days between Nehru and the Sheikh. By this time, the Sheikh was spending more and more time behind bars, and Farooq would often be taken along to sit and chat with his father, to share a meal with him or catch him up on his daily life. His first real exposure to political life came when the Sheikh met with Mohammad Ali Jinnah (these were the days before Partition and Independence, of course, for Jinnah died in 1948) and Mahatma Gandhi. They each represented two different ends of the Indian political spectrum and Farooq was vastly impressed by both: by Jinnah's elegance and articulation and Gandhi's undoubted political and spiritual depth.

The end of his early schooldays coincided with the invasion of tribals from the Northwestern Frontier Province into the Valley. Integration, transfer of power and accession are all events that are spoken about and detailed elsewhere, and this book does not profess to deal with those events. But it is a fact that Farooq was, by then, ten years of age and old enough to remember Dakotas landing at the Srinagar airport as Indian troops arrived on the ground. Sheikh Abdullah was in charge of the emergency administration at the time, and his hands were overflowing with the troubles in Kashmir. So bad did things get that for a time, the family had to leave Kashmir to seek refuge in Delhi and then with the Begum's brother in Indore. Farooq was too young to be told the extent of the troubles, only that the maharaja had fled, leaving his people to face trouble alone. But his father's role in the state's politics would only become clear to him years later.

For his matriculation, Farooq attended the Tyndale Biscoe School, which was behind Pratap Park in the heart of Srinagar. A year senior to him was Ranga Trilochan Bedi, whose parents were extremely close – because of their leftist progressive leanings – to the Sheikh and the Gandhis. Pyaare Lal Bedi (BPL Bedi as he was known) was a communist leader in Punjab, and ideologically, he fit right in with the Sheikh's own left leanings. It was BPL Bedi who drafted the NC manifesto of Naya Kashmir in 1931. BPL's wife, Freda, was also leftist and in Kashmir she encountered a state that had had enough of the maharaja and wanted a new beginning for itself. Freda was also a member of the Women's Defence Cadet Corp in Kashmir before she became a Buddhist nun, and was a friend of Indira Gandhi's. Other than Ranga, the Bedis had two other children – the more famous Kabir, and Gulhima, a daughter born in the hills.

His school's motto was typical of the adult Farooq: 'They say what they say. Let them say what they say, for they say what they say. And in all things, be men.' It was a school that Farooq enjoyed, for it combined a healthy mix of the physical and the intellectual. It was here that the qualities that would mark him as a leader emerged: he was decisive, imperious and incredibly kind with his friends.

After his matriculation, Farooq went to SP College, from where he obtained his intermediate degree that was then called the FSc. After this, he had decided to go to medical school. But this trajectory was interrupted – as life often was in the Valley – by political events larger than Farooq. These were the early 1950s, and relations between Delhi and Srinagar were beginning to backslide. As prime minister of Jammu and Kashmir from 1948 to 1953, the Sheikh implemented a vigorous programme of land reforms, which saw the abolition of zamindari, implementation of land ceilings, transfer of land to the landless, and equitable tenurial arrangements. However, trouble was brewing with Delhi. The Sheikh wielded enough influence over New Delhi for Nehru to concede a 'special status to J&K' via Article 370 of the Constitution of India. It guaranteed a separate flag, constitution and autonomy. Except for defence, communication and external affairs, Jammu and Kashmir was autonomous in all other respects. The Sheikh was in total control through these provisions, but still pressed on for more and more autonomy to implement his vision of Naya Kashmir (New Kashmir).

There are many stories about the senior Abdullah – one of which includes the US presidential candidate Adlai Stevenson. It is said that in May 1953, Stevenson came to Srinagar, where he had a long meeting with Sheikh Abdullah. Following this meeting, in July that year, the *New York Times* published an article on the story, hinting at independent status for the Valley. Reports suggested that the Sheikh actually said, 'A time will come when I will bid goodbye to India.'

Farooq vehemently denies this story. He has told me that Stevenson – a mutual friend of both Nehru and the Sheikh – had certainly come to visit Srinagar, where he had lunch with the Sheikh. Then he was to take the flight back to Delhi. Farooq tells me that the plane – the old Dakotas they used in those days – couldn't take off. The Banihal pass was closed due to bad weather. The Sheikh, when he heard Stevenson was stranded at the airport, telephoned him and asked him to come back home for a cup of tea. In Farooq's version, the sensational stories of the Sheikh's secessionist tendencies spring from these mundane circumstances – and were not true at all.

Jawaharlal Nehru's last foreign secretary, Y.D. Gundevia, asked the Sheikh in Jammu and Kashmir House in September 1949, 'Sheikh Sahib, why haven't you thought of independence?'

'No way,' the Sheikh said immediately. 'These guys [Pakistan] attacked us once. They will chew us up next time. And how can an independent Kashmir survive in the middle of two huge powers? How will the economy run? Where will we get our defences from? How will we survive? Pakistan will take over Kashmir very quickly once India leaves.'

Farooq agrees with that version. For both the Abdullahs, secessionism has never been a thought or a wish. Doctor Sahib himself has borne out the truth of that. In 1995, at a time when Delhi was all for mainstreaming the separatists,

Farooq asked me, 'I know that you guys are talking to Yasin Malik. Can I meet him?'

'Sir, whatever you want – but are you sure you want to meet him?' I asked.

'Yes, I'd like to meet him.'

Farooq met with Yasin Malik in a safe house operated by the IB in Mandi village. I wasn't there myself, but I'm told that he pulled Yasin outdoors and gave him real hell, about the JKLF's use of violence in Kashmir and about the JKLF dream of *azaadi*. '*Kis duniya mein rehte ho?*' he demanded. '*Kaunsi independence chahte ho? Hum independent reh sakte hain? Humein koi rehne dega independent?*' (What is this world you live in? What independence do you dream of? Do you think they'll let us be independent or that we can ever be independent?)

So effective was the rocket he gave Malik that I'm told that Malik didn't touch his food for the next two days.

That was how firmly both father and son banished any thought of secessionism. Yet, back in the 1950s, Prime Minister Jawaharlal Nehru was growing increasingly disillusioned with Sheikh Abdullah's refusal to commit to India and curb secessionist tendencies in the state. Tempers were running high in the Valley, and Farooq recalled a young boy at college telling him bluntly that the Sheikh had 'sold Kashmir'. The details of how his father could possibly have done this eluded him, and his mother would give him no clear answers, for he was as yet too young. It was a question that troubled Farooq, even as a boy. To his (correct) knowledge, the Sheikh was even then a legendary figure. He was 'the voice of the people'; the 'most revered and loved leader' of Kashmir.

But on the night of 23 June 1953, the telephone rang – and changed Farooq's world forever. The telephone used to be kept in Farooq's room, and if the call was important, he would take the phone in to his father. This time, it was from the health minister, Shyam Lal Saraf, who wanted to speak to the Sheikh urgently. He was calling with bad news.

In the days to come, Sheikh Abdullah was unceremoniously arrested and dismissed from office, as part of a coup engineered by dissidents in the national government. It was the beginning of a new age in Kashmir – and for young Farooq Abdullah, it was a personal political baptism by fire. He responded to that crisis in his life as he has always done – with decisive action. Perhaps it was a trait engendered in him in Biscoe: where, if you became stuck during a hike, you did not cry, you merely bent your mind to the most resourceful way to get moving again. He did the same now: starting a campaign to drum up public support against the imprisonment of his father. It was a searing initiation into politics.

When Delhi arrested the Sheikh and involved him in conspiracy, Farooq realized that all Kashmiris had come under that same cloud of suspicion. There they would remain ever since, but in the high-strung days following his father's arrest, Farooq plunged headlong into a spree of public speeches, seeking support for his imprisoned father. But if he thought his father would be delighted, he was severely mistaken. 'This is not the time for you to become involved in politics,' the Sheikh told him angrily. 'It is the time for you to study.' When Farooq remonstrated, his father ended the discussion with his usual firmness, 'God will take care of you. Have faith in Him and you will come out of this. But first study, first make yourself worthy, complete your education. Then the sky is the limit for what you want to do.'

For Farooq, to whom his father was an icon worth aspiring to, these words were both balm and incentive. He bid goodbye to his family – and applied for medical college in 1955. The desire was not his own, but his father's. The Sheikh had always wanted his sons to become doctors – a dream that he himself had had to put aside. Farooq made it through to the interview stage – where he found himself nose to nose with the very man who had politically felled his father: Bakshi Ghulam Mohammad. Still, his answer, when he was asked why he wanted to study medicine, was a cool and calm one. 'I want to serve my people,' he said. 'I feel doctors only make money and they don't pay attention to the poor. But I would like to help the poor.' He selected Indore as his first choice and Delhi as the second.

I will not go into the details of Farooq's medical career, but suffice it to say that in these early years of his medical training, he travelled across India, working with the poorest of the poor – and still finding time to act as a kind of intermediary voice between his father and Nehru.

To be fair to Nehru, he wanted to forgive his old friend, the Sheikh – and he did eventually, but by then, the damage to Kashmir had been done. It is remarkable that their friendship stayed intact, but it is one of the great characteristics of the Sheikh – one which Farooq has inherited – that he lacked both bitterness and rancour towards Nehru, despite the years of incarceration. In fact, the Sheikh later told his son that when he met Nehru in 1964, Nehru had told him of the pain he had suffered all those years, knowing that he had locked up his friend, and that it had not been right.

For Farooq, the prime minister of India was a kind man, genteel and erudite. His interactions with Nehru were, according to his biographer Aditya Sinha, evocative of a father–son relationship, similar to the one that Farooq unconsciously feels he has with Rahul Gandhi today. It was his interactions with Nehru that gave Farooq the sense that, unlike the angry slights hurled at him after the Sheikh's arrest, he was a part of India – an Indian in every sense of the word. It was also Nehru who taught Farooq the inimitable quality he possesses even today: a true democratic ability to listen to all points of view, to take every perspective under advisement even as he follows his own path.

These early experiences taught Farooq invaluable skills, including ways of doing politics that are, in this day and age, a dying art. 'Oh yes, I did [advise Farooq to join politics],' Sheikh Abdullah once admitted with a twinkle in his eyes and a sly smile. 'I told him that this is a constructive phase and he can help the country by running a hospital! But politics is more glamorous than anything else. The question is, we want to hand over to young people. They must take responsibility. Now, there should be a young man who has a popular base, whom the young support. And there was a demand for Dr Farooq from all over the party.'

It would take some time for that to happen.

Farooq took seven years to complete his medical training. He was in his last year of training in Jaipur when China invaded India in October 1962. Farooq and his friends were of the opinion that if the war continued, they would all volunteer to go to the frontline and offer their medical expertise, such as it was. Fortunately, the war was a short, though humiliating, affair, and Farooq finally became a doctor. He returned to Srinagar, where he took on the job of senior house officer (a resident doctor) at the SMHS Hospital, attached to the professor of medicine.

Life settled into an uneventful routine: Farooq would get on his scooter, go to the hospital, attend to patients, and return home. As Kashmir went through its own political evolution, Farooq told his father that having completed his training in India, he wanted to go to England to continue his studies. He did so in 1965, and with an ocean between himself and the Valley, settled down to a good life. Indian doctors who were in England at the time recall that Sheikh Abdullah's son was known for being fun-loving and not having much patience for politics back home.

It was here, though, that Farooq encountered a trainee nurse named Mollie Pritcher. He was immediately smitten by her. She was reserved and calm – and, in fact, she initially refused to even date Farooq! He became more determined in his efforts to woo her. The path of true love was proverbially difficult for them, for Mollie's family panicked at the idea of a Muslim – one from a politically active family at that – wanting to marry their daughter. On Farooq's side, Aditya Sinha – in his biography, *Kashmir's Prodigal Son* – writes that he himself faced a tricky situation because, before he had left for England, Farooq had been engaged to a cousin: the seventh daughter of his father's second brother, Sheikh Ghulam Mohiuddin. Not surprisingly then, the news of Farooq's desire to marry Mollie broke as a storm over the Abdullahs' heads. Sheikh Abdullah was furious. He told his son that since it was his choice, he would have to inform his uncle and break the engagement. 'You will have to apologize to them,' he said to Farooq. 'I'm not going to, it is you who must.'

The awkwardness was tided over, as it happens in families, with time. Mollie and Farooq were married in England on 14 September 1968, and came to India in 1969 for a simple *nikaah* ceremony, conducted by Sheikh Abdullah, in Srinagar. After the ceremony, the happy couple returned to England. Farooq's biographer makes the claim that post his marriage, the Sheikh's son did not see a future for himself on the subcontinent – at least not immediately. Yet, having seen a different, far more developed world, and having noticed where his own people stood in comparison, Farooq began to have second thoughts.

From here, we know the history of Farooq's return to Kashmir and his arrival on his home state's political stage. It was against this backdrop that I met Farooq in 1987, and came to know what a caring doctor he really was, despite the colourful canvas of his family. The Abdullahs dominated Kashmir's political landscape. Of that, there was no doubt. For the most part of the last five decades, under their aegis, the NC has been synonymous with Indian politics in Jammu and Kashmir. Yet for years the same family has faced the wrath of Kashmir's citizens, as well as the separatists, for their loyalty to India. At the dawn of the armed rebellion that began three decades ago, an NC leader was the first political leader to be killed by the rebels, who, since my time in Kashmir, have killed several hundred NC party workers. Sheikh Abdullah himself had died in 1982, some six years before I arrived in Kashmir.

Khalida was the eldest of Sheikh Sahib's five children; his other daughter Suraiya was the youngest. Khalida was also her father's favourite. When she was only fourteen, in 1948, she was married to a man twice her age, Ghulam Mohammed Shah, otherwise known as Gul Shah. He was an NC loyalist, and in Sheikh Sahib's emergency administration in the immediate years post-Independence, he had served as the controller, food and civil supplies. When Sheikh Sahib returned to power in 1975 after two decades of imprisonment, Gul Shah served in his state cabinet as a minister in charge of important portfolios such as food and civil supplies, transport, works and power.

To some, including Shah himself, it seemed he would inherit Sheikh Abdullah's political mantle. But what Gul Shah did not count on was that after the 1977 assembly elections, in the final five years of Sheikh Sahib's life, it was Begum Akbar Jehan Abdullah whose power grew. She wielded a lot of influence in Sheikh Sahib's last days. She became a member of Parliament after Sheikh Sahib returned to power in 1975, and during his final years, there were many rumours of corruption in his government that dented his image as a statesman, and somehow many of those rumours could be traced back to the Begum and her coterie.

Begum Abdullah was old-school, and an extremely charming and elegant lady, but she didn't talk much. She was careful about what she said. During my days in Srinagar, whenever I heard her, she showed great respect for the Nehru–Gandhi family, but in whatever she said she was definitely part of the older guard, the more conservative part of the NC. I was not in Srinagar in the days when political machinations derailed personal dynamics in the Abdullah family. The greatest and most public example has been Farooq's spat with Khalida's side of the family.

Gul Shah might have been a smarter politician than Farooq, but he was widely regarded as a bully. Another factor that might have swayed Sheikh Sahib was the fact that Gul Shah ill-treated Khalida; she would come home and complain to her parents about it. Thus, ultimately, it was the Begum who tilted the balance, and Farooq was appointed president of the NC in August 1981. Sheikh Sahib passed away in September 1982, and Farooq took over as chief minister.

Farooq planned his succession meticulously, with all the love for political theatre that ran in his veins. Days before the ceremony, he personally mobilized the cadre to make it a memorable event. Volunteers were sent to the lanes and by-lanes of Srinagar with posters and banners to decorate every inch of available space. They were told to rally people from every house and make them flood the streets. Nobody really needed to be encouraged. Who doesn't love a good, chaotic celebration? Even on the night before the event, Srinagar's streets were chock-a-block. An undeclared holiday was observed in all offices and educational institutions to mark the 'national festival'.

Farooq started the day by leading a noisy and unruly procession through the main streets of the city. A vast crowd followed him, cheering loudly. Groups of men danced to the beat of 'National, National. All are National'. A visibly pleased Farooq egged them on, waving his arms in rhythm with the beat of the chants. The ageing Sher-e-Kashmir watched his son's advent through the streets with pride. From the balcony of the Lal Rukh Hotel, he gathered flowers in his hands and showered them upon Farooq. Later, he was called upon to give his last presidential speech. He spoke with barely concealed delight, 'After 50 years ... I get a chance on this historic moment to transfer to the younger generation the trust handed over to me by martyrs – I lighted this torch, and many a storm could not extinguish it until today when [I] transfer [it]. Fervently, I hope that Dr Farooq shall prove worthy of the trust. I transfer my presidency to him.'[1]

Delegates and party workers might have cheered this rise of the son, but there was trouble within the family. Gul Shah felt cheated; he had had a long innings in politics, and he was senior to his brother-in-law both in age and in politics. He was unhappy at being overlooked for the job. Sheikh Nazir, the Sheikh's adopted son and the provisional president of the party, was also muttering. Farooq, he felt, was still not ready for a big step like this. In due course, Khalida's family and Farooq's family drifted apart. It would culminate in the ugly coup against Farooq in 1984, which is the story in the next chapter in this book.

When I came out to Srinagar in the spring of 1989, the Begum was running a kitchen cabinet of sorts. Farooq, for his part, would 'mummy' her and keep her in good humour, but she did not meddle too much in day-to-day affairs. She was also walking the difficult tightrope between her daughter Khalida and son-in-law Gul Shah, and her son. Though she was often around when I visited Farooq's residence, she never spoke while her son was speaking. It was a tacit, often implicit dynamic, but despite its existence, both mother and son were very close.

The early days of my assignment in Kashmir marked the heyday of Farooq's cinema-style chief ministership. His constant high jinks led to disapproving murmurs from within the family. Farooq, they said, knew everything, but he wasn't serious about the mantle he had inherited. But Farooq's nature was such that he really never gave a damn, even if he heard the talk behind his back. He was building a new Kashmir in his way, and in his own style. He didn't feel he needed to justify how he was doing it. He was determined to play as hard as he worked – that joie de vivre was an inherent trait in his personality, and it stays with him even today.

I remember M.K. Narayanan saying dryly that the chief minister of Jammu and Kashmir was 'mercurial'. It's an apt word; Farooq was still growing into his many-splendoured personality in those days. There is no doubt, despite the whispers, that Farooq was a man who loved his family. There had been a time when he was warned by his dearest friend and one of his 'ideal human beings', Mridula Sarabhai, as she lay dying of cancer, that he was to look after Mollie.

'Be good to Mollie,' she had adjured him. 'Don't let her face the same tragedies that your mother has had to …'[2]

It was perhaps these words that guided Farooq through his life. He was an undoubted family man, and he unequivocally adored his children, Omar, Safia, Hinna and Sara. There was little that he would not do for them and for his wife. Take, for instance, the meltdown in state order in 1989–90. Farooq, as you know, left shortly thereafter. It felt right to do so at the time. Not only had Delhi not had his back, he felt, but above all else, he felt he had to prioritize the safety of his family. He articulated his feelings about it at a function in honour of the Urdu writer Mazhar Imam, at the Iqbal Academy, on 9 July 1988: 'I have a lot to attend to on the domestic front which has suffered due to my heavy political preoccupation … I am also one of those who like to pack up after some time and relax by playing golf and being with one's family.'[3]

Family for him has always come first and always will. Yet, inevitably, there was no denying that when Kashmir was at its worst, Farooq's family was affected. His children were young in the late 1980s, and they were often upset by the blaring of the pro-azaadi messages at the mosque Farooq had had built just below his house on Gupkar Road. With the atmosphere being what it was, he eventually decided to send them to school outside the state (to Himachal Pradesh). It was a course of action that Paran and I would follow with our son and daughter as well. But my point in all of this is that in return for Farooq's constant efforts to do his best for his family, Mollie has been his anchor. I don't think anyone else would have suited Farooq in quite the same way.

Theirs was a simple existence. In maintaining the mundanity of the everyday, it helped that Mollie was totally apolitical. She hadn't wanted to come out to Kashmir so soon after their marriage, and for as long as I knew her in the early days, she stayed in the background, busying herself at the nearby hospital on Gupkar Road. She was shy and quiet and though she never took interest in politics, if she needed to accompany the chief minister somewhere, she would. Not that she went with any great amount of joy. Her first priority was always her work and her family, and she would often say to me, 'Politics doesn't interest me so much. This fellow drags me all over the place.'

'Madam, you're the chief minister's wife,' I would tell her. 'You have to go.'

'Yes,' she would agree morosely. 'That's why I do go.'

Now that I look back over the years, I understand that it was Mollie's practicality and her matter-of-factness that kept the Abdullahs grounded. They needed someone like her: calm and pleasant and down to earth. Politics in India, as you know, is a heady business, and in Kashmir, there's always an edge of danger to it. But with Mollie around, Farooq found it easy to be himself, while never getting swept away by the euphoria of it all. In return, I noticed that Mollie always kept a step behind Farooq whenever they were touring together. It was, I felt, a tacit acknowledgement that in a public and political setting, Farooq was the leader. Mollie might be the leader at home, but out here, among the Kashmiri people, he was the figure of authority. No doubt she enjoyed being the chief minister's wife, but she left Srinagar in 1990 when things went out of control. It had become too much for her and she told her husband that it was no place for their girls to go to school. (Omar was already in college in Bombay.) First she spent some time in Delhi, at her mother-in-law's house in Safdarjung Lane; then she left for England.

Mollie has not changed since that time. As Khalida told me in the summer of 2024, 'Mollie is the most admired in the family. She's the most selfless, having given Farooq a kidney. But Farooq? He's the most lovable!'

Today, after all these years, Mollie comes to Kashmir for the winter even now, and goes to England for the summer. The trammelling of politics has not changed her. She remains simple and without frills. She has never wanted anything more than she has, though I know of plenty of chief ministers' wives who would have automatically wanted more. That's human nature, after all.

But not Mollie.

She has always loved England as much as she loves Kashmir, and one of her favourite places remains her little home in Southend-on-Sea in Essex. She has never questioned Farooq's desire to be present in Kashmir, to be present in politics. In fact, she has made it a point to be there for her husband and their children. In 2020, she returned to England only after Omar and Farooq were released. Only then did she consider her duty done. But for herself, she doesn't like too much pomp and ceremony. I remember when Delhi was trying to get back to Doctor Sahib, and he came to Delhi after his release in July 2020, his pretext was that he had come to see off Mollie, who was then on her way back to England. The national security advisor Ajit Doval knew of Mollie's plans, and he helped them with her passage, with the bandobast of details. She wasn't too happy about it.

Mollie isn't a bandobast person. She's very much her own person, happy with her routines and quiet ways. Even now, when I met her at Omar's swearing-in ceremony in October 2024, she was here only for the winter.

'Madam, I might need a favour from you,' I told her.

With a little smile, Mollie said, 'I make no promises, but as they say here, Inshallah.'

That's Mollie for you.

In the early days of my time in Kashmir, Paran in particular became good friends with Mollie, and they spent a lot of time together while I was at work. Paran had no friends in Srinagar, so who better than the chief minister's wife? As they got to know each other, it also helped me professionally. It was only after a few months into living in Kashmir that I understood just how caring Doctor Sahib could be. I wasn't feeling well at one point, running a slight fever. I had gone to see Farooq for some work, and he noticed that I wasn't looking too great.

'What's the matter?' he asked keenly.

'It's nothing,' I said, trying to brush it aside. 'But I haven't been feeling too well today.'

Immediately, his medical instincts kicked in. Farooq got up and came around his desk to where I was sitting and conducted a quick preliminary physical examination. Then, signalling to me to keep sitting, he called his brother-in-law, who was also a doctor, to come in with a specific prescription.

'Sir, you don't have to do that,' I protested.

'Don't be silly,' he said gruffly. 'Take these medicines and you'll be fine.'

The other time that Farooq helped me was when he helped my entire family. It so happened that my sister and her family had come to Kashmir to visit Paran and me. My son was also home for the holidays then and the kids were all in their college-going years. It was a rambunctious young crowd, and naturally, plans were made for fun and games. One night, the youngsters, including a few friends of Arjun's, who were staying with us, went to a party at Muzaffar Ali's place. Arjun had not gone out with them that night. In the manner of youngsters, four of them decided spontaneously to drive to Pahalgam after dinner. Close to Pampore they realized that Pahalgam was too far away and decided to turn back. There, the car spun out of control, turned turtle and my nephew, Aditya, bore the brunt of the accident.

Still being new to Srinagar, we didn't know who to turn to, until Paran walked across to Doctor Sahib's house to seek help from Mollie. Instead, she met Farooq at the gate, who told her not to worry, but to have Aditya transferred to the Soura Medical Institute – the equivalent of AIIMS in Srinagar – where doctors would take care of him. They did indeed, because Aditya, who had suffered a serious head injury, regained consciousness after two days and recovered thereafter.

Farooq offered his own helicopter to my sister to take Aditya to Delhi if she preferred, but Poma (my sister) said that she had full faith in the Kashmiri doctors in Soura. To this day, Poma has never forgotten that moment. To her mind, Farooq – among the skilled doctors and nurses at the hospital – was the man who saved her son's life. Doctor Sahib, too, has not forgotten Aditya, and enquires about him at every opportunity. He also attended Aditya's marriage some years later.

I have never forgotten that moment either. It was an example of how great this man is, and the kindness he is capable of. He really didn't have to go out of his way to help my family – but he did so, and he did it as a matter of course, rather than as a favour which required a reciprocal transaction. He showed the same kindness when I contracted COVID in 2021. It was luckily a mild attack, but my daughter insisted that I be admitted to hospital. I wasn't too happy about that, I can tell you, and created a bit of a ruckus. At her wits' end, Paran rang Farooq, 'Look at how your friend is behaving,' she said. 'Please speak to him!'

When he spoke to me, he said, 'Come along, you must focus on getting better. Between us and Allah, we'll have you out of there in no time.'

After that, he called me every day to find out how I was doing. It cost him nothing, but to me, it was a remarkable gesture – of faith and goodwill and simple humanity, from a man whom I had known for over three decades. Farooq has shown that faith in me too many times for me to count. He has come for every book launch I have had – whether it is in Delhi or in London. Indeed, he flew down to Delhi in May 2024 for the launch of my book, *Covert*, at the India International Centre (IIC). It was the day that Omar's constituency in Baramulla went to the polls for the parliamentary elections, and at first, I had been unsure that Farooq would come.

'No, no, of course, I'll come,' he reassured me. 'It is Omar's election. Ours in Srinagar is already over.'

It is in moments like these where I have seen what lies below the veneer of Farooq's political façade. He is, as I have said countless times, India's tallest politician – certainly its tallest Muslim leader. But in acts like these, I realize what Mehbooba's daughter, Iltija, meant when she told me that while she agreed that Farooq was the tallest leader, he was, she said, 'the nicest'.

The Chief Minister and the Spy

'Nice' is the mildest word you can use for a man like Farooq. He is a deeply complex man, with a peculiarly simple heart. He is known, like I said, to be unpredictable and imperious. You rarely know where you are with him. Yet, 'nice' is the most apt description of his nature. I have seen Farooq angry; I have seen him at his loneliest and most exhausted, particularly in the years after the abrogation. I have seen him excited like a child – like he was when he called me jubilantly after the NC carried the assembly elections in October 2024. I have seen him being cool and impatient, as well. But through it all, Farooq has never lost his streak of kindness, that innate humanity that characterizes the man. There is a depth to Farooq that many people – politicians and civilians alike – underestimate: a compassion that lies under the gruff exterior that I have seen not just towards myself but towards other people as well.

There was, I remember, the case of an officer who wanted a transfer to a particular station and had gone to Farooq with *sifarish*. When Farooq mentioned his case to me, I said, 'Sir, his case is not exactly deserving.'

'*Kar do*,' Farooq said. '*Mere paas do baar aaya hai.*' (Do it. He's come to me twice.)

You see, he found it extremely difficult to say no to anyone, and went out of his way to help whoever it was.

3

1984: The Coup

Let me go back to before my time in the state, to tell you the saga of the coup that was engineered to unseat Farooq in 1984, and the disastrous fallout of this act on Delhi's part. I thought it well to write about it, for you cannot fully comprehend the political legend that is Farooq Abdullah without the coup of 1984.

B.K. Nehru had refused to do it. That's why Jagmohan was brought in as the hatchet man to dismiss Farooq on 2 July 1984. Always referred to simply by his first name 'Jagmohan' – few were aware of his surname 'Malhotra' – the bespectacled, capable but combative civil servant was known for his shrewdness. It was under his tenure as governor of Jammu and Kashmir that the authority of the Centre was indelibly stamped on Kashmir.

That is why, in the preface of his book on the subject, *My Dismissal*,[1] written with Sati Sahni and published in 1985, Farooq said that he wanted to set the record straight. More importantly, he said, he had written the book to inform his fellow countrymen of what Farooq Abdullah was all about. For him, this dismissal was both political and personal – and at each level, it was a betrayal.

It was a blow from a group of legislators who hadn't ever got used to the fact that they had been denied ministerial berths – and who had, in turn, been promised these coveted jobs by Farooq's estranged brother-in-law, Gul Mohammad Shah. In the process, Farooq's own 46-member legislature party had been reduced to a minority group of 34 in the 78-member house. As the conspiracy began spiralling out of control, Shah was in the driver's seat with the support of 26 Congress (I) members.

Those were the political dynamics of it.

At a deeper, more personal level, it was the last and most spectacular round in a long-running family feud, which had begun in the last year of Sheikh Abdullah's life. Farooq had won the first round in 1981, when the Sheikh appointed him as the president of the party. And his mother, the Begum, wholly supported him after his father's death. In 1984, it was clearly Shah's turn.

Farooq threw in his lot with young leaders as soon as he took over. He made it clear that he needed to replace the old with the young. 'I will induce a larger number of youth to join me in the organizational set-up,' he said. The party's old guard did not take the statement kindly, particularly the band of old loyalists who owed allegiance to Farooq's brother-in-law.

1984: The Coup

The coup was hence born from the breast of Gul Mohammad Shah, who had consolidated his hold over the party network in the six years during which the Sheikh Abdullah government was in power following the Indira–Sheikh Accord of 1975. He had shadowed the Sheikh closely, and in the eyes of the NC workers, he was the Sheikh's natural successor. Farooq's return to Kashmir had dashed the hopes of many of these men, but the question of who would take on the Sheikh's mantle was still an open one in those days. After all, the Sheikh had occasionally hinted that his daughter Khalida's husband would be a better fit for the chair. Perhaps he did it to preserve peace in the household; perhaps he didn't think his son was ready as yet. We will never know.

It was not an easy time for Farooq in those days. Apart from wrangling within the party, Farooq faced an imminent threat from the dominant Opposition party in the state: the Congress. It was in power at the Centre and virtually controlled the political process in the Valley. He had been back only a short time from England, but Farooq was also aware that though the Abdullahs needed the Congress's support to stay in power, the grand old party could not be trusted fully. It was a learning curve for Farooq, and the beginning of Delhi's uncertainty about the Sheikh's son and heir. Time and again, Delhi would try to bury the hatchet with Farooq – and sooner than later, hostility would again bubble up from below the surface.

Farooq, even then, showed quite publicly that he was not his father. He didn't want confrontation with the Centre; he wanted to try and work with it. At a huge rally on 21 August 1984, as crowds turned hostile and began chanting, 'Where is Congress? Where is Congress?' Farooq intervened quickly. 'I am totally for conciliation and not for confrontation with the Centre and all others. Confrontation leads to destruction as was witnessed in 1947 when India and Pakistan confronted each other.'

He reminded the crowds that despite constant strains in ties, there had always been a personal and historic connection between the Abdullah and Gandhi families. 'Rajiv Gandhi telephoned me and wished me well. You know, there has been a lifelong relationship between Pandit Nehru and my father, and also with the late Feroze Gandhi and Mrs Gandhi. I want to further my friendship on a similar pattern with Rajiv.' His most dramatic exclamation came at the end of this speech, when he turned towards the old Sheikh and declared, 'I will not be your son if I do not shake all of India.' After that, it was not surprising that Sheikh Abdullah should have chosen Farooq to be his heir. A helping hand, of course, was given by Indira (as explained elsewhere in the book). But Indira's persuasion only served to seal what the Sheikh was already thinking.

The choice of Farooq angered Shah, who had long believed that the chief minister's chair was his for the taking. Looking back at the two men, they couldn't have been more different. Shah was hot-headed, stubborn and arrogant, a man consumed by the virtues of his own ideas and principles, guided by an unrelenting sense of his own self-importance.

1984: The Coup

Some said, 'His background led him to feel that he was indispensable to the Sheikh. He was obsessed by the idea that he should be acknowledged as the chief minister of the state.' Others said, 'He is a man of principle who will not compromise where he sees it is not in the interest of his people.'

A profile in *India Today* by veteran journalist Suman Dubey described Shah as having a 'leaden public image'.[2] Short and stocky, with his eyes always shaded behind heavily tinted glasses, Shah was impatient and vigorous. He was rarely charming, though his oratory could move crowds. 'Shah's tantrums are legendary,' Dubey wrote. 'He has physically manhandled people – a school teacher here, a bus conductor there, a junior police official or an executive engineer, to name some recent cases – situations which were saved only by the Sheikh's personal intervention …' The controversies birthed the image of an unpleasant person who lacked mass political and popular appeal. 'Essentially, he is an organisation man, and has spent his energies honing the NC according to his lights, raising funds for the party and building a base in the legislature party … he rules with a heavy hand, is intolerant of disagreement and is generally kept at a distance by one and all.'

Farooq's image, on the other hand, was almost a polar opposite. He was seen as merely affable, charming and humorous. His supporters say this was due to Shah's interference in the party which reduced Farooq to a *'darkhast* president' – simply forwarding petitions to the government.

He sang ghazals melodiously and loved a good game of golf. 'I'll try and play golf every day to keep alive,' he said on his way to attend office on his second day as health minister.

Those were the days of Farooq being known as the 'disco chief minister'. His critics were quick to portray him as a frippery fellow, more interested in glamorous film actresses – Shabana Azmi and Rekha being a few that come to mind! All of this only heightened whispers that here was a playboy masquerading as a chief minister. Farooq, in his characteristic way, didn't give a damn. He seemed, on the other hand, to mischievously revel in it. *Let them say what they want to say*, this was always his attitude to life. Unlike other politicians, he has never hidden that part of himself. His life, as it were, has been an open book. Yet, to look at Farooq casually, to read the legends that exist about him in the public domain, is to dismiss his great legacy.

Farooq himself is inured to public scrutiny. 'The first rule for a First Family is to understand this: public scrutiny of how you walk, live, talk and dress will happen every day. And so, like the Kennedys (Jackie's style), the Thatchers (Dennis's drinking) and the Gandhis (Sonia's Italian connections), it must be endured. The second rule, therefore, follows: zip your mouth, seal your lips, be tolerant of the inquisitive and the jealous,' he said once, in his inimitable style.

Star & Style, in its 16 March 1984 issue, in the column 'Frankly Speaking' by the late Devyani Chaubal, described him thus: 'Farooq Abdullah, Chief Minister of Jammu and Kashmir, stretched out on the sofa of the Rajput suite at the

1984: The Coup

Taj Hotel discussed outdoor shootings in Kashmir, Rajesh–Dimple's impending divorce, *Filmfare* awards, and wondered why there were no awards for Chief Ministers. Then he discussed women, the "difficult" ones, those who he said are difficult for nine days, to finally give in on the tenth day, etc. And all this after he had spent his only night in Bombay with Goldie Anand till 2 a.m. ...'[3]

This was silly journalism, the kind that brings down politicians' approval ratings in a jiffy. Another example was the March 1984 issue of the *Onlooker*, which showed Farooq sitting cosily with actor Dev Anand and three starlets. The photograph was reprinted, without any explanation, by a local newspaper. This kind of sensationalism did Farooq no good in the eyes of his electorate. When he began dancing with the television personality Hasina Akhtar at a dinner for 650 travel agents at his official residence, the media picked it up instantly.[4]

The most famous incident, of course, relates to the film actress Shabana Azmi. Farooq had gone up to Gulmarg on his motorcycle – here again, the bike was a point of raised eyebrows. Chief ministers in India do not customarily zip around on bikes. Ostensibly, Farooq had gone to do a flying check on the local administration. It was one of his quirks – he liked to carry out these checks randomly, for he felt that if he followed protocol and let an entire chain of authority – from the deputy commissioner to the superintendent of police onwards – know that he was coming, he would never really know the truth of how things were being done in his state.

The Chief Minister and the Spy

According to his biographer, Aditya Sinha, Farooq's random check led him to the swanky Highland Park Hotel for tea. Since the hotel belonged to his uncle, his having tea there was nothing unusual. But while he was there, he ran into V.V. Purie, Aroon Purie's father, and Shabana Azmi, who was shooting for a film in Gulmarg. When she met Farooq, she jokingly remarked that though she had been on many motorcycles, she had never yet ridden pillion behind a chief minister. Naturally, that was enough for Farooq. His instinctive charm asserted itself. 'It's the chief minister's duty to serve the people,' he remarked, telling her that he'd be glad to give her a ride. And so, off they went to the Golf Club. Purie took a photograph of the two – but though he told Farooq it was for his personal collection, that same photograph soon appeared in *India Today*.[5] Farooq's detractors were livid. From here, it was a short step to real viciousness.

Dilshad Shaikh, the widow of his dearest friend, Javed, and the sister of film actors Feroz and Sanjay Khan, has been a good friend of Farooq's, and remembers him endearingly today. She says that Farooq is a 'darling of a man, a gem of a human being. Nobody can doubt the purity of his soul.' According to her, all of Kashmir has nothing but love for him. In Charlie Chaplin's words, you need power only when you want to do something harmful. Otherwise, love is enough to get it done. What Dilshad said reminded me of that saying. Incidentally, Dilshad always loved Farooq but was never *in love* with him.

1984: The Coup

With age, the boy in the chief minister who offered Shabana Azmi a lift on his motorcycle in Gulmarg is beginning to fade, if not tire. Doctor Sahib's younger sister Suraiya, not having witnessed his intensity from close quarters, maintains that Farooq knows more than anyone else, but the disco chief minister was not always so serious.

He was no great public speaker in those days, having only recently started speaking at meetings in Kashmiri and Urdu. But there was an indefinably regal air about him. Those who looked upon him saw the Sheikh in his bearing. Farooq has always found it easy to make friends and influence people. But in those days, even his most ardent supporters murmured anxiously about how it would be a long time before he made the cut as a politician. Despite his occasionally brow-raising behaviour, he was likeable, open and fresh, but could he be the shrewd political chess master that Kashmir required? As Thakur Baldev Singh, then the president of the Bharatiya Janata Party (BJP) and an MLA from Hiranagar, put it, 'Experience is a good school, but the fee is very, very heavy.'

Just how heavy it could be was something Farooq would learn in the years to come. But as the Sheikh watched his son, he probably realized that here was a young man who might – with proper training and direction – become more acceptable to Delhi. Farooq had the edge of novelty helped by a natural charisma and his willingness to be flexible with the Centre. In fact, that is an attribute that has persisted, I think, over the years. I see Farooq as the last of the real giants among politicians. Here is a man who has stayed true to the Nehruvian way of doing things: of living his life, yet serving his people. Of loving his state, but having a deep curiosity for the rest of the world and its ways. Of listening and encouraging multiple points of view – and still doing his own thing. Any opponent to Farooq must present a style and vision that is larger than his – and that is a difficult task to do.

G.M. Shah, his brother-in-law, a veteran of the days when the Sheikh was in favour of plebiscite to determine the state's future, undoubtedly failed to endear himself to New Delhi when he spoke about the controversial Resettlement Bill enacted by the state assembly to permit genuine state subjects settled in Pakistan to return to their ancestral homes and lands in Kashmir. Farooq, in contrast, was already trying to build bridges with New Delhi. This was apparent when he was at the forefront of the mourners who brought Sanjay Gandhi's ashes to immerse in the Jhelum in 1980.

Just as the Sheikh had had close ties with Nehru and Mrs Gandhi, Farooq was a regular visitor to 1 Safdarjung Road, and a confessed admirer of Rajiv Gandhi. If anyone was wondering about his political shrewdness, it became apparent in the way he declined to follow Shah's lead and discuss the Resettlement Bill. In his unspoken opinion, that was an issue best left undisturbed, and it underlined his need for good relations between the Centre and the state. Indeed, one of Shah's reservations about Farooq was that he might be too soft in Centre–state questions, to the state's detriment. That, in my eyes, was never an issue with Farooq. His motive

1984: The Coup

from the start was to disarm any hostility that the Centre might have for Kashmir. After all, Jammu and Kashmir is no ordinary state. It has a historical importance that has to be understood and respected when its leaders reach out to Delhi. Even today, these issues are relevant, for in India, history is never a dead subject. In that context, Kashmir's accession to India has constantly been questioned by Pakistan; its territory acrimoniously divided; its emotional integration with the rest of the country remains less than desirable; and it reverberates with parochial problems of community, language and region that seem to be barely under control.

Aside from all of this, however, Shah was Khalida's husband. For Farooq, family was always apart from political dynamics. Perhaps that's why he never saw the coup coming – and also why, over the years, he has put it aside completely. For him, family is paramount.

The planning for the coup began on 28 June 1984, when a group of potential deserters gathered furtively in the rooms of the newly opened five-star Centaur Hotel in Srinagar on the eve of Eid. The venue and timing were significant: a gathering of this kind would not be unusual, considering that it was Eid. To further camouflage their intentions, the dissidents went and greeted an unsuspecting Farooq before getting down to business. That very day, a letter was drafted and signed by 10 of the 12 MLAs, informing the governor of their decision to withdraw support to the NC.

The Chief Minister and the Spy

Earlier, on 23 June, Mufti Mohammed Sayeed, the state Congress (I) chief, had been summoned to Delhi and ordered to support a dissident government headed by Shah – should it come into being. With the ball set in motion, the dissidents were taken in three groups to different hideouts in the city by Shah's 28-year-old son, Muzaffer, while Shah closeted himself at home and his top advisors D.D. Thakur and M.N. Kochak – both former ministers in the Sheikh's cabinet – went off to Pahalgam, ostensibly on a fishing holiday.

The unsuspecting chief minister, meanwhile, played a leisurely round of golf on Eid, and on 1 July, when the drama behind the scenes was reaching its climax, he had driven out of Srinagar, to personally take some timber smugglers by surprise!

On the evening of 1 July, the conspirators assembled at the home of a friendly industrialist, from where at a quarter past 11 at night, Shah telephoned the governor, Jagmohan, to let him know that he would bring over the 12 MLAs who had withdrawn support from Farooq. He was advised to wait until dawn; what Jagmohan really wanted to do was to consult with the Centre as to his next moves.

Clearly, Jagmohan got the green light.

Instructions from Delhi were to swear in Gul Mohammad Shah, even though Jagmohan himself was in favour of Governor's Rule. Within the next six hours, he acted swiftly. Requisitioning over 2,000 soldiers from the Border Security Force (BSF), the CRPF and other paramilitary units, he even alerted the Indian army. The efficient dispatch of forces, from places as far away as Madhya Pradesh, was evidence enough that Delhi was taking more than a routine interest in Jammu and Kashmir's internal security. In fact, Indian Airlines was obliging enough to disrupt its commercial schedules to ferry troops into Srinagar on four Airbuses and two Boeings. The entire incident was reminiscent of yet another topple, three decades ago, when the Sheikh had been arrested in 1953.

The next morning, while Farooq sipped a cup of tea with Mollie, Shah and the rest of the defectors sped up the drive of Raj Bhavan in a convoy of four cars. It was not even 6 a.m., and the BSF had already arrived, taking up strategic positions across Srinagar. Jagmohan had taken the precaution of requesting Lt Gen. Hoon, then the corps commander of the Indian army in Kashmir, to be available for consultation. Another letter, confirming withdrawal of support, was quickly written and signed in Jagmohan's presence. Maulvi Iftikhar Hussain Ansari, leader of the 26-member Congress (I) group, also arrived and handed over another letter assuring his party's unconditional support to Shah.

At a quarter past seven in the morning, Jagmohan summoned Farooq and handed him a letter, which read, 'Thirteen MLAs of the Legislative Assembly of Jammu & Kashmir have approached me in person this morning. They told me and have given in writing that they have withdrawn their support to your government and pledge their support to G.M. Shah, MLC ... I am satisfied that you no longer enjoy the majority support of the Assembly and have, therefore, forfeited the right to continue as chief minister and to head the Government. I, therefore, regret to inform you that I have dismissed you from the chief ministership of the state and dissolved the council of ministers headed by you.'

Dumbfounded, Farooq looked around the room. His eye fell on Ghulam Mohammed Shah. According to the journalist Prabhu Chawla, who wrote about that fateful morning in *India Today*, he thumped the table angrily, telling Jagmohan, 'Do what you like but don't let that man become chief minister,' gesturing in Shah's direction. Despite his impetuous anger, Farooq remained ever alert to what his state needed. Two hours later, he sent Jagmohan a long letter advising him to call the assembly so that he could prove his majority. In the letter, Farooq maintained that the 13 defectors had lost the right to vote. He asserted: 'I, therefore, reiterate that the Assembly be summoned forthwith so that on my failure to demonstrate confidence of the House, we can next consider the options available to us under the Constitution of the state. If, however, you do not want to conform to this democratic method, I on behalf of my cabinet would request you to accept our advice of dissolving the Legislative Assembly so that we can go back to our people.'

Naturally, this did not happen, but Farooq had put on record his willingness to play by the rules, even if the rules had the tendency to change at lightning speed.

With the split in the NC providing a cover, no one in the Congress (I) was willing to admit to Delhi's hand in this particular toppling operation. Yet it was clear that the high command had acted for a variety of reasons.

1984: The Coup

Farooq had never wanted a confrontation with the Centre. He had wanted to be a bridge between Srinagar and Delhi. Like his father before him, Farooq had been able to provide a stable government with the solid backing of 46 members in the 78-member state assembly. He wanted to ensure that his state remained on the right side of Delhi. His father had taught him always to keep the idea of India alive. He had told me once, 'The nation, the *country*, is what is important. Communalism is the monster that is ruining the country.' It is an ideal that he has always lived by.

Yet again, it comes back to the fact that Delhi has never really understood Farooq Abdullah or his ideals. This is a sad truth despite the fact that the relationship between the Abdullahs and the Nehrus goes back to the 1930s, to the days of the Sheikh and Panditji. For his part, Farooq had always tried to maintain that special bond. When Mrs Gandhi was defeated in the general elections of 1977 and came to Kashmir to seek his father's advice, Farooq had taken her around the state personally. In that brief space of time, Nehru's daughter had seen the potential in the Sheikh's son. It was Indira who had pushed for Farooq to become the Sheikh's successor, to become Kashmir's young chief minister. Naturally, then, between the two of them, there was always a special relationship, a family relationship.

The questions of India, Delhi and politics were the ones that stood between the two of them. In 1974, Farooq had visited Pakistan-occupied Kashmir (PoK) in order to understand it better. He would go on to write that pro-

Pakistan elements had always existed in the region since 1947. After his dismissal in 1984, his frustration led him to Punjab. Here, his meeting with controversial preacher Jarnail Singh Bhindranwale led to allegations that Farooq was a Khalistan supporter. Much was made of the meeting and he was accused of supporting Sikh separatism, even as the Akalis and Sant Longowal, who would later sign an accord with Rajiv Gandhi, thought he had come as an emissary of Mrs Gandhi.

Farooq was always pro-dialogue. When he visited Delhi, he spoke to Mrs Gandhi about his talks with Sikh leaders and pleaded with her that these talks should continue. Farooq also met the leaders of the All India Sikh Students' Federation (AISSF), though only local issues were discussed, not Punjab politics. A lot has been made of his contacts with the AISSF leaders, but truth be told, Farooq always had good relations with Sikhs, including their student leaders who brought their demands to him. He was charged with not taking any action against Sikh extremists. He never accepted Khalistan; in his mind, a high number of Sikhs were reasonable and highly patriotic. They were not Khalistani or Pakistani, but Indian.

Faced with criticism, Farooq forcefully denied any collusion between Sikh extremists and the Jammu and Kashmir government. Even so, Delhi's only agenda was to paint him as antinationalist, pro-Pakistan and pro-Khalistan, to buttress the case for his dismissal. The Congress calls itself a secular organization, but there have always been people in the party who thought communally.

1984: The Coup

Post-1980, Mrs Gandhi had become Brahmanical and pro-Hindu, thanks to the coterie around her. The great divide between the Congress and Mrs Gandhi on one side, and Farooq and the people of Kashmir on the other, had begun in 1983. During the upcoming elections of that time, the Congress had wanted to ally with the NC. Farooq had refused. His reason was that the NC should retain its own Kashmiri identity, in keeping with his father's values. But the Congress in Kashmir has long been known for its tricks. The Gandhis are friends and continue to be so, but their politics has often been difficult and offensive. The Resettlement Bill – passed during the Sheikh's day and age – was what created the initial misunderstandings between them. Introduced on 8 March 1980, the bill became a law in April 1982, when the state legislative assembly passed it. B.K. Nehru returned the bill on 18 September 1982, seeking 'reconsideration'.

A handful of days later, on 4 October 1982, both houses passed it without any change. Though the governor gave his mandatory assent to the bill on 6 October 1982, the legislation had been sent on 30 September 1982 for a Presidential Reference to the Supreme Court, under the provisions of Article 142 (1) of the Constitution by the then President Giani Zail Singh. The idea was to seek the Court's opinion 'as to whether the bill or any of the provision thereof, if enacted, would be constitutionally invalid'.

Anyway, the refusal to ally with the Congress was the domino that began the great fall.

The second issue was Farooq's cabinet. To start with a clean slate, he had dropped some of the ministers from Sheikh's cabinet. What was more, he did not oblige his sister, Khalida, and his brother-in-law G.M. Shah to include their cronies in the cabinet. Despite standing firm, he still had to give in to family somewhat – inducting some friends of Shah's, who ultimately proved to be liabilities when they defected.

Then there was his friendship with the Mirwaiz Maulvi Farooq, leader of the Awami Action Committee, whose politics had long been suspect in New Delhi's eyes. With that, Farooq ended more than 50 years of *sher–bakra* enmity in the city, but he was accused of tying up with a communal party by doing so. Strange – when Congress approached the Maulvi, he was termed a nationalist, but when he befriended Farooq, he was a separatist and a secessionist.

In the aftermath of this division in 1983, Farooq was accused of rigging the elections, which the NC won hands down. With his customary insouciance, Farooq told Jyoti Basu, 'Rigging may have happened in one or two seats. What's all the noise about?'

Truth be told, the Congress – led by Mrs Gandhi – was unwilling to live with rival centres of power in Jammu and Kashmir. It didn't help that the small coterie of people surrounding the prime minister didn't allow Farooq to build the bridges he wanted to. In those days, the principal actors within the Congress who wanted Farooq's dismissal were Arun Nehru, M.N. Fotedar, Ghulam Nabi Azad and Mufti Mohammad Sayeed. This cast was presided over and

1984: The Coup

directed by Mrs Gandhi. The same cast, albeit minus Mrs Gandhi, was responsible for Farooq's removal, once again, in 1990. Jagmohan was the convenient pliable instrument in both the cases.

In 1984, the transfer of B.K. Nehru should have been a clear signal to Farooq that the days of his government were numbered. But he was still naïve in politics.

If Delhi had been feeling a natural and normal process of loss of faith in his government, it need not have been done in the darkness of night, as the *Guardian* would report it to be, treating Kashmir as the colony which Delhi would have to pay for one day. The deal *had* to be done in the dead of night, simply for the fear that it might come unstuck.

Jagmohan had come to Kashmir with the reputation of being a 'fixer' for the Congress. Mrs Gandhi used all her might, devious methods and money to defeat Farooq. The Congress contrived, planned and executed this conspiracy, giving support to a minority government. But it could not escape the fact that Farooq's efforts being nationally recognized had yielded him handsome dividends. He received solid support from the entire national Opposition.

In a meeting in Delhi on 11 July, the Opposition expressed solidarity with Kashmir. In a letter to Farooq, it said, 'Your leadership and conduct have made an immense contribution to national integration.' Among others, this letter was signed by Jyoti Basu and Atal Behari Vajpayee. Even the BJP, to which Farooq was anathema, adopted a resolution condemning Jagmohan for imposing a 'rump government' on the state. In another unprecedented move, BJP president Vajpayee moved a resolution in the Ministry of Home Affairs' (MHA) parliamentary consultative committee meeting, demanding Jagmohan's recall. The West Bengal cabinet was furious about the installation of a government of 'stooges and defectors'. The constituents of the United Front dispatched a six-member delegation including, among others, I.K. Gujral and West Bengal finance minister, Ashok Mitra, to Srinagar to convey to Farooq their unequivocal and total support.

But the damage had been done.

Delhi was gleeful. It had split the formidable Sheikh family, winning Khalida, G.M. Shah and Tariq Abdullah to its side. Many questions were raised about the role played by the old Begum. It was said that she was anti-Mrs Gandhi. But that's preposterous to even consider. Under the circumstances, all she could do as a mother was to stand by her son, her daughter and her son in-law. But even if Delhi had not tried this tactic, it would have succeeded some other way. Mrs Gandhi was hell-bent on it.

After his dismissal, fearing a backlash, the authorities moved in with an indefinite curfew to keep irate and potentially violent mobs indoors. Farooq himself stayed indoors for the first 24 hours, fearing that his presence might worsen things. Even so, over 2,000 people spurned curfew restrictions to crowd at the gates of Farooq's residence and express solidarity with the deposed leader. Seeing the support for him, Farooq remarked, with typical sarcasm, 'Here is a

1984: The Coup

chief minister who can't move without gun-toting cops in a city which he claims is his.'

On 5 July, Farooq addressed a huge rally in Mujahid Manzil, the NC's double-storeyed wooden office in old Srinagar. 'We are not alone in this hour of grief of the Kashmiri people,' He roared. 'We have the entire nation behind us.' Accompanied by his mother, Farooq roamed through the Valley in his Matador. At her first public meeting in Pampore, a tiny hamlet 11 kilometres from Srinagar, the Begum declared: 'Nobody can rule over you from outside. The Congress (I) has been able to instal a puppet government with a few *quami gaddars* [traitors] but their rule will not last long.'

That might have been true, but the entire incident left a scar on Farooq's psyche that has never fully healed. For him, his dismissal was the betrayal of a lifetime – not only was he betrayed by Indira Gandhi, but he was betrayed from within his family.

I don't think he has ever recovered from that.

Nor do I think he ever will.

4

Conversations and Confidences

In 1990, things were going badly in Kashmir.

The IB's sources were dry – non-existent. Nobody would talk to us. Jammu and Kashmir was on fire – and Pakistan was enjoying the spectacle. I may have been thrilled to get the hell out of there, but I knew the Valley was in trouble. The scent of *azaadi* was fresh in the air. I've written about this in *The Vajpayee Years*:[1] that insurgency in Kashmir, in the 1990s, was masterminded by General Zia ul-Haq and his men. It was revenge for Bangladesh. The bait that was cast for Kashmiris was simple: if they began something big enough, the Pakistani army would come to liberate them from India. Kashmiris swallowed it, hook, line and sinker and began crossing the border in droves.

After my Kashmir posting, I was in Delhi, posted to counter-intelligence.

Delhi had changed under V.P. Singh's short-lived government – and so had IB headquarters. Farooq had left

The Chief Minister and the Spy

Srinagar too, and had come to the capital on his way to London. He would leave for England in April 1990, but as long as he was in Delhi, we continued to meet and talk. He was staying at 9 Safdarjung Lane, in the house allotted to his mother, Begum Abdullah. We enjoyed our meetings in these surroundings, which were free from pressure. These were the days when our friendship really took root, and when both of us seemed to realize that this was a bond worth nurturing. I had known Doctor Sahib all of two years at this point, and in some very difficult circumstances. Yet, the bond was already developing into a strong one.

From what I had seen of him, in the last two years of my service in Srinagar, Farooq was a staunch nationalist, particularly when issues of national security were involved. Many people have doubted Farooq, even prime ministers such as Narasimha Rao and Vajpayee, but I have known that of all Kashmiris, Farooq is the one Kashmiri who was always there for India. He has said time and time again that Kashmir's accession to India is final and irrevocable, the only Kashmiri to do so. It is a pity that that steadfast support has been battered time and again over the years.

In those transient months of 1990, nobody really came to visit Farooq, apart from myself and a couple of other people. I would meet Maulvi Iftikhar Ansari and Professor Riyaz Punjabi there frequently. Other than them, there was only the ubiquitous Rashid Baba, Farooq's Man Friday, putting on the lights in the evening.

Nobody else.

That's how it is when you fall out of power as a political leader – nobody really cares. Farooq, as I recall, was not upset at the turn that events had taken. He was quite calm, steady in his belief that this was as it should be. But we continued to meet and I continued to encourage him on the subject of Kashmir. Sometimes Dr Saifuddin Soz would also be present. One evening, we were at dinner at Sagar Suri's house on Tilak Marg. It was a small gathering, and as I recall, among the guests were myself, Farooq and Soz.

Soz was a strange character: he would never look anyone in the eye when he spoke and instead direct his gaze at a point just above one's head. I instinctively didn't trust him, and rarely went out of my way to organize meetings with him. But Rajiv was close to Soz, and since the man was an English-speaking professor, the prime minister found it easier to chat to Soz than to Farooq.

It was irritating for Farooq, and though he never said a word, I could see that Rajiv's actions were beginning to affect his relationship with Farooq. Like I said, Farooq had, even when his father was alive, tried to show that he was open to not just talking to Delhi, but working with Delhi. I still recall that the two families, the Abdullahs and the Gandhis, went on a holiday together to snowbound Gulmarg once the Rajiv–Farooq accord had been signed. It was a visit that gave media mills much grist. The optics were great, of course: both men were young, English-speaking, said to be great friends and had attractive foreign wives. A big reason their relationship worked is that M.K. Narayanan went out

The Chief Minister and the Spy

of his way to make this happen, and Narayanan, as you might recall, got on excellently with both prime minister and chief minister. But with Soz's continuous presence on the scene, even after the accord, Farooq never got time with Rajiv – or, should I say, he never got enough time.

Farooq didn't seem to mind either. He, too, was close to Soz in those days, for reasons beyond my understanding. Nevertheless, for the people of Kashmir, it was hardly flattering that while Rajiv seemed to have little to no time for Farooq, he seemed to have plenty of time for Soz. For the IB also, it was not really helpful, particularly since the Srinagar desk's brief was to stay close to Farooq. Here, then, was the prime minister, who was talking to Soz instead!

Farooq, unsurprisingly, was furious at this. I eventually mollified him – but it was beginning to seem to me that Delhi was giving Farooq a hell of a lot of reasons to require mollifying. Farooq was known to be volatile, but in this one respect, he had remained steady and constant. Yet Delhi didn't seem to understand him at all.

This was to become the core behind many of our interactions. It was, I suppose, a necessary and inevitable core, given my job and given his position in politics. Farooq could easily have treated me as Delhi's extended limb. After all, in many ways, the IB *is* the Centre's arm in Kashmir. Everyone knows that. But Farooq never treated me as anything more than a working professional in the early days. He knew what my brief was, but he never reminded me of it. The only maxim that he insisted on was that I always tell the truth to

Delhi, no matter how bitter it might be. In the same vein, if I represented Delhi's views to him, as was my job to do, he always listened, and though he might harrumph or snort, he usually came around to what I was telling him.

But in 1989–90, our dynamics were shaped not just by Delhi but by the rising bloodshed and violence across the Valley.

In the winter of 1990, Soz came to see me. He wanted my help to release a friend of his who was in jail. 'Please help him, he's a personal friend of mine,' Soz said. 'And he could be of use to you also.'

Now, Soz's friend was a prominent businessman, who will remain anonymous. He was one of those who were funding militancy – and from whom money was being extorted. There was plenty of that happening in Kashmir at the time. In fact, some of these business people with links across the border were pivotal in sponsoring terrorism. They were also oddly paradoxical, because it was these same people who would help us in our fight against militancy. They were easier to find and cultivate, at least as far as the IB was concerned, and we cultivated a nice little quid pro quo situation with them. Some of them came to us; some we heard about and approached on our own; some became friends quite organically. In this case, Soz's friend was in jail because Jagmohan, in his time in Kashmir, had gone after those he suspected of funding militancy in the Valley. It was this businessman who told me honestly, 'If Delhi is serious about a dialogue with Kashmiris, then Shabir [Shah] is the right person.'

Shabir would turn out to be the entirely wrong person, in fact – but that was much later. To return to Soz himself, I found myself at this dinner, trying to talk to Farooq and being constantly interrupted. Soz kept hinting broadly that Farooq needed to leave – he was due at Rajesh Pilot's home for another dinner. After a while, Farooq left with Soz, leaving me annoyed. Who the hell was Soz anyway, I fumed to myself.

The next day, when I met Farooq, I asked, 'How close is Soz to you, sir? How much do you trust him?'

Doctor Sahib eyed me. 'I trust him fully. Why? Don't you trust him?'

'No, sir. Soz Sahib never looks anyone in the eye. He looks above your head and it gives me a queasy feeling.'

It was a little more than that.

Soz was facilitating discreet dialogue between Kashmiri separatist leaders and the Government of India. The interesting thing here is that when the nineteen-day Vajpayee government collapsed in 1999, it was due to one vote: that of Saifuddin Soz. He voted with the Congress and against his own party, triggering government collapse. He would go on to join the Congress in 2003. Farooq called me the evening Soz voted with the Congress, 'Come here,' he said. 'I want to talk to you.'

When I got there, he was smiling, '*Tumhe yaad hai tum uss din keh rahe the, "do you trust Soz?" Theek keh rahe the, yeh toh haraami nikla. Ulta nikla!*' (Do you remember the other day you were asking me if I trusted Soz? You were right. He turned out to be a bad egg.)

'*Sir, yeh toh theek kiya usne, par aap usko kitna trust karte ho, woh alag hai!*' I laughed. (Sir, he's done the right thing in this case, but my question was how much do *you* trust him!)

Interestingly, Soz comes up again – during the abrogation of Article 370 in 2019. Farooq was cut up that the Congress had not joined the People's Alliance for Gupkar Declaration (PAGD). When the PAGD meetings were taking place, I decided to call Soz to find out where matters stood.

'*Soz Sahib, kya ho raha hai aaj kal?*' I asked. (Soz Sir, what is happening these days?)

'*Kuch nahi ho raha,*' he replied, a little petulantly. '*Koi poochhta hi nahi hai humko.*' (Nothing is happening. Nobody asks me anything.)

'*Aap Doctor Sahib se kyu nahi milte ho? Aap PAGD mein kyun nahi ho?*' (Why don't you meet Doctor Sahib? Why aren't you in the PAGD?)

'*PAGD toh party ka faisla hai.*' (That's the decision of the party.)

'But why don't you meet Doctor Sahib?' I insisted.

'*Mujhe yaad hi nahi karte,*' Soz said. '*Bulaate hi nahi.*' (He doesn't remember me. He doesn't call me.)

The next time I telephoned Farooq, I told him that Soz had complained that Farooq never took any notice of him.

'He's not worth taking any notice of,' snorted Farooq dismissively.

I smiled. The response was so typical of Doctor Sahib.

'*Sir, bula toh lo usko.* [Call him at least.] Call him for a cup of tea.'

Farooq agreed – but he never called Soz. Today, Soz is a spent force. It's a pity. I was never an admirer of Soz, but he was a person who was always very close to Farooq and the Congress, and could have been useful had the cards been properly played.

When I was meeting Farooq in 1990, there was never a time limit to our meetings, nor were they official in any capacity. They were long, meandering evenings, and sometimes when I stayed longer than I ought to have, I would take my evening walks within his compound. Through all of this, I was aware that the Valley needed Farooq to return. I didn't know when or how – but to my mind, that conviction must never leave Doctor Sahib. Once the V.P. Singh government fell, Mufti Sahib too started saying – not once but quite a few times – that Farooq was the only answer to Kashmir.

The IB knew that I was in touch with Farooq after his exit, because I constantly provided a stream of information to headquarters. DIB R.P. Joshi encouraged me to maintain contact. In fact, I was advised to speak to more people than Farooq, since it was assumed that I must know some people by now, though the fact was that, in those days at least, I knew nobody apart from Doctor Sahib. I was told: '*Ab tum toh Srinagar mein rahe ho.* [You have spent time in Srinagar.]

You're more contemporary. Why don't you talk to these fellows?'

Talking to 'these fellows' would become the principle with which I lived my life in Srinagar, and in that respect, I think Doctor Sahib and I shared that trait. We both believed far more in the power of dialogue than in the zap of a bullet. I might have got the hell out of there, but somehow Kashmir hadn't let go of me. I was still thinking about it, still thinking about ways to get Farooq back in the driver's seat. My short time in the state had shown me that despite the traits for which he was reprimanded or was notorious, Farooq was the one leader that Kashmir needed. The people responded to him, to the legacy of his father, and to the legacy of the NC. Even in the 1990s, the party was a shadow of itself without Farooq.

Luckily for me, in those days, the IB was helmed by a man who believed in the same things as I did. I liked R.P. Joshi. He had come to the bureau late, and as a result he wasn't like those of us who had been earmarked right at the beginning of our service. He had entered the IB at the level of deputy director. In itself, this was quite amazing, because the IB likes to nurture and encourage people from within the organization. But in Joshi's case, it gave him the advantage of having served in another field: the police. Combined with his experience was an innate honesty and directness, and an inclination to take a risk if he felt that it was the right thing to do. Joshi was a relaxed guy, but he was intelligent. He was aware of the fact that, after 1989, the IB's status in Kashmir had tanked – disastrous for an organization that already had a poor reputation in the state since the days of the Sheikh himself.

In response to this failure, Joshi advocated that Delhi continue talking to Srinagar, and that the IB continue building its presence in Kashmir. It was a policy of ongoing engagement and dialogue, despite some pretty heavy odds. I liked that model and the optimism that lay behind it. I've never believed in closing doors, especially if they are doors of communication. You can only move forward by talking to someone.

For myself, I had been transferred to counter-intelligence the minute I came back to Delhi, and truth be told, for most intelligence officers that would have been the end of their Kashmir experience. Meanwhile, the spike in militancy after Farooq's departure meant that Delhi was forced to call in the army to contain the violence. The Indian army was willing, but it would have been fighting blind if it hadn't been for the IB and the intelligence it was continuing to provide. I was a distant spectator to these events, and as the days passed, I watched as some militants were killed, some disappeared and others slipped over the border to Pakistan. The shifting grounds in Kashmir encouraged separatists like Shabir Shah and militants like Firdous Syed to come out of the shadows.

After Farooq left for London in the summer of 1990, I hardly had any interaction with him. But in Delhi, the process for getting the political system in the state up and running again never stopped. These are the wheels that keep turning in the background, the spinning of which goes unseen and unnoticed by those who are not in the know. Largely though, I focused for a few months on my work in counter-intelligence, which spanned countries from Pakistan to China. I enjoyed myself, but to be honest, the political atmosphere was such that Kashmir would never be on the back-burner.

Eventually, the political winds began to change in Delhi. V.P. Singh's government fell and Chandra Shekhar became the new prime minister with the support of the Congress party. One of his first actions was to bring Narayanan back as the director of the IB. As soon as that change was effected, Narayanan called for me. 'You've had enough of a holiday,' he told me genially. 'Now come back and do some serious work. I want you to come back and look after Kashmir again.'

That was how I returned, metaphorically speaking, to Kashmir.

I never left it again.

In December 1990, I was put in charge of the IB's Kashmir Operations Group, known jocularly as the K-Group. I was still in Delhi, but this posting was a milestone for me. For eight years, until I went across to the R&AW, I worked on nothing but Kashmir. I've written about this before, so I won't go into it again in too much detail, but in essence, there were three types of actors in Kashmir, in my observation. One type was on the periphery of the movement in Kashmir. They were, to put it simply, hangers-on: supporters and sympathizers but not active within the movement itself. The second type was the political prisoner. By early 1990, the former Muslim

United Front leaders who would later form the All Parties Hurriyat Conference, or the JKLF boys, were in different jails across the state. A captive audience, if you don't mind me saying so. The IB thus had the chance to establish contact with whomever it chose, which is how we began talking to Yasin Malik and Shabir Shah.

The third category consisted of the militants. This was a slightly more difficult group, for how do you get to some boys who are in the field, or underground? Simply put, the answer lay in nurturing and cultivating relationships. It's a difficult process, though it sounds easy enough.

With Shabir, it was a long and circuitous dialogue – ranging from topics like the futility of violence to an honourable peace. It would take a considerable amount of time before we could even begin speaking about some kind of settlement with India. In the case of Farooq, it was equally long, though of course the approach was very different. It was based on our existing friendship. But since he was away in London, the best I could do was to begin laying some kind of foundation on the basis of which he might be induced to return to the Valley.

Then, in 1991, Delhi changed yet again. After the collapse of governments headed by V.P. Singh and Chandra Shekhar, over 500 million voters were given the chance to elect another new government. These were difficult elections for many reasons, but primarily because the country was deeply polarized along religious and communal lines. The move to implement the recommendations of the Mandal Commission for 27 per cent reservation for the Other Backward Castes (OBCs) in government jobs led to protests across the country. Then, there was the Ram Mandir–Babri Masjid issue in Ayodhya, which had already sparked violence in the years before 1991. The BJP was using the Ram Mandir as its major election manifesto, while the ruling Janata Dal campaigned on the plank of implementing the Mandal Commission report. Then, a day after the first round of polling took place on 20 May, former Prime Minister Rajiv Gandhi was assassinated as he campaigned in Sriperumbudur.

His death brought the country to a halt – and changed India's political future forever. Freshly leaderless and shaken to the core, the Congress (I) reached out to P.V. Narasimha Rao. Previously denied a Lok Sabha ticket and having already packed his bags to return to Hyderabad, Rao was now the prime ministerial candidate. Backed by a wave of public sympathy and grief, the Congress (I) formed a minority government supported by the Janata Dal.

Change was in the air.

Narasimha Rao was a veteran at balancing people. In 1993, for instance, US Assistant Secretary of State Robin Raphel had questioned the finality of Jammu and Kashmir's accession to India; at the same time, Pakistan's permanent representative to the United Nations, Jamsheed K. A. Marker, told the General Assembly that the Kashmir dispute was an 'unfinished business of Partition'.[2] Both statements came during a high-profile stand-off between the army and JKLF militants at the Hazratbal shrine on the outskirts of Srinagar. Rao's brainwave was to send a delegation to Geneva headed by the leader of the opposition, Atal Behari Vajpayee. The delegation included Farooq.

Doctor Sahib's presence was despite the fact that the prime minister didn't necessarily see the Abdullahs as any kind of prime movers in the revival of democracy in Kashmir. He wanted to talk to all Kashmiris, and as I've written in *The Vajpayee Years*, he didn't mind if that included separatists or militants. As far as this delegation was concerned, the prime minister's main intention was that India must present a united front to the world on Kashmir.

Of course, the state was just one of the prime minister's concerns. India was staring down the barrel of an impending economic crisis. With Dr Manmohan Singh's able assistance, Rao brought in the economic liberalization reforms for which his administration is known today. He energized the national nuclear security and ballistic missiles programmes, which resulted in the Pokhran nuclear tests in 1998. His PMO authorized an increase in military expenditure, and set India on course to fight the emerging threats of insurgencies and terrorism. It was Rao who handled the Indian response to the occupation of the Hazratbal shrine in Jammu and Kashmir by terrorists in October 1993. He brought the occupation to an end without damage to the shrine. Similarly, he dealt with the kidnapping of foreign tourists by a terrorist group called Al Faran in Kashmir in 1995. Although he could not secure the release of the hostages, his policies ensured that the terrorists' demands were not conceded to, and that the action of the terrorists was condemned internationally, including by

Pakistan. Rao's term was hit by violence across India with the demolition of the Babri Masjid in 1992, and a massive corruption scandal (in the form of the stockbroker Harshad Mehta's actions).

In the middle of this extremely eventful tenure, Kashmir became Narasimha Rao's prime focus. By 1993, the government had pressed the accelerator on its policies toward the state. Militancy had been growing in the early 1990s, inspired by the Palestinian intifada and the Russian evacuation of Afghanistan. Rao began to feel that there was a need to make a change in Kashmir in the hope that the separatists might be brought into the political process. In the course of time, he also realized that Kashmir had had enough of Governor's Rule and elections were necessary. Unfortunately for Delhi, the separatists were still not willing to participate in elections or the democratic process, and as always, the only fallback position was Farooq. That is when we had to start working on Farooq. The PM and the IB were hoping for Shabir's involvement in the democratic process. The reality was that we had no option other than Farooq Abdullah. That's when I began devoting most of my time to him.

In January 1993, Rao initiated a major reshuffle of his Council of Ministers. In what I think was a smart move, the prime minister carved out a separate Department of Kashmir Affairs, which he headed. He appointed his trusted and proactive colleague, the young and clever Rajesh Pilot, as minister of state in the MHA and allowed him to engage in dialogue with all sections of people in Jammu and Kashmir.

In addition, he brought in the former cabinet secretary, Naresh Chandra, as a special advisor. Chandra brought with him his vast experience as a former home secretary, as well as that of having served briefly as an advisor in Srinagar during President's Rule in 1986. The prime minister also began involving Finance Minister Manmohan Singh in the Kashmir affairs discussions. Perhaps this was intended to put before the people of Jammu and Kashmir a credible political face as and when required. Apart from Dr Singh, I don't think anyone in Delhi really understood Farooq in Rao's administration.

All in all, though, I frankly felt that Narasimha Rao was a canny fellow with an open approach to dialogue. He wasn't too impressed with the IB or the work that it did, and if there was one thing that I found irritating it was his idea that he knew it all – anything the IB had to tell him was nothing new. I took it in my stride, since the prime minister's main goal was to open up Delhi's engagement with Kashmir. He was fed up with Governor's Rule in Kashmir, and he was determined that from 1994 onwards, democracy must be revived in the state. If Kashmir had to be normalized, if the security threats within the state had to be dealt with, this was the only way.

It was the beginning of a political reorientation towards Kashmir, on Delhi's part. Rao instructed his principal secretary, A.N. Verma, and other officials in the PMO to work with the media in Jammu and Kashmir. Rajesh Pilot –

the new minister of state for home – was asked to take stock of the supplies of essential commodities to the Valley.

It was clear that Rao was seeing Kashmir as a distinct security problem that Delhi had to handle tactfully – and immediately. After all, it had been under Governor's Rule since 1989, and militancy aside, the people of the state were dissatisfied with the limbo in which they hung and by the seeming lack of federal funds being disbursed by Delhi. To increase the people's dissatisfaction with the administration, the terrorists were attacking vital facilities such as health and educational infrastructure. Militancy was a huge concern for Narasimha Rao's administration. In his view, militancy had succeeded in shutting down democratic political activities, and both local and national political parties had succumbed to the militants' threat and abandoned their political activities altogether. The prime minister wanted to revive the Congress in the state and work with other parties to restart regular political processes. This was proving to be a tough task on the ground, as his own party people such as the state Congress unit president, Ghulam Rasool Kar, feared for their lives. As long as the local Congress party was politically inactive, Narasimha Rao knew that reviving democracy in Kashmir faced a hopeless future.

Now, the process of engaging with Kashmiris gained momentum. Farooq had to come back into the picture. Of this, I had always been convinced, but my efforts became pronounced now. In September 1993, I was in London to attend an intelligence-liaison conference. I had three nights, so I thought I should call on Farooq who was in England those days. He did go to Kashmir, but he never stayed long. After all, he was number one on the terrorists' hit list: we had heard that the ISI's largest bounty was being offered for Farooq's head.

One day, I found myself with some time on my hands. I called Farooq and said, 'Sir, I'm in London.' He was not living in London, but in Southend-on-Sea, in Essex, an hour and a half's drive east from London. 'Will you be coming into London?' I asked.

'I'll come to London whenever you want,' Farooq said. 'But first you must visit us at home.' Farooq and his wife lived in a modest corner house near the beach. There was nobody there but them. I was rapidly learning that that was the kind of man he was, adjusting from the good life in India quite easily to a more frugal one in England. I noticed that, surprisingly, there seemed to be no security, considering how much we Indians are obsessed with it. 'Do you have no security at all?' I asked.

'Sure,' he said. 'The police know I'm living here. They've given me a number that I can call in any emergency; they'll come immediately. They have their own way of doing this thing, so I'm not worried.'

Farooq, Mollie and I went to a club for lunch. When we returned home I sat in the drawing room while he went into an adjoining room and came back with a whole stack of literature. He handed me something by Hashim Qureshi, the pro-independence Kashmiri leader and one of the founders of the JKLF.

'This may interest you,' he said. 'Okay,' I said, thumbing through Hashim's writings. 'He may be useful to you,' Farooq continued, for he knew that Rao's government was pro-separatist, and as a result, much of my job at the K-Group involved speaking to the separatists as well. 'Why don't I get him to speak to you?' Then Farooq called up Hashim and we exchanged greetings.

Our friendship was always as simple and basic as that. There would be many times when Farooq would drop a careless tip in my lap. Equally, there would be many times when I would be the only person he seemed to listen to, especially when he was in one of his angry moods or when he was pissed off with Delhi. There came a point in Kashmir's troubles and in Farooq's life that he grew to rely on me. You might have thought that he would not exactly want to entertain a fellow from the IB at a time when he had deliberately chosen to step away from the ruckus of Kashmiri politics. Farooq is nobody's fool and he must have known that I was coming to see him with some kind of idea in mind. But he was ready to meet, ready to chat, ready to play the kind host. It helped me lay the foundation for Farooq's return to Kashmir – which was on his mind as well.

Meanwhile, in Delhi, our relationship with Shabir Shah had progressed to such an extent that, by 1994, the prime minister was fondly dreaming that Shabir would enter the democratic process. Rao didn't like Farooq too much, and he felt that Kashmir needed a fresh start. As we all know now, that was a blind alley. But it was an alley in which Rao believed. Before he left for a foreign tour in November 1995, the IB director sent me off to brief Rao on Kashmir.

It was the first time I had ever met the prime minister. He reminded me of Soz, in that he didn't look me directly in the eye. But he asked me quietly, 'How necessary is Farooq for the revival of the democratic process in Kashmir?'

The question crystallized what I had been suspecting. Narasimha Rao was obviously looking towards a state assembly election in Jammu and Kashmir the following year and it was clear that he was placing great hope in Shabir.

I was frank. No separatist, Shabir included, was ready to hitch their wagon to Delhi. Moreover, I insisted Farooq be given a strong chance as well. After all, the NC was now back in the picture, pressurizing Delhi to give it something that it could sell to its electorate during the upcoming elections. There were critics of Farooq's mindset and strategy, of course. Rao's aide and advisor, S. Narendra, for instance, has argued in a 2023 book that the NC was 'blackmailing' the Centre, 'since its participation in the poll was essential in view of the separatist parties' call for a poll boycott'.[3]

In all honesty, one could not have expected Farooq to take part in a fraught electoral process – particularly when he knew that Rao and his government had been encouraging separatists to enter the mainstream in the Valley – without giving him something in return. As he candidly told me, '*Kuch toh dena hoga.*' (You'll have to give me something.)

Rao's prime ministership was a period that marked Delhi's attempts to rehaul its policy in Kashmir. That translated into a tense period of waiting for me and Farooq. I had to ensure that Farooq stayed in the game, that he didn't run out of hope or steam or optimism to rejoin the political race in the Valley. Much of this involved dialogue and more dialogue, of course. Farooq was now back in the country, tempted by the thought of power. He was, after all, a politician to the core. In his own eyes, he was a general called to war. 'Generals choose the time and place. I'm a general. I will choose my time and place. And my party workers will become active when the general's bugle sounds.'[4]

He was not worried about whether the NC might have become irrelevant. 'The NC will not die for a million years. You [the media] wouldn't be talking to me if I were irrelevant. You know how relevant we are and without us you have no one else. I bet on this. You have no other organization more nationalistic than the NC,'[5] he would insist. 'Farooq Abdullah has a past, a history that can never change. A past which is written on granite. The NC freed people from autocratic rule, raised them from the ground to the sky and gave them honour and this time, too, we will restore that honour.'[6]

In that remark – and he has made several similar ones over the years – I have found a strange similarity between father and son. Farooq has always disavowed any sameness between himself and the Sheikh, yet for both men, the honour of their homeland has always been paramount. The old Sheikh's

The Chief Minister and the Spy

fight was always for Kashmir's pride and prowess. So, too, for Farooq. Nor did he feel he had made any mistakes in Kashmir before he left. It was that devil-may-care attitude coming to the fore. That attitude has saved Farooq from moments and incidents that would have confused a lesser mortal. His single largest mistake, if he was pressed to name one, was 'being too naïve and too trusting. I trusted people more than I should have'.[7]

Despite his disillusionment and his obvious cynicism with a political process that had constantly let him down, his first thought was always how to get back into the saddle as soon as possible, and to get out there, doing what he loved best. At no point had he discouraged the Centre or me from talking to the separatists, even though it would have gone against the grain for him. He was no fan of anyone who believed in carving up the Valley in any way: 'I will continue to fight them [the separatists]. They have to be fought continuously.'[8] In Farooq's mind, talking of *azaadi* was akin to flogging a dead horse. He made a clear distinction between *azaadi* and autonomy even then, and to that principle he has stayed true till today.

In the early 1990s, Farooq was constantly watching Delhi and seeing what Rao's tactics could achieve. In February 1994, Farooq gave an interview to *India Today* – Harinder Baweja had to really chase him for it, for he was not an easy guy to pin down! – in which he was unusually serious. 'I feel that the Government of India is finally serious about doing something. The situation is very grave. It's about time we got on with our job,' he told Baweja.⁹ This was a clear-eyed Farooq, one who had been away long enough to notice what the world was thinking about Kashmir. In 1994, the US changed its position on Kashmir by openly declaring it a disputed territory. This was a change from its previous stance, which was to not publicly challenge the legitimacy of Kashmir's accession to India. Pakistan was also very much in the picture at the time, having moved a resolution at the United Nations Human Rights Commission (UNHRC) in Geneva to send a fact-finding mission to Jammu and Kashmir. The allegation, as always, was India's violation of human rights in the state.

In those days, every soldier in Kashmir was supposed to carry a laminated card in his pocket containing the 'Ten Commandments' on human rights issued by army chief, General B.C. Joshi. Among its first three elements were: no rape, no molestation, no torture resulting in death or maiming. It enjoined personnel to respect human rights in general and uphold dharma, defined as an 'ethical mode of life – the path of righteousness'. It was during his tenure that the army also tightened its procedures to punish wrongdoing by its own personnel in Kashmir. Even then, as poet Agha Shahid Ali wrote, 'Srinagar hunches like a wild cat; lonely sentries, wretched in bunkers on the city's bridges, far from their homes in the plains, licenced to kill ...'¹⁰

In this backdrop, Pakistan was taking India's 'severe' human rights violations in Kashmir to the United Nations in early 1994. In response, Rao responded by passing the

Kashmir Resolution on 22 February 1994: 'On behalf of the People of India, the Indian Parliament firmly declares that The State of Jammu & Kashmir has been, is and shall be an integral part of India ...'[11] Five days after the Indian Parliament's resolution, Pakistan tabled a resolution at the UNHRC in Geneva through the Organization of Islamic Cooperation (OIC) that condemned India for human rights abuses in Kashmir. If passed, the UN Security Council would have imposed economic sanctions on India.

Pakistan's global campaign came at a time when India was grappling with weak polity, poor economy and stunted security. To counter the move, as mentioned earlier, Rao dispatched a team led by Opposition leader Atal Behari Vajpayee to Geneva. Salman Khurshid (then deputy to Foreign Minister Dinesh Singh) and Farooq (as the point man) were named as emergency emissaries in Vajpayee's team, along with I.K. Gujral. The Indian delegation performed brilliantly, with Farooq being – as Shekhar Gupta described him aptly – 'full of beans and banter'.[12] He wasn't scheduled to speak, since Gujral was to be the prime mover in advocating India's cause. But, as he told me later, Gujral shook his head at the end, '*Aap baat karo*,' he told Farooq. (You talk.)

Farooq's diplomacy at the moment underlined a conviction that I have always had – he would have made a superb external affairs minister. Administration after administration has had the chance to give him that portfolio. He is erudite and eloquent and balances it beautifully with his natural humour and charm. The fact that he is a Kashmiri Muslim can only be in India's favour – and would have been a masterstroke in subverting Pakistan's narrative about Kashmir that it peddled at international fora.

At a time when India and Pakistan's diplomatic volleying was at its most tense in the marbled halls of the United Nations, Farooq retained his wit and presence of mind. As the discussions were ongoing, he nonchalantly told everyone, 'We will sort out this problem soon. Then you come down to Srinagar for a round of golf. The view is beautiful.'[13] A delegate would recall that he offset this sangfroid by challenging his opponents to 'speak Kashmiri with him, to prove their Kashmiriyat'.[14]

Not many politicians today have that kind of aplomb. Farooq has never been a starched-shirt public servant. His flash and fire are part of his public and political persona, as much as his erudition and charm.

Yet, all through, his mind was ticking fast and furiously. He knew that this was the right time to return. Nothing that I could possibly say would have worked quite so well as Farooq himself realizing that Kashmir needed him. He returned to the Valley soon after, insisting that things were going rapidly out of hand, and the NC needed to step in as soon as possible. There was, even then, some bitterness about the way he had been treated by Delhi. 'I accept my responsibility for being stupid and for having an accord with the Centre, hoping that they will help me remove the misery of the people. The Centre is the one which has reduced my honour and dignity.'[15] But he was clear that in politics, one could not keep carrying a grudge. It was yet another example of the greatness of the man – Farooq has never believed in closing a door, as I have said before. It has been the cause of his greatest betrayals and let-downs.

In 1994, his greatest priority was to ensure that peace prevailed once more in the Valley, especially given the international attention on Kashmir. 'I don't want a situation like that of Afghanistan. I have seen the destruction of Afghanistan.' He told the press upon his return to the Valley, 'I have seen a position where the land has disappeared, where the people have disappeared. Afghans are killing Afghans, and I don't want that to happen in my state. If we don't act now, it'll be too late.'[16]

It appeared, from his words, that the efforts to keep Farooq in conversation about the need to return were bearing fruit. 'Farooq is not as useless as you Indians think,' he insisted. 'When Farooq comes out to fight, you will not know in which corner to hide.'[17] He was playing to the gallery here yet again, and it was effective. He insisted that what the people of Kashmir wanted was peace, and that the NC would enter the electoral race on the plank of autonomy.

'Do you really think people will accept that?' he was asked.

'I cannot tell you. I don't know how many takers there will be, but at least it will be something for us to go ahead with,' Farooq responded.[18]

Farooq's ability to take risks is what makes him a true politician – he is unafraid to gamble if the need arises. But he was belligerent at the outset – another characteristic that he is unafraid to espouse. When Harinder Baweja asked him what role he was envisioning for himself in the state in the upcoming elections, he 'shouted and thundered': 'Are you going to get me murdered and my party members murdered by asking this question? I don't know what role I see for myself as yet. I've just come back. For God's sake, allow me to study the situation. Ask me this question in three weeks.'[19]

Behind the drama, there has always been a keen-eyed strategist. Farooq had been away from Kashmir for three years. He had come back to find a situation on the ground that required an experienced hand. There was a distinct weariness among the people towards violence and guns, and the army's presence. He could see it and he knew the task ahead of him was an intimidating one – but Farooq's sense of hope is rarely extinguished permanently. He was aware that a sense of 'alienation' persisted, 'but I still say, despite that alienation, we have not reached the point of no return. We can still turn the clock around'.[20]

Farooq has never believed that matters can ever be at a dead end. No matter how difficult the circumstance, he has retained faith in finding a solution. This is not to say that he has not experienced momentary bouts of defeat. But he has always managed to surface from them. 'Golf, actually, is in many ways like politics. If you don't hit the ball to the hole, you are over,' he would say. 'The only good thing is that you have to be a gentleman in golf, but in politics the quality of gentlemanliness differs.'[21]

To those of his critics who felt that he had run away four years ago and only returned at a time when it was suitable for him to take power again, Farooq was dismissive. 'Damn hell, I belong to that land [Kashmir], I belong to those people. I'm part of those people ... Four years ago, I did not leave. I was made to leave, otherwise I would have met the same fate as Mirwaiz Maulvi Farooq, and they would have buried me. I am not ready for burial as yet. I will bury others before I go.'[22]

I have raised the matter of Mirwaiz Umar Farooq with Doctor Sahib many times, because I felt that he still had a key role in Kashmir. Farooq's answer was always, 'Why not? We could always join together.' After all, he had had an alliance with Mirwaiz Maulvi Farooq, in what was then referred to as the 'Double Farooq Accord'.

Interestingly, two senior leaders of the NC, Mustafa Kamal and Ali Mohammad Sagar, had once indicated that a 'Double Omar Accord' (a reference to Mirwaiz Umar Farooq and Omar Abdullah) was in the interests of both sides. The fact is that I would never suggest anything to Farooq, knowing that he might disagree with it. I knew that he would agree with any reasonable political suggestion. My idea – I was on the same page as Delhi on this matter – was to mainstream Kashmir. To do this, the Mirwaiz was a key figure. So, one way was to get the separatists to join the democratic process, which was not that easy because of Pakistani pressure. The other way to go about it was via the NC itself. Today, it is in the interest of Kashmir and the separatists themselves to join hands with the NC.

He was unrepentant about having had a good time and living his life while he was away. 'I was enjoying myself. With nations, four years don't make a damn difference ... At that time, there was no other way but to go.' To interviewers who might have brought up the issue of his love for golf and travel, Farooq was defiant, 'I will never stop playing it whether you like it or not. At least I'm a gentleman when it comes to sports. I will continue to visit God's earth – whether it is Europe, China or Africa ... And let me tell you, I will still go to London. My children are studying there and I cannot ignore them.'[23]

That was Farooq for you. He refused to be any less than what he was, to be compartmentalized into a box for the sake of the conventions of public and political life.

For me, Narasimha Rao's strategies were a welcome change from previous policies. I wasn't exactly sure what results could be achieved from talking to militants or separatists, but his policy encouraged an open door for all parties, which was more than what previous prime ministers had done. But even so, his statecraft could not prevent major mishaps like the 32-day siege of Hazratbal between 14 October and 16 November 1993, and the destruction of the Charar-e-Sharief township after a protracted stand-off between the security grid and the militants, mostly non-native Pakistanis, on 11 May 1995. All the holed-up militants in the Dargah

Hazratbal were given safe passage as part of the negotiations between the government and the militants.

I was beginning to up the ante, as far as leaning on Farooq was concerned. I could see what Delhi was trying to do: to make Shabir feel that the engagement was getting serious, that Narasimha Rao was keen on him. It is another matter, of course, that not only did Shabir not take this bait, but was a thorough let-down in the end.

On a visit to the African nation of Burkina Faso, Narasimha Rao made the statement that has gone down in history. The government was willing to discuss any kind of political arrangement with Kashmir; any quantum of *azaadi*. 'In a pre-election gesture, Prime Minister P.V. Narasimha Rao today offered a political package to Jammu and Kashmir on the basis of the Indira–Sheikh Abdullah accord and said the centre has no objection on the use [of] the title of *Wazir-e-Azam* for the Chief Minister and *Sadar-e-Reyasat* for the governor of the state legislature so desired,' *Hindustan Times* reported from Ouagadougou on 4 November 1995. 'Mr Rao assured the people that Article 370 shall not be abrogated, that a package would be worked out to ensure time bound revival of Kashmir economy and that measures had been taken to ensure peaceful conduct of elections, the dates of which would be announced by the Election Commission.'

The prime minister went a step further. 'The sky is the limit,' were his famous words. The reason for this was that by the time Rao left for Burkina Faso, the reality was beginning to dawn on him that the separatists were never going to make it. So if the Kashmiris wanted autonomy, the sky would have to be the limit.

It defined much of what would come next – but by the end of November 1995, all seemed to be in jeopardy. The NC had backed out of the elections. 'The only reason why we have backed out is that the package of autonomy that we had asked for has not come forth,' Farooq told *India Today*.[24] He wanted Kashmir's status to be restored to what it had been in 1952.

I told him that the prime minister had said what Farooq wanted. Farooq said, '*Kehne se kya hota hai?* [What do words mean?] We want a conversation on that matter with us. *Upar hawa mein baaton karne se kya fayda?* [What is the point of merely saying something?]'

Farooq was smarter than everyone else. He knew that autonomy was a ticklish issue, but what he wanted at times of his political need was for the matter to be raised to make Kashmiris believe that he was doing what they wanted. You see, even in 2000, when the Jammu and Kashmir Assembly passed the resolution seeking autonomy, and wanting to go back to 1952, Brajesh had asked me what my friend, Farooq that is, was up to. I told Farooq that Delhi was a bit worried. He said don't worry, the resolution won't be passed. But it was passed, perhaps deliberately so. What Farooq wanted was a word from the home ministry that they were examining it, because he needed it for the 2002 elections.

In July 1952, the Indian government and Kashmir signed the Delhi Agreement, which gave the state autonomy within India and within itself. The agreement also gave the President of India the power to declare a state of emergency in the state. In November that year, the Constituent Assembly abolished the monarchy and replaced it with an elected Sadr-e-Riyasat, or Head of State. Karan Singh, the son of Maharaja Hari Singh, was elected as the first Sadr-e-Riyasat. In fact, the Sheikh obtained a few more concessions – the right to resettle refugees from PoK in the state, and a separate flag. On 7 August 1952, the Indian Parliament approved the agreement. Farooq was going back to history, to a world before the betrayals of Kashmir began. 'Restoration of pre-52 status is not a precondition but a representation of the aspirations of people of Jammu and Kashmir,' he insisted.[25]

Rao, on the other hand, dug his own heels in – and insisted that if anything, Kashmir's status could only go back to 1975, during the days of the Indira–Sheikh Accord. Farooq wasn't having it – and he pulled out of the running for the parliamentary polls upcoming that winter.

There was uproar.

'Kashmir continues to be a textbook example of opportunities missed, frittered away or shamelessly sacrificed at the altar of political expediency and emotive chauvinism,' Inderjit Badhwar wrote scathingly in *India Today*. 'The spurning of Prime Minister P.V. Narasimha Rao's pre-election package by the NC, and the subsequent cancellation of the loudly ballyhooed elections, is but another example of a sham in which Rao has lost face.'[26]

That presented yet another dilemma. The question, as it always had been, was whether the clock could be turned back

Conversations and Confidences

enough for Farooq to come forward and stay in the political game. He was adamant – the people's honour and aspirations for autonomy had to be respected. The then governor, Gen. K.V. Krishna Rao, wrote in his book, 'I met Prime Minister [P.V. Narasimha Rao] on 25 March and he was keen that the National Conference first participate in the elections and the autonomy issue could be resolved after the elections.'[27] But obviously, Farooq did not want to move ahead without some resolution on the issue.

Kuch toh dena hoga. (They have to give us something concrete.)

This Gordian knot would take another few months to untangle, and it only underlined Farooq's integrity and his commitment to the cause of Kashmir. It also illustrated the need to hold early assembly elections as soon as possible.

This, then, was the run-up to the 1996 elections, and it formed yet another context in which the friendship between Farooq and me began to deepen. The assembly elections would be a milestone for Kashmir, a milestone for Farooq. 'We never asked for *azaadi* but for our rights to be returned.' He would tell the media years later, 'He promised. It's on that promise [that] I went to the polls and carried people with me.'[28]

More than anything, it was a milestone for me and my work with the K-Group. All through these difficult years, the idea had been to ensure that Farooq stayed on course to return to Kashmir, despite his mercurial temperament and the numerous provocations provided not just by conditions within the state but from the Centre too.

The Chief Minister and the Spy

I'll discuss the 1996 elections in the next chapter, but when Farooq came back to Kashmir as chief minister, it was almost as though it was the start of a new era in the state. For Farooq and myself, it was the beginning of a new era, certainly. I like to call it the golden period of our friendship. In those days, I could have said anything and asked anything of him, and he would not have refused. But, you see, Kashmir was always the backdrop.

5

1996: A Pivotal Election

I often refer to the days after the 1996 assembly elections in Jammu and Kashmir as the best days for Farooq and myself – and I don't say it lightly. That time saw our association at its peak. Much of this stemmed, of course, from Farooq's return to power in the state, after a long period of living away from Kashmir, in London. It also stemmed from the work that the K-Group (myself included) was doing to speak to separatists and militants to convince them to come to the political table.

As I've said before, I kept up contact with Farooq during the transitional period before 1996. I don't see my keeping in touch with him as being particularly extraordinary, to be honest. Yes, I did think he was the best candidate for leadership in the Valley. That's an opinion I still hold, but quite apart from that, it is the job of a spook to keep in touch with your contacts and with those who have let you in. Good spying, if I can call it that, comes down to maintaining dialogue, maintaining contact and relationships. I don't

The Chief Minister and the Spy

mean this in a transactional way. Human nature, after all, is about giving and receiving. You must give in order to get something from another person – whether that be trust or information. I think that Farooq and I share this belief. He is as open to keeping in touch with everyone as I am. It made life much easier as a spook, certainly, but it also made it easier to become close to Farooq. And Delhi certainly didn't mind. It was not often that the MHA and the IB were on the same page, but in the days before the 1996 elections, this was the case. In fact, nobody really knew where the dice would fall at the time.

I recall going off to Srinagar with a special secretary in the MHA, known as 'Jain Sahib', before the elections. I don't want to take names here but some advisors of the government at that time – it was Governor's Rule – went to the extent of suggesting that Kuka Parray (the founder of the Jammu and Kashmir Awami League) might become chief minister! I told them frankly, '*Aap log paagal ho gaye hain!*' (You guys have lost your marbles!)

To me it was obvious that if the NC contested the 1996 elections, the party would win comfortably and Farooq would return as chief minister. In a sense, this was Delhi's problem with Farooq. While desperately trying to get him to contest the election, Kuka Parray was fielded as an alternative chief minister.

Jain Sahib called me into his room at the Nehru Guest House later that evening, and laughed and laughed. '*Tumne*

1996: A Pivotal Election

achchi sunayi!' (You gave them a befitting reply!) he grinned. 'These guys really have lost their marbles!'

Given this unpredictability, Narasimha Rao was a man who had come to the Kashmir table without any baggage. He had a strategic vision of what Kashmir could be and where Delhi could help it along. Dr Manmohan Singh, his finance minister, was assisting him in shaping Delhi's policy towards Kashmir. I was speaking to the likes of Shabir Shah, Firdous Syed and Abdul Ghani Lone. It is a testament to Farooq's omnipresence and stature that his name rarely left any political conversation or equation. For instance, when Shabir was ready to hold talks with Delhi, Narasimha Rao sent me to meet Dr Singh to let him know. This instruction confused me for a moment. Why was I being sent to meet the *finance* minister, when Dr Singh wasn't remotely involved with Kashmir? Later, I realized that it was a measure of how much Rao trusted Manmohan Singh.

When I went to meet Dr Singh to let him know, I was taken aback by his brevity and directness.

'Does Dr Abdullah know about this?' Dr Singh asked.

'No,' I replied, 'he doesn't.'

'Well, don't you think he should be informed?'

I laughed. 'Dr Farooq doesn't need to know everything, sir.' We left it at that, but it highlighted Dr Manmohan Singh's consciousness that Farooq was the big leader in Kashmir and that we shouldn't have been bypassing him the way we were at the time.

Delhi had focused a lot of its energy on a man like Shabir – though I had long suspected that he wasn't the man to last the home stretch.

Events in 1996 and afterwards would prove me right, but for now, I was very intent on bringing Farooq back as a political player. Since I had re-established contact with him in 1993, I had been focusing all my energies on him.

Now, obviously, Farooq did find out that we were talking to the separatists. I don't think that he particularly liked the fact that the separatists were now involved but, as I say, he is a man who understands that politics is a ball that must be kept rolling. He never enquired into my conversations with Shabir, for instance. He was too magnanimous for that. '*Kar lo baat*' (Talk to them) was a phrase he was fond of using in this context. *If you can swing something with the separatists, so much the better.* You see, he could afford to be open to the prospect of talking to the militants and the Hurriyat – because at the end of the day, Farooq believed in his people.

For him, Kashmir reigned supreme, over and above everything else. It was a belief that was ingrained in his very bones, and it was inevitable given his father's importance in the Valley. Farooq had grown up in the shadow of Kashmir and had learnt, over time, that there was nothing quite so important as to ensure the state's best interests. He knew that the people would be angry with him and he would have to explain himself, and prove to them (not with words, but by deeds) that he was still their best bet. But first, the ground had to be prepared. For those reasons, before the 1996

1996: A Pivotal Election

elections, Farooq was all for mainstreaming the separatists. He would never stop anyone from speaking to anyone he didn't agree with ideologically or see eye to eye with. It is an important quality in a politician: to never close a door just for the heck of it, or because you're too obstinate or rigid. Farooq has always been open to all possibilities, while maintaining firmly that he is in Delhi's corner.

In that same spirit, I was continuing to speak to the NC leaders as well, sounding them out for a possible return to power in 1996. It was a typical pattern, representative of the fact that for Delhi, Farooq was always a fallback option. To prepare the ground for his return, I would meet often with Mohammad Shafi Uri Sahib – who was deputizing for Farooq – and once or twice with Abdul Rahim Rathar as well. Shafi was quite clear, 'What Delhi wants is fine,' he would tell me. 'But everything depends on the return of my leader – and on what he thinks.'

What *did* Farooq think?

It was, to be honest, anyone's guess. That's the thing about Farooq – you are never sure where you stand with him. That has been Delhi's biggest concern as well, and one of the biggest causes for the misunderstanding between Delhi and Srinagar, as far as Farooq has been concerned. Even with me, though we were drawing very close in those tricky days of negotiations, I never made the mistake of believing that I fully understood Farooq. Yet I was sure that Farooq Abdullah would be chief minister in 1996, not Shabir Shah.

The Chief Minister and the Spy

I had continued to call him after I met him in England in September 1993, but he was somewhat non-committal. Eventually, as the pressure increased on the idea of bringing the NC back into the political game, Farooq returned to India. This was the moment at which I decided that the time had come to lean on Farooq just a little more heavily. I cast about in my mind for a suitable person who could speak to Farooq without losing his interest. I was already hitting a bit of a dead end as far as my conversations to persuade him were going. I needed third-party intervention, someone who would be both sympathetic and empathetic to the cause of the NC – and to Farooq himself. I hit upon a DG of police, A.M. Watali, who was posted in Srinagar.

Because my friendship with Farooq was always based on a fair amount of honesty as to motive and agenda, I put the idea to him – albeit in a roundabout way, 'Sir,' I said one day, 'We need more people involved. *Watali Sahib ko bula lein Kashmir se?*' (Should we call Watali Sahib from Kashmir?)

Farooq, I knew, would never say no. There are those who have plenty of difficulty in saying *yes*, but there are those who have an equal amount of trouble refusing anyone. Farooq belonged to the latter category. It's an excellent quality in a politician, for if you combine it with an open mind (which, also, Farooq possessed) and a willingness to take a bit of a risk and a gamble, you can actually work a fair bit of a miracle!

True to form, when I suggested that we bring in Watali, Farooq was amenable, '*Haan, haan,*' he said agreeably. '*Bula lo!*' (Yes, yes. Call him.)

I lost not a moment of time, because with Farooq, you can never take anything for granted. I telephoned Watali immediately, keeping the tenor of the conversation affably vague, '*Watali Sahib, aap Dilli aa jaiye, aapki zaroorat hai. Doctor Sahib aa gaye aur unse milne ki bhi zaroorat hai.*' (Watali Sahib, please come to Delhi. We need you. Doctor Sahib has returned and it's necessary to meet him as well.)

Watali responded instantly. 'Of course,' he said. 'But what's the problem?'

There comes a time to stop beating about the bush and be direct. That time, in this case, was now.

'Doctor Sahib is indecisive,' I said frankly. 'He's dilly-dallying a bit with the idea of participating in the elections. I thought you could persuade him.'

Watali was immediately on board with the idea, '*Haan, main karta hun baat.*' (Yes, I'll speak to him.)

He asked me not to come with him, so that he could speak to Farooq 'Kashmiri to Kashmiri'. Now, of course, since he was close to the Abdullah family, perhaps he might have felt that, in return for this role as emissary, he might be accommodated as a minister of state. Be that as it may, he *did* speak to Farooq.

'Sir,' he said gently, 'Things are changing. *Aapko election ladna chahiye. National Conference ki government aani chahiye Kashmir mein phir se.*' (Sir, things are changing. You should fight the elections. The National Conference should form the government in Kashmir once again.)

And so it was, that with a little bit of the right persuasion, Farooq was brought back into the game in Kashmir. Truth be told, of course, he'd never really left. It was often said in those days that Farooq was interested in everything else apart from politics in Kashmir: that he was always away, on holiday or philandering. It is true that while he was in England, he was living a wholly different life with great zest. But that's the strength of the man – his ability to compartmentalize his life. Farooq loves life as much as he loves Kashmir and the fact is that there was never anyone in the state's modern history who was more involved with Kashmir and its political future.

When he came back to campaign for the elections, it was a time of great change within the state. The reigning impression was that the NC, which had been targeted by militants since 1990, was almost a negligible power in Kashmir, especially after Farooq had left for England. It was felt that people in Delhi, including the prime minister, were hoping that the separatists could be roped into the elections. It was unsurprising, perhaps, but then, that was also why we were so keen to get the NC on board and contest the elections.

Then there were others like Muzaffar Hussain Baig, who was the state's advocate general in the late 1980s (and who would in 2002 join the PDP and become deputy chief minister). In 1996, he joined Abdul Ghani Lone's party, the People's Conference. Lone himself was upset to see Farooq contesting the elections. He approached Farooq to urge him not to participate. But once Farooq gives his word, it is as

1996: A Pivotal Election

good as set in stone. He could see Lone's point, but he had, by this time, committed to Delhi's ideas for Kashmir. So, to Lone, he was forthright but apologetic. 'Can't back out,' he told Lone. 'I've given Delhi my word.'

Those elections, it is fair to say, broke the back of militancy in Kashmir and brought democratic processes back into the state at a time when all hope seemed lost and when the politics of the state were drifting aimlessly. Had Farooq not agreed to participate – had the elections not been held – militancy would have continued for another ten years, perhaps. (This is not the same, however, as saying that Kashmiris were politically satisfied.)

Under Farooq's magnetic leadership, the NC – hitherto dispirited and low on morale – revived magically. Over time, I have come to believe that Farooq *is* the NC. It is difficult to imagine what would remain of the NC if Farooq was not around. In the Kashmiri mind, it would be nothing short of an earthquake.

Time and time again, when it came to the question of national security or helping the intelligence agencies, Farooq was always there – always present with an offer to help. This was an undoubted risk to take. But Farooq had realized that with Narasimha Rao's policy of talking to the separatists, he would need to present an alternative. If the NC was going to be that alternative to separatism and to militancy, then he would need to work with not just Delhi but the IB as well. He would also have to take into account what the average Kashmiri wanted. That was going to be a delicate

The Chief Minister and the Spy

and dangerous tightrope to walk, but Farooq didn't lack the courage. It helped that Delhi (and I) had been making the right noises about granting 'peace with honour' to Kashmir. But what did that mean?

It was that year, while we were laying the ground for Farooq and the NC to return to politics, that Narasimha Rao finally exited. Now came the turn of the reserved H.D. Deve Gowda to be prime minister. Born in 1933 in Mysore, Gowda earned a degree in civil engineering and worked as a contractor for a while before entering the INC, where he stayed between 1953 and 1962. He then abandoned the party, and was elected to the Mysore state legislative assembly for four consecutive terms. In 1994, Deve Gowda assumed leadership over the Janata Dal and became Karnataka's chief minister. In the parliamentary elections held in 1996, the United Front (a Janata Dal–led 13-party coalition) formed a government at the centre with the support of the Congress (I) in order to prevent the BJP from coming to power. Gowda was sworn in as the new prime minister. He was a simpler kind of man as compared to Rao – though I must say, he wasn't as simple as he seemed! But what was good for Kashmir was that he kept his politics very simple. Most of my dealings with him were through a minister from Bangalore, C.M. Ibrahim.

Ibrahim was of the belief that nobody knew more about Kashmir than he did. He thought he was the cat's whiskers, an attitude that pissed off quite a few Kashmiris because he would often ponderously quote from various religious scriptures to astonished and outraged maulvis. So annoyed were they that one day, one of the maulvis demanded of me, *'Yeh kaun le aaye ho aap saath mein? Yeh humein sikha rahe hain?'* (Who is this that you have brought with you? He's trying to teach *us*?)

Despite his undoubted smugness, Ibrahim and I became good friends, because in those days, while he was Gowda's sidekick, he still needed me to report to Gowda about Kashmir.

I remember one day Ibrahim asked me what I thought about Dr Abdullah. I knew he knew that I held Farooq in very high esteem.

'*Aap batayen?*' I replied. (You tell me.) 'I think he's the best we have.'

'I'm asking you because the prime minister has a lot of faith in him, and in his thinking, Farooq is Kashmir. We don't need to do anything. We will leave it to him to deal with things as he sees fit.'

I laughed. 'That's perfect. I don't think Farooq would like anything better than that!'

It was a good sign and it was, in a nutshell, Deve Gowda's policy towards Kashmir. And that was why Farooq was most comfortable with him. There was no meddling in Jammu and Kashmir's affairs. That was the best thing from Farooq's point of view. There was no panic in Delhi when Farooq's government set up the State Autonomy Committee, because for somebody like Deve Gowda, who came from state politics, and whose government was a united front of regional parties, discussing how to expand a state's autonomy was the most natural thing in the world.

I should tell you something of how Deve Gowda helped the IB to begin preparing for the assembly polls in 1996 in Kashmir. Deve Gowda's biographer, Sugata Srinivasaraju, has written that Kashmir had a special place in the new prime minister's heart.[1] When Deve Gowda visited Kashmir for the first time as prime minister, and as the cavalcade passed the Dal Lake to reach the Nehru Guest House, he wished romantically that he had brought his wife along. It was a curious thought from such a prosaic man, but then, Kashmir has a way of getting to you. From there, it was a short step to beginning to work to understand the real issues that haunted the Valley.

In retrospect, Deve Gowda's prime ministership was a special one for the Kashmiri, coming as it did during a time of real jadedness. His agenda was not just to restore political normalcy in the state, which he did, but to aim for a pragmatic solution to the vexing international issue Kashmir had become since India's independence. In the 11 months that he lasted at the helm, he visited Jammu and Kashmir four times. This was unprecedented, given that no Indian prime minister had visited the Valley in nearly a decade. He was not afraid to look Kashmir in the eye, and that was a quality that Farooq respected. Deve Gowda might have lacked political experience at the national level, but where he compensated for it was his sincerity, particularly in the conduct of the state assembly elections. His United Front

The Intelligence Bureau (IB) centenary celebrations in Srinagar, 15–17 October 1988. Director of the Intelligence Bureau (DIB) M.K. Narayanan presents a memento to Chief Minister (CM) Farooq Abdullah in the presence of Governor Jagmohan.

Farooq and his wife Mollie Abdullah entering the function

Farooq and Mollie at dinner

Mollie with Ammu, M.K. Narayanan's wife

Farooq with Mrs Narayanan

Sara and Farooq at our 50th wedding anniversary at the Ashoka Hotel, Delhi, 2016

Farooq with Paran and me at our 50th wedding anniversary

Farooq with Paran and me at one of many parties

At the launch of my book, Kashmir: The Vajpayee Years, *in 2015*

At the launch of The Spy Chronicles *in 2018, Farooq shares the stage with Hamid Ansari, Manmohan Singh and Yashwant Sinha*

Farooq in a thoughtful mood at our residence in December 2024

With cricketing legend Sunil Gavaskar at our common friend Peter Hasan's place in 2024

With Mallikarjun Kharge, Farooq and Ali Mohammad Sagar at tea after Omar's swearing-in as CM in October 2024

At lunch the same day with Priyanka Gandhi (left), Mollie (centre) and Nidhi Razdan (right)

With Farooq

Farooq, Omar and Prakash Karat at dinner on the day before Omar's swearing-in

The Gandhis and the Abdullahs being photographed together after the swearing-in

With Farooq (left) and Sara (right) at dinner

With Farooq at O.P. Bhutani's 96th birthday in Delhi in February 2025

1996: A Pivotal Election

government moved fast on the Kashmir issue, realizing that the baggage it carried over from the Rao administration was particularly heavy. Once again, the central government initiated talks with Farooq. But there was also the BJP to deal with now. As a home ministry official at the time put it, 'The new government may have the right intentions, but because it is a minority government, it will have to keep in mind the political implications of the BJP's stated position on the abrogation of Article 370.'[2]

'Kashmir for Gowda was beyond politics,' was how Srinivasaraju put it. 'It was a surprise passion and an exploration of his own statesmanship.'[3] As a first step, he fixed a date to visit the Valley. Intelligence and security officials met with the cabinet secretary and the prime minister's principal secretary to make their individual assessments. In the initial stages of planning, the visit was deemed a high risk to Deve Gowda's life. The prime minister seemed to accept this – but not for long. It wasn't many weeks later that he revisited the subject, with a question that was hard to ignore: 'If Kashmir is an integral part of India, why should a prime minister be afraid to go there?' After consulting his astrologer, he fixed the official date for his visit as 6 July 1996.

Simultaneously, he called up Gen. K.V. Krishna Rao, who was governor of Jammu and Kashmir, and asked him to extend an open invitation to all political parties, Kashmiri organizations, including secessionist groups, to come and make their case before him. There would be no formalities and no protocols involved. 'Anybody can come and see me.

Whoever wants to talk to me can walk in,' he said.[4] This was unheard of inside and outside of Kashmir. Free access to India's prime minister, that too in a troubled territory, instantly created a favourable impression about Deve Gowda.

'Gowda went about the task without resorting to any theatrics. He refrained from invoking any catch phrases like "jamhooriyat, insaaniyat and Kashmiriyat" to woo the people. Neither did he resort to chanting mantras of "vikas and vishwas" while promising a better future for Kashmiris. Instead, the prime minister put it across in plain terms that they promised a free and fair election. At the end of the day, it was Deve Gowda's down-to-earth approach that struck a chord with the people in the Valley,' reported Ajith Pillai and Masood Hussain in the 19 June 1996 issue of *Outlook*.[5]

This attitude elevated Deve Gowda in Farooq's eyes. Here was a prime minister who clearly knew his way around diplomacy and an urgent subject like Kashmir. From playing hardball on the issue of the assembly elections, Farooq began to calm down. It helped that when the two men finally met in Delhi, Deve Gowda ensured that the best kebabs, from the nearby Hotel Ashoka, were laid out. Facilitating the smooth conduct of the elaborate luncheon was Deve Gowda's troubleshooter, Civil Aviation Minister C.M. Ibrahim. From being a little-known politician who had accidentally become prime minister, Deve Gowda had suddenly acquired character. Farooq was impressed.

'[Narasimha] Rao never accepted our views on autonomy,' he told journalists. 'Deve Gowda believes in making India a

1996: A Pivotal Election

federal country and this is a major departure from the past 50 years. Deve Gowda is talking of strong states and a strong Centre and that makes a world of difference ... We've always gone on the basis of trust. Deve Gowda has assured not just Farooq Abdullah but the whole nation. He's a new man, a farmer who has risen from the grass-roots level. He wants to strengthen the roots and I have no reason to believe yet that he makes backroom deals.'[6]

After that first visit, *India Today* wrote: 'The signs of hope are unmistakable. There was silent admiration in the war-weary Valley after the first visit by a Prime Minister in nine years brought about the improbable ... Schools which admitted children only after parents signed indemnity bonds are now taking them to Gulmarg and Pahalgam for weekend holiday camps ... In the coming months, Deve Gowda's political acumen will be put to test – by the militants and a people who, with hopes rekindled, are in no mood for another round of games.'[7]

Farooq was in a buoyant mood. I have never seen him quite so hopeful – perhaps only the second time was when he laid eyes on Rahul Gandhi during the Bharat Jodo Yatra of 2023! 'I am not frightened. The only heartening things I see are the strong bridges that have been built on which we are going to cross the hazards. Unlike the past, the nation is now solidly behind me. Farooq Abdullah is not alone today. He is not afraid of death but he's not a fool to put himself before a bullet.'[8]

The Chief Minister and the Spy

Shortly thereafter, the NC joined Deve Gowda's United Front coalition. The more Farooq heard Deve Gowda's intentions towards Kashmir, the more he liked what he was hearing. The prime minister was on the ball when it came to local issues – like the economy, unemployment, poor tourism and abject poverty. He announced a loan waiver in Parliament so that the Kashmiri economy could limp back to normal. 'It was my administrative style to take decisions then and there, not procrastinate. In this particular case, it had helped create tremendous confidence among people in the Valley,' Gowda recalled.[9]

This was exactly Farooq's style too. He was no fan of red tape, and had even less time to waste on formalities and protocol. Deve Gowda was showing him what Delhi had not been able to show Farooq for a long time: that he was capable of swift moves in favour of Kashmir. Take for instance, the prime minister's second visit to the state, which happened within a month of his first, on 5 August 1996. Deve Gowda visited Leh, Kargil and Jammu, and addressed a public meeting in Rajouri. From Rajouri airport to the town where he was to address the meeting, he wanted to be taken in an open jeep so that he could wave at people assembled on either side of the road. It was a short distance – just about two kilometres – and the area commander, my friend, Lt Gen. J.S. Dhillon, was aghast at the thought. But Deve Gowda insisted, 'Nothing will happen, don't worry. You drive and I'll sit next to you. Assume somebody lobs a grenade; both of us will die. Where is the question of you being hanged?'[10]

1996: A Pivotal Election

It was, if you recall, very similar to the theatrics that Farooq enacted in August 1989 when he slow-marched over the small distance instead of riding in a jeep. Small wonder then that Farooq liked Deve Gowda as much as he did. They were two different personalities, though paradoxically they were cut from the same cloth.

Amid all the trust-building activities, Farooq could see that Gowda's mind was constantly preparing for the assembly elections in Jammu and Kashmir. On 2 August 1996, he had ended his speech in Parliament, saying, 'I would like to take this opportunity to reiterate the government's commitment to give maximum autonomy to the state. Once an elected government is in place, we would hold consultations with them to arrive at a consensus.'[11]

There was a mention of Kashmir and elections in Gowda's Independence Day address too: 'I visited Jammu and Kashmir twice and met the people of the state and felt their aspirations. The conditions are changing there ... We will complete the task of restoration of normalcy and return of a popular government in Jammu and Kashmir.'[12]

In June 1996, the assurance of 'maximum autonomy' generated hope and discussion in the Valley. Gowda himself recalled: 'I remember the Hurriyat leaders were stubborn. They said let the Centre keep railways, highways, currency, defence, foreign affairs and let us manage the rest. I never discussed [Article] 370; I discussed only autonomy. I did five rounds of talks but did not give any publicity. My strategy was to solve it like I had solved the Idgah Maidan issue in

Hubli: quietly. One of my conditions to the Hurriyat was you should not discuss anything with the media, and I too will not speak to them.'[13]

Outlook reported the mood on the ground, 'The winter of political deadlock in Kashmir is not quite over but the first signs of the ice thawing are visible. The promise by the United Front (UF) Government that it will give "maximum autonomy" to Kashmir is being widely seen as a positive signal that could end the strife in the Valley and restore peace. Suddenly everyone – from the All Party Hurriyat Conference (APHC) to Farooq Abdullah's National Conference (NC) is ready to talk and though the different political groupings may differ on the modalities to resolve the crisis, they are all agreed that the new Government in Delhi does hold out hope.'[14]

In Gowda's eyes, a state assembly poll without the NC, the main political party participating, would not make sense. It was a line that he had been pegging since the days of Narasimha Rao's administration, when he had personally telephoned Farooq to persuade him to return to India. 'Your father was like a lion. What is wrong with you? Why are you staying away? You should contest. Your party will sweep the polls.'[15]

Now, Farooq was convinced. As he joined hands with the United Front and began to look ahead, he was more confident than he had ever been in the past. He knew that militancy would not immediately vanish but, as he said, 'A clean political process will build confidence in the people and that will gradually silence the gun. Then our neighbour [Pakistan] too will realise the futility of their proxy war. For God's sake, a beginning has to be made. We should all keep our fingers crossed. This is an opportunity which can turn the tide and we should all work towards it.'[16]

To critics who felt that he was betraying not just Kashmiris but himself by allying once again with New Delhi, Farooq was blunter still: 'I do not bother about what the Kashmiris feel about it. This dual attitude of being with India and yet keeping a distance will never help us. I have to be part of India. Otherwise, how am I going to take my state forward? ... I won't walk into the traps of the past. This time I did not promise anything to the people, unlike the 1986 elections. I did not raise their hopes because I knew the promises of New Delhi were never fulfilled and we fell flat every time. Now all that I am saying is that we will only try to get things done.'[17]

I was glad to see this change in Farooq. It was as though a new man had returned to the Valley, the one time where he finally seemed to be finding his political feet after a period of uncertainty and insecurity about himself and his role in Kashmir's politics. Here, at last, was the fighter that I knew he was, with that courage of his that could be dauntless in the face of adversity.

We began to prepare for the polls.

'After almost seven years of separatist rebellion, at least 14,500 deaths and the destruction of a thriving tourism industry, Indian officials hope the election of a new state government here will restore democracy and normalcy to the disputed Himalayan state of Jammu and Kashmir.' The *Washington Post* summed up the situation nicely.[18] The big question on everybody's mind was if they would be free and fair, as Delhi had promised. Deve Gowda immediately set to work, to make these wonderings stop. His diplomacy was, if I say so myself, quite sterling. He called ambassadors of a few countries for a breakfast meeting and asked them if they would act as observers and dispatch independent reports to their respective countries and international agencies. They agreed.

Deve Gowda took another major decision, which was to allow international media to freely travel anywhere in Jammu and Kashmir and report. 'I had nothing to hide, I had nothing to fear,' he recalled later to his biographer.[19] The NC, in its discussions with Delhi leaders, had also insisted that elections to the state assembly be held in the presence of independent observers.

The Election Commission on 7 August 1996, two days after the prime minister's second visit, announced elections in four phases in the month of September. Deve Gowda was in touch directly with Lt Gen. Dhillon, to ensure that not only was law and order maintained, but that everyone involved understood that the 'image of the nation' was at stake. As Ajith Pillai wrote in an article in *Outlook*'s June 1996 issue, 'In sharp contrast to the Delhi media, I recall ordinary folk and journalists in Srinagar telling me that their own assessment was that the new prime minister was sincere and had his heart in the right place. He was someone who could be trusted and was not given to making tall claims that he could solve the Kashmir problem overnight. All he was promising for a start was to hold a credible election in a strife-torn state.'[20]

All these ploys worked.

The NC swept the polls as predicted. Farooq was shaken to his soul, despite his confident exterior. It was almost, I think, too much for him to bear. The inner confidence, that inner steadiness – that faith about how it would all go eventually – that was missing, despite what he showed the people. He talked about it to me, because in those days, Farooq was at his most vulnerable and at his frankest with me. Before the swearing-in took place, he and I met for lunch at the Taj.

'You have to come for the swearing-in,' he told me, like a child.

'Of course we'll come, sir,' I assured him. 'There's no question about that.'

Before the 1996 elections, the DIB had lost his job and Arun Bhagat was the new DIB. He didn't know the ABC of the IB at the time, but what happened then was that the Cabinet Secretary Surendra Singh, the Home Secretary K. Padmanabhaiah and the DIB, all got on very well. Surendra Singh was a fine gentleman and while Padmanabhaiah was haughty, he was one home secretary who devoted himself to Kashmir and whose door was always open to all Kashmiris. Now, because of my affinity with Farooq, I fitted into this whole network.

The Chief Minister and the Spy

Not only did I go to the swearing in, but Arun Bhagat too went by my advice, as did Ajit Doval. Doval was joining his post in Srinagar at the same time. This was a time when I was telling the director what we should do. I had also told Doval that he could do things his way and I had no doubt that he would deliver.

As for Farooq, he was leaning on my advice for even the formation of his cabinet at the time. 'I'm told that in 1983 when you formed your first government, you had only a handful of ministers and it made a huge impact,' I said, during the course of the meal. 'Why not do that again – keep the cabinet small, and afterwards you can expand it?' Farooq agreed.

Home Secretary K. Padmanabhaiah gave him a slip containing two or three names, and suggested that these names might be suitable for Farooq as the state's new chief secretary. Farooq gave me the slip of paper.

'What is this, sir?' I asked.

'Your home secretary gave it to me,' he said. 'See what you think.'

Now, the old Farooq would have torn up the slip of paper. He would have said, why do I need this?

So that's what I mean by the uncertainty that seemed to dog Farooq's footsteps. He leaned on me heavily at this moment. I sometimes think that he perhaps hadn't even believed that it might come to this. So my job had transitioned in a manner of speaking – I was not only keeping an eye on him for Delhi, but I was also his confidant, his comforter in times of need. I demanded why he was carrying around the slip of paper. 'You want Tony Jaitly to be your chief secretary, don't you?'

Farooq nodded. 'Yes, I do.'

'Well, then, the matter ends there.' I said, 'Just tell Padmanabhaiah that you have your own chief secretary and he will not say anything after that.'

Once that matter was settled, there was the tricky affair of choosing Farooq's DG. At one stage, Tony Jaitly came to see me and said, 'The boss wants you as DG. Will you consider that?'

I said, 'Tony, I haven't done a police job in years, apart from being an ASP [assistant superintendent of police] in a subdivision. I have no idea how things are right now. Besides, it's not fair to the force, of which I know only a few officers. I will be an outsider. I'm an intelligence officer, who will be more useful to you in Delhi.'

This was when Farooq called me and asked for help in finding a new DG. I told him that M.N. Sabharwal was the seniormost and the force was quite happy with him. Farooq retorted, 'The force may be happy, but I am not! You will have to find me a new DG.'

Once again, Jaitly had a list of Muslim officers all over the country. But I told Farooq, 'If you want an outsider, please don't look beyond Punjab, which has dealt with insurgency and knows about these matters.'

That was how Gurbachan Jagat was brought in. There were a couple of people in the police force with whom Jagat felt uncomfortable. He wanted them out. I was especially called from Delhi for a meeting with the chief minister, the chief secretary and Jagat. Farooq said to me, 'I want you to sort this out. Jagat is not very comfortable with these guys.'

I said, 'Sir, Jagat is a leader. He's come from the Punjab, where it's much tougher. Now, they are his officers. It'll send a very bad signal, both to the J&K Police and a signal about Jagat's competence that he can't deal with his own people.'

I don't know if Jagat liked what I said, but Jaitly supported his cause. Jagat made an outstanding DG and went places after that, ending up as governor in Manipur. Farooq supported him at every step.

But at that moment in that room, I was the person to whom Farooq had turned, 'If you feel so strongly about this, then Suri [A.K. Suri] and Aivalli [Veeranna Aivalli] are decent people. But we can tell Delhi to get one person – preferably Aivalli – moved.'

Unsurprisingly, Aivalli was not thrilled about this, but my point is to highlight Farooq's insecurity and uncertainty in these circumstances. Even for trivial matters like press interviews, he relied on me. I was his main man. To cover the swearing-in, NDTV had sent a couple of journalists, one of whom was Sonia Singh. I knew her because her uncle, Peter Malik, was a good friend. Sonia got in touch with me, 'Uncle, please get me an interview with Dr Abdullah.'

'What's the problem?' I said jovially. 'Farooq is all over the place.'

But she insisted that I speak to Farooq personally and arrange it for her.

1996: A Pivotal Election

I organized an interview for her at the Centaur Hotel, where the press corps was staying. He was quite happy to speak to her. You see, we had moved beyond our professional designations: we were almost friends at this point. I have often wondered to myself what has enabled us to keep our friendship alive under such difficult circumstances. I may have represented Delhi in my official capacity, but as far as Farooq was concerned, he was also someone I admired and deeply respected, even then. He trusted me – and for me, that trust was a rare gift. It is also naturally why whenever I was reckoned to be close to Farooq, my stock in the IB would inevitably rise. As you can imagine, in 1996, Arun Bhagat was very happy with me!

It's just how things were at the time. I must admit that I began to enjoy it, for I had never been given so much importance.

The swearing-in ceremony was held in the Sher-e-Kashmir auditorium on 10 October 1996, and was attended by the Congress president, Sitaram Kesri, along with former Prime Minister V.P. Singh, Union Ministers Ram Vilas Paswan, C.M. Ibrahim, B.S. Ramoowalia, Communist Party of India-Marxist (CPI-M) leader Harkishan Singh Surjeet, CPI leader M. Farooqui, former Union Minister Rajesh Pilot, Kamal Nath and Sanjay Singh. I also went, and I took along my IB colleague, Ajit Doval, who was being posted to Srinagar and whom I wanted to introduce to the new chief minister.

The oath of office and secrecy was administered by the governor, Gen. K.V. Krishna Rao. As Farooq came on stage, the audience stood up and gave him a standing ovation. He became emotional and began calling people to join him, '*Tum bhi aajao*', and in the end around 20 fellows got sworn in. Among them was one non-NC member: Iftikhar Ansari, who was in the Congress party.

During the ceremony, Farooq asked Kesri: '*Inko humare saath aane dijiye.*' (Let him [Iftikhar Ansari] come with us.)

Such was the goodwill that Kesri immediately agreed, and said, '*Inko National Conference mein le lijiye.*' (Take him into the National Conference.)

Farooq took in 12 ministers of the cabinet rank, some ministers of state and two deputy ministers, one of them a woman.

At the conclusion of the ceremony, the chief minister pledged that Kashmir had to be restored to its old glory and asked Pakistan to keep off from the internal affairs of the country.

On 2 October 1996, Deve Gowda congratulated the people of Jammu and Kashmir by saying: '[They] have not only elected a government of their choice but have also shown where their heart lies.'[21] Unfortunately for Farooq, Deve Gowda's tenure was short-lived. In April 1997, the Congress (I) withdrew its support for the coalition. The reason given was that, despite being dependent upon the Congress, the prime minister did not consult it regarding important matters.

1996: A Pivotal Election

On 11 April 1997, Deve Gowda lost a no-confidence motion in the Lok Sabha by a wide margin; I.K. Gujral, then minister for external affairs, was chosen as the coalition leader. Farooq got on well with the stoic Gujral as well, especially since Gujral had a particular skill for looking in the other direction when it was required.

Promptly after the assembly elections, on 29 November 1996, the state government set up the State Autonomy Committee with the following terms of reference:

- To examine and recommend measures for the restoration of autonomy to the state of Jammu and Kashmir consistent with the Instrument of Accession, the Constitution Application Order, 1950, and the Delhi Agreement, 1952.
- To examine and recommend safeguards that be regarded necessary for incorporation in the Union/state constitution to ensure that the constitutional arrangement that is finally evolved in pursuance of the recommendations of this committee is inviolable.
- To also examine and recommend measures to ensure a harmonious relationship for the future between the state and the Union.

While this rolled ahead, Farooq employed his most trusted bureaucrats to help him administer Jammu and Kashmir. It was at this time that our friendship, now at its zenith, began making a lot of people – in Delhi and Kashmir – uncomfortable. I was in Kashmir a lot in those days despite my work in Delhi, and Farooq and I often spent long, convivial evenings together. He also helped me with my golf game, I must say.

I had learnt golf in Srinagar, from a seasoned pro at the old course on Maulana Azad Road, which was burnt down during the militancy period. Farooq loved his golf and any time he could squeeze out he would be on the golf course.

The Golf Club was a place for great kebabs and I also knew a couple of people in the air force and in the army who were keen on golf and who got me to learn. Of course, Farooq was a 4 or 5 handicap, whereas I had a handicap of 24 or so. I never had to lug a golf set up to the club. He always had three or four sets lying at home and would give me one. He would teach me, saying 'this is what you're doing wrong', 'this is what you're supposed to do'. I used to tell him I was spoiling his game, but he was patient. He was a good teacher and I picked up a few things from him.

One of these days, Farooq and I were sitting together on a flight from Jammu to Delhi with his principal secretary, B.R. Singh, sitting behind us. Farooq suddenly turned and told Singh that only one thing remained on his agenda, and that was to get me to Raj Bhavan as governor. I laughed.

Yes, that was a different Farooq: slowly gaining confidence as the days passed, always ready with the 'beans and banter' that Shekhar Gupta described him as possessing. I have never really seen that Farooq ever again.

The fall of the Deve Gowda government was a lost opportunity to build a real bridge between Delhi and

1996: A Pivotal Election

Srinagar. Most importantly, given the international and national context reigning at the time, it would have been a good chance for Delhi to reduce the superfluous army presence in the Valley. The moment to have done this was ideally after the 1996 assembly elections, when a democratic government was in place and Farooq was on good terms with Delhi. The army had done a damn good job of containing militancy in the early 1990s, but now it was time for it to be pulled back and gradually withdrawn. Doing so would have opened up more space for political activity, which in turn would have further marginalized the separatist movement.

Yet the army did not want to cede the power it wielded as head of the unified command, and insisted that only it could be in charge; Farooq wanted it headed by his DGP. The compromise was that the name of the set-up was changed to the unified headquarters headed by the chief minister, who was assisted by the two corps commanders deployed in Jammu and Kashmir. Farooq agreed with this – though he would then blame all the law-and-order problems in the state on the presence of the Indian army.

Still, as long as Deve Gowda was prime minister, Farooq was content. Theirs is a relationship that has flourished across the years as well, a testament to how much Farooq believes in maintaining ties with those who have treated him and Kashmir well. There are many who say that Farooq is nobody's friend, that he is selfish and only cares for those who can offer him something beneficial. I don't agree with that – I have seen Farooq being a friend to those he really didn't have any investment in, just because he liked them or something about them appealed to him. He is not a fair-weather man. If you are his friend, he will stay with you through thick and thin. In June 2024, he flew to Bangalore to meet with Deve Gowda. Though both sides maintained that this was not a political meeting, Farooq spoke to the press afterwards in his forthright way, 'I was here to thank him (Deve Gowda) for what he did as Prime Minister of India and for what he did for my state. We had a free election. When nobody wanted to come there, when people were afraid of terrorism, he as PM came, inaugurated many development projects there. He also went to Rajouri and many places close to the border to show the world that Kashmir is part of this nation.'[22]

To him, that has always been important: that Deve Gowda stood by him and pushed for Kashmir's cause with as much honesty and integrity as he did. It was not often that Farooq came across a prime minister in Delhi who believed in Kashmir as much as he did. Over the years, that bond would only grow. In fact, when Paran and I went for Omar's swearing-in as chief minister after the assembly elections of 2024, Deve Gowda had just been holidaying with Farooq in Srinagar!

But that's a story for another day and another time. For now, the halcyon days of our friendship were at their peak – though they were shortly to be hit by crises beyond our control.

6

Power Plays and Betrayal

As early as 1990, Farooq had said that Kashmir needed to be on the right side of Delhi. This was a repetition of his first political statement, made in 1981, where he had said that he wanted to be a bridge between Srinagar and Delhi.

What happened in 1983, now that we think back on it, was that Farooq turned down Mrs Gandhi's offer of an alliance. It is often said that Farooq acted imperiously in this case, but we would do well to remember the context in which this refusal took place. After all, Farooq was the Sheikh's son, and he had seen a whole flood of people who had come for his father's funeral. He needed no further evidence of the Sheikh's popularity. In his own mind, he admits that he was naïve in trying to improve upon his father's image during his first chief ministership. But in Delhi, the real tragedy began with Mrs Gandhi's dismissal of Farooq.

Farooq never got over that betrayal. It was politics, sure, but it was also personal. After the Emergency, she had come to Kashmir and met with Sheikh Sahib, and told him that she was seriously considering quitting politics.

'How can you think that?' he had demanded. 'You are Pandit Nehru's daughter. How can you quit?'

She stayed in Kashmir for a few days thereafter, being escorted to temples across the state by Farooq himself. She returned to Delhi a different woman. I'm only mentioning this because in Farooq's mind, Indira's dismissal of him was not just sad, but stunning, given that she was the one who pushed and prodded the old Sheikh to decide on his successor, to choose Farooq. To her, he seemed to be the more trustworthy option. Perhaps she was swayed by Farooq's modern outlook, his foreign exposure, and his ease with English as well as with Kashmiri and Urdu. We'll never know for sure, but for her to have dismissed him after this deep personal context was a betrayal he would always carry in his heart.

To be sure, her treatment of him has often been repeated thereafter. It was the problem with Narasimha Rao, as much as it was with Vajpayee. The latter was far too smart as a politician. He would never show that he didn't want Farooq. But Narasimha Rao had planned the whole business of separatists joining the elections in 1996. Each politician was different in his method of handling Farooq, but the ultimate outcome only proved the same thing: Delhi never understood Farooq. There was something about him that was simply beyond the capital's comprehension. He was always the more difficult option because even when Delhi had other preferences, because of its limitations, Farooq would become the fallback option. But he was a difficult option because he could not be pushed around, neither could he be controlled.

So when, in June 2000, the assembly in Kashmir convened for a week-long special session to discuss the Autonomy Committee's report and pass a resolution to accept it, Delhi was suspicious. It had its reasons. In its report, the committee recommended the restoration of the 1952 Delhi Agreement, in which the only areas that the Union government would be in charge of would be defence, external affairs and communication. It also recommended that Article 370 of the Constitution, which grants special status to the state, be made a 'special provision' in the Constitution instead of 'temporary provision'. This was the last thing the BJP and its allies wanted. The party has always stood for the abrogation of Article 370 and for putting Jammu and Kashmir firmly at par with other states in the Union. Similarly, the NC has always walked this tightrope. Notwithstanding his popularity, Farooq needed Delhi's understanding, if not support, in fighting the elections. Looking ahead to the 2002 assembly election, Farooq knew he had to deliver on his promises well on time.

I had heard from our man in Srinagar, K.M. Singh, that Farooq had told him that he had contested the 1996 elections because the Government of India wanted him to contest, and at that time he had told the government that he needed a plank to fight the elections. Autonomy had been that plank.

I think there was no better plank for the NC to fight the 2002 elections. Farooq said to me very honestly one day, 'What is this whole hullabaloo about? All we wanted from Delhi was a statement that the resolution was being examined. The problem is that Delhi never understands us.'

Delhi wasn't pleased.

'What is your friend up to?' Brajesh Mishra asked me. I was at this point heading the R&AW.

When I rang Farooq to speak with him, and to let him know that Delhi was concerned, he told me that he had been pleading with New Delhi to also appoint a committee, which could have a couple of cabinet ministers on it. However, there was no response to his suggestion from the National Democratic Alliance (NDA), and left with no choice, Farooq was forced to move this resolution in his assembly.

'Why are you worried?' Farooq asked. 'Everybody has to be kept happy. Tell them not to worry, the resolution won't get passed. *Kuch nahi hoga.*' (Nothing will happen.)

But when the resolution *was* passed by the Jammu and Kashmir assembly, Farooq merely sent it on to the Union home ministry. He knew that the home ministry was headed by L.K. Advani, and he knew that with Advani in charge, nothing would happen. It gave him, he figured, some time to breathe as well as an election plank. But the thing was that Delhi was supremely unhappy. Members of the NDA government were upset, and a cabinet meeting was immediately called. It summarily threw out the resolution, saying it was not acceptable.

Farooq was infuriated.

Yet again, it was, in his eyes, a question of Delhi not understanding him or the games he needed to play to keep the NC in the political running in Jammu and Kashmir. Delhi, he felt, was being far more hardline than was necessary. Kashmiris were once again being shut out, with not even a chance at dialogue. The thing is – you cannot push Farooq around.

I watched as the Delhi–Srinagar relationship became strained once again. I suppose, in retrospect, it did not help that Farooq was unpredictable enough to keep Delhi on its toes. One day he might be taking a sail down the calm waters of the Dal Lake with Home Minister L.K. Advani, even flying to Leh to welcome him and Prime Minister Atal Behari Vajpayee for the Sindhu Yatra festival. Soon after, he would be lashing out at Advani's ministry for conspiring against him. But that is Farooq's nature. It cannot be changed and nor should Delhi have expected anything other than volatility from him.

In one respect, Farooq has remained consistent: his demand for autonomy. In many ways, his autonomy package mirrors his father's demands as early as 1953. Belligerence often characterized Farooq's dealings with the Centre, but when he made his latest move, Delhi was not ready for the denouement. This despite the issue being debated in the Jammu and Kashmir assembly for five days, with Farooq often spitting fire, with noisy verbal debates and walkouts. When the resolution was eventually passed, it was received in Delhi with shock and disbelief. But even here, Farooq left room for negotiation. Though he upped the ante and threw the ball in Delhi's court, making it clear that it could cosy up to parties like the Hurriyat only at the cost of the NC, he left the door open for dialogue with his trademark belief in 'consensus, not confrontation'.

'Nothing has been spelt out yet.' He told *The Statesman* airily, 'Talks are still in its preliminary phase. There is no use talking about it at this stage. Nothing has gone beyond Mr Advani's statement. We have to see what they are ready to give us. We have placed our report before them. There is world pressure to settle the Jammu and Kashmir issue. While we settle it, let one thing be clear. We have to win the hearts and minds of the people of the state. Granting autonomy to the people can help bridge the gap.'[1]

Delhi, however, was having none of it.

Furious, Farooq threatened to resign. A tense meeting of the NC MLAs was held to determine what the next step should be.

Then, the morning after the meeting, on 11 July 2000, Begum Abdullah – that elegant, wonderful old woman – passed away of a cardiac arrest.

As I've written before, this was a personal tragedy for the Abdullah family – but for Delhi, it was a political opportunity. K.M. Singh, my colleague in Kashmir, rang me up, 'Things are very bad here,' he said. 'Farooq is threatening to leave the NDA. Now he's lost his mother. If the prime minister were to come here for the Begum's funeral, it will resolve everything.'

I went straight to Brajesh Mishra.

'*Haan*,' he said. '*Advaniji jaa rahe hain.*' (Yes, Advaniji is going.)

I said, 'Sir, maybe something more than Advaniji going should happen. Perhaps the prime minister can go.'

Brajesh looked taken aback. 'You really think so?'

'Yes.'

So Brajesh asked Vajpayee if he would consider going. Unsurprisingly, the prime minister was quite open to the idea.

It was, in retrospect, a terrific idea.

A thaw between Delhi and Srinagar set in immediately after. Farooq and the Abdullahs were touched – and in a way, the whole of Kashmir was touched. After all, it was a rare gesture for a prime minister to come to Kashmir at this moment of grief.

I went, too, of course – and I saw just how shaken the Abdullahs were. Perhaps the biggest sign of how emotionally devastated they were was that Omar hugged me as I got off the flight from Delhi. He is not a physically demonstrative boy and for him to have made this gesture meant a lot.

So when we come to 2002, I wonder now, in retrospect, if I was brought into the PMO after retirement as special advisor on Kashmir only to facilitate Farooq's shift from Srinagar to Delhi. I joined on the first day of 2001, and it could not have been more innocuously put back then. I remember asking Brajesh what I was supposed to do. 'Anything you like,' Brajesh said. 'But we want you to focus on Kashmir.'

A few days later we had a longer chat and I asked, 'Okay, what in Kashmir?'

'Elections are coming up next year,' he said. 'We want as much participation as possible, as many people as you can get in. Try and get these separatists in.'

What more could one ask for? Kashmir had always been my favourite subject, and now I would be devoting all my time to it. I had already built up considerable experience discussing the state's political future with the separatists. In addition to all of this, between the autonomy resolution in the Jammu and Kashmir assembly and the vice-presidential elections in August 2002, much water had flown down the Jhelum. The Agra summit had taken place, as had the 9/11 attacks on the World Trade Center in America. Closer home, we had seen the terrifying attack on our own Parliament and India's subsequent military mobilization along the western border.

The assembly elections in Jammu and Kashmir were next in line.

Vajpayee and Brajesh Mishra had tasked me with overseeing a completely free and fair Jammu and Kashmir assembly election, if possible with the participation of the separatists. Getting them into the electoral process was another matter altogether because they were so tightly controlled by Pakistan, but that was my brief. The historic Agra summit in July 2001 had a positive fallout in Kashmir, for when things are going peacefully between India and Pakistan, that is when the Kashmiri feels the most optimistic, and this helped in the run-up to the 2002 assembly elections. Other factors also paved the way, such as the Hizbul Mujahideen's chief commander Abdul Majeed Dar's return from Pakistan and announcing a ceasefire and Vajpayee's unilateral Ramzan ceasefire in November 2000.

At this time, I suggested to Brajesh that Vajpayee begin taking Omar – then a minister of commerce – along on his foreign trips. 'He looks good, he speaks English and he's a Kashmiri.' I said, 'It gives him good exposure and it also sends a positive signal.'

Brajesh was agreeable, and on the next trip, Omar went along. Then he went again. And again. Vajpayee was impressed with what he saw. At that point of time, the prime minister became more of a father figure to Omar than his own father. Omar was moved to the Ministry of External Affairs, where he was made a junior minister. Omar was now Delhi's choice, something I facilitated in a way.

At a meeting with the prime minister, I mentioned the possibility of Farooq becoming vice-president. Vajpayee said to me, '*Woh aapka idea achcha hai. Usko pursue karo.*' (It is a good idea. Pursue it.)

The offer of vice-presidency was made at my residence by Brajesh Mishra, later reaffirmed, according to Farooq, by Home Minister L.K. Advani, and of course the prime minister himself. Farooq was elated. His life's ambition had been to one day become president of India, and this was the penultimate step to that goal. But you see, everything was a scheme, from Delhi, to get Farooq out of the way.

The Chief Minister and the Spy

Sometimes I had no idea about it. Sometimes, I indirectly contributed to these plans.

Farooq, being Farooq, went along with the game. He knew pretty quickly what was happening.

A year before Kashmir went to the polls, in February 2001, I went to Jammu to deliver the Amar Kapoor Memorial Lecture. Kapoor had been an Indian Police Service (IPS) officer of the Jammu and Kashmir cadre from the 1964 batch, a year senior to me. He was the additional DGP when, four years before, he had died suddenly of a heart attack. This lecture had been instituted in his memory. My topic was 'Kashmir: The Way Forward', and it is well to remember that when I went to deliver it, I was still with the R&AW.

At the time, Gary Saxena, the former R&AW chief, was the governor, and he insisted that I stay at Raj Bhavan. On my way to the lecture, I stopped at Farooq's house, where I made the unsuccessful case that the former militant Firdous Syed be given another term as a member of the legislative council. Firdous had come overground and had found accommodation with the NC in the past.

Farooq was presiding over the lecture that day, and he wasn't too happy during its course, because I was quite vocal about the need for dialogue with, and the involvement of, separatists. This was exactly the kind of situation that the NC was wary of: being replaced by the separatists. Now, Farooq, as I have mentioned earlier in this book, was never closed to the idea of dialogue. He was an open-minded politician in that sense of the word, but not everybody is Farooq.

Power Plays and Betrayal

As the leader of his party, he had to make sure that the party line was being followed, at least in semblance. Our dialogue with Abdul Ghani Lone was making him anxious before the 2002 elections. During the lecture, I happened to refer to Lone as 'Lone Sahib'. A few NC people pointedly didn't stay for tea, though they were polite enough to stay for the duration of the lecture. But it was clear that they were not happy.

'*Yeh Lone kab Lone Sahib ban gaye?*' one of the NC fellows asked me later. (Since when did Lone become Lone Sahib?)

'It was only out of respect for age,' I said. 'He's older than me.'

Gary Saxena read about it in the papers the next day. He understood what was going on and complimented me. '*Tum achcha bole,*' he said. '*Bara balance kar ke.*' (You spoke well. It was a balanced speech.)

Farooq was not happy, but he didn't say a word about it to me. He didn't have to. I knew his feelings on the subject, just as I knew that he had the gift of being balanced in his political approach. When Farooq is quiet, it is because he knows Kashmir and Kashmiris better than anyone else and he has that confidence as well.

Meanwhile, the elections were growing. A whole lot of people were filing nominations. This is what the NDA wanted, but it also wanted Omar Abdullah as chief minister. Farooq had his own view: 'You know he's my son,' he said to me on several occasions. 'He has to succeed me and I would like him to succeed me. But I would like him to first learn the ropes.'

This was a time when Omar could yet not stand up to his father. On one occasion, just prior to the elections in 2002, Doctor Sahib wanted to introduce Omar to P.S. Gill, his favourite candidate as the next prospective DG. Omar was neither comfortable with the idea of meeting Gill, nor with having Gill thrust upon him as DGP. He wanted me to be present. It was an occasion where I felt for Omar. Much as I liked Gill myself, I felt it was premature to thrust a DGP upon Omar even before he became chief minister.

Farooq's plan was that Omar would be a minister in his government for a year or two, as an apprentice of sorts, and then take over as chief minister for the rest of the term, at which point Farooq would withdraw. 'Let him learn,' he said.

In a sense, he was hedging his bets, because it was now dawning on him that Delhi intended to make Omar chief minister, but it would never make him vice-president of India.

Brajesh, on the other hand, was very clear about going ahead with the switch to get Farooq out of Kashmir. So when participation in the elections grew beyond expectations, he asked me: 'Omar is all right, no?' What worried Brajesh was that even people on the fringe of the Jamaat were jumping into the elections. Anything could happen.

The thing was that all these fellows had a reservation at the back of their minds, that the elections would be fixed, that the NC would return no matter what they did. It was in order to allay that fear and extract greater participation through transparently free and fair elections that the Vajpayee government made a suggestion to Farooq. It came up during the time that Farooq was promised the vice-presidency. In those days, Brajesh and Farooq talked openly and freely because Farooq was going to be vice-president.

'Doctor Sahib,' Brajesh said. '*Aisa hai*, this time we want the elections to be free and fair. Omar *toh* chief minister *banega hi*, but we want the elections to be free and fair, so we would like to have it under Governor's Rule.' (Omar will definitely be chief minister.)

Luckily, he'd caught Farooq in a good mood. Farooq's amiable response was, '*Theek hai, laga dena uss time.* [All right, put Governor's Rule in place at that time.] If we are on the same page and I know where we are headed, then okay.'

For that brief moment, perhaps, Farooq believed that he might actually be made vice-president of India.

But it was an illusion.

Around May that year, the whispers began in Delhi. That month, I was in Srinagar and received a message that the chief minister wanted to meet me at 11 in the morning. I took it for granted that I had been called home, but I was told, '*No, sahib ne office bulaya hai*,' which is very unlike Farooq.

At his office, he sat me across the desk and asked me point-blank, 'What are Delhi's plans? Do you believe that these guys will make me vice-president?'

'Why not?' I asked.

'I don't believe it, that's why I'm asking you.'

'What do you believe?' I asked. 'Sir, you've spoken to the home minister about this, haven't you?'

Farooq said yes.

'And you've spoken to the prime minister about this?'

'Yes.'

'If both have given you their word then you will be the next vice-president,' I said.

'But I don't trust them,' Farooq said. 'I don't trust Delhi.'

As it turned out, he was right.

There are always wheels within wheels, not the least being that the Rashtriya Swayamsevak Sangh (RSS) was no fan of Farooq's.

The facts are well-known: in 2002, Vice-President Krishan Kant was on course to become the 11th president of India. Such a promotion to Rashtrapati Bhavan was a tradition, and in this way, six previous vice-presidents had gone on to become president. At the time, Vajpayee and Sonia Gandhi were both agreeable to Kant's candidature – he was one of the Congress party's original 'Young Turks' and a member of the 1977–80 Janata Party government. His name had been announced as such.

Several members of the NDA government, like Home Minister L.K. Advani, however, remembered that along with Madhu Limaye, Kant had been responsible for the fall of the Janata government over the issue of dual membership in the RSS.

So they opposed Kant.

Vajpayee then had to propose long-time civil servant and Tamil Nadu governor P.C. Alexander as the NDA's candidate, but the Congress vetoed the idea. Ultimately, A.P.J. Abdul Kalam became president and proved to be the most popular one India has had. Two days after Kalam was sworn in, a broken-hearted Kant passed away, the only vice-president to die in office.

The moment Kalam was sworn in, Farooq's fears were confirmed. The president and the vice-president of India could not both be from minority communities. He was proven right.

The result? Farooq had to be ditched. The NDA leadership had obviously said to Farooq whatever they had said, but they had not been sincere about what they had said. As before, betrayal came easily in politics. It didn't matter to anyone that they had made certain promises which they were now breaking.

That was that.

So when the whole plan eventually began to fray, when Farooq began to see that things were not going his way and that there was no way he would ever be vice-president of India, he rejected what he'd previously agreed to in his conversation with Brajesh.

This loss was the great tragedy of Farooq's life, after his dismissal by Mrs Gandhi.

It was an outright betrayal.

Now, Delhi's challenge – and mine – as we headed into the assembly elections in Jammu and Kashmir was to keep things as lawful, free and fair as possible. That was going to be easier said than done.

On 31 July 2002, Fayaz Ahmed Bhat, who was set to resign from his government job to contest as an NC candidate, was shot dead. A week later, Ghulam Hasan Jan, another potential candidate, met a similar fate. Farooq was furious and made it clear to the public that this was an election being fought against Pakistan. He couldn't have put it more aptly. No sooner had Delhi set the ball rolling on the poll exercise – staggered over four phases to ensure unprecedented security against militant threats – Pakistan upped the ante. President Musharraf was at his acerbic best when, in his 14 August speech, he called the elections 'a farce'. For us, then, it became imperative to have the elections as free and fair as possible, not only to call Islamabad's bluff on Kashmir but also to show the disenchantment with the decade-long violent secessionist scourge – all with maximum participation of candidates and voters.

Farooq was again pushed to the wall. 'Pakistan has threatened us against holding elections. We will show our neighbours that the elections will be held … They may do anything. We are not scared. We will get on with this [elections]. Inshallah, we are all raring to go. We have made enough sacrifices and are ready for more.'[2] Throughout, he insisted on maintenance of autonomy, and on allying with the Centre as much as possible. He refused to listen to criticism, saying memorably, 'Farooq Abdullah is like a raincoat – rain falls on it and runs off and doesn't stick to it.'[3]

The elections to the 87-member assembly took place over four phases in September and October of 2002. They were widely seen as credible, though there was a lot of violence before the elections. Nearly 600 deaths occurred. The verdict that the people delivered saw the NC lose power.

On Thursday, 10 October, three weeks short of the NC's 55th anniversary, the Sheikh's grandson, Omar Abdullah, was defeated in Ganderbal. The NC itself was reduced to 28 seats in a legislative assembly of 87. In the Valley, where the NC had won 44 of 46 seats in 1996, the party was down to 18. Omar, who had taken over as NC president from his father, had been undone.

The media reportage, as usual, was savage. 'The first, most simplistic factor was good old anti-incumbency. Farooq's government paid for six wasted years, a period in which it promised much, delivered little and had the chief minister dividing time between foreign holidays – he left for South Africa after the third of the elections' four phases – and the golf course, with occasional visits to the state secretariat … That aside, Omar's distaste for his father's flamboyant ways – he moved out of the chief minister's residence a few weeks ago – and alienation of the NC's old guard didn't help. The new NC chief replaced a third of his party's sitting MLAs. Yet, of the party's 30 new faces, as many as 21 lost. What's more, the displeased veterans only fuelled rebellion and ate into the NC vote in constituency after constituency.'[4]

From where I stood, one way of looking at the betrayal would be that Vajpayee had played a deep game when he offered Farooq the vice-presidency. He liked what he had seen in Omar, and he wanted to switch up the father–son combination by bringing Farooq to Delhi and putting Omar in Srinagar.

It was a masterstroke that whetted Omar's appetite for power. When Farooq's term as chief minister ended, he never became chief minister again, even though he was publicly willing to do so in 2008.

All in all, for Farooq, 2002 was a terrible year. He did not get the vice-presidentship. There was a lot of talk that he would be inducted into the cabinet as a Union minister. After the elections, I asked him, 'What happened, why did you refuse a ministership here?'

'Which ministership?' he asked.

'Weren't you offered a ministership?'

'What rubbish,' he said. 'Nobody's offered me anything. But now that you are talking of ministership, at least get me a house. I don't even have a house in Delhi.'

You see, he had not even got that. On the other hand, since Omar had been allotted a house on Akbar Road, Farooq was told: 'Your son has a house, why do you need one?' It was unsurprising that he was disappointed and disgusted.

There was nowhere for the party to turn to, because at that time, the Congress was not going to support the NC. The Congress plus PDP together tallied 36 seats and, with the support of smaller parties and a handful of independents, it crossed the halfway mark of 44 seats (in fact, the Congress–PDP combine mustered a total strength of 57 seats when it went to the governor to stake claim to form the next government). The tie-up was natural in many ways for, after all, Mufti was originally a Congressman.

Farooq was furious at his party's loss. On the day of counting he had flown in from London and sent me a message to come over and have breakfast with him. I reached his place about 10 a.m., by which time the results had started coming in. He was taking a shower, and after he got ready, he stormed into the room where I was waiting.

'Now I know what you guys have been up to,' he snapped.

There was nothing I could say. He had lost out on the vice-presidency and now he had lost his state.

No, it was not a good year for Farooq.

The postscript to all this was that in the aftermath of the elections, word began to circulate in Kashmir – driven by many angry NC leaders – that Delhi had conspired to dethrone the party. I was portrayed as the villain of the piece.

'*Isne karaya hai,*' they said. (He's the one who did it.)

I took it quietly for as long as I could, then, when I could stand it no more, I went to Farooq.

'Sir, everybody's saying that you blame me.'

'Who's saying that?' Farooq demanded.

'It's not a question of who told me,' I said. 'It's a question of do you believe this to be true?'

Farooq looked at me. 'Not at all,' he said simply. 'You're like my younger brother.'

That was good enough for me.

7

Father and Son

The father–son relationship is never an easy one. As Richard Nixon once remarked, 'To have a father – to be a father – is to come very near the heart of life itself.'[1]

Omar was born in England in 1970, at a time when his grandfather, Sheikh Sahib, was exiled from Kashmir. Those were difficult days for the state. After Nehru's death in 1964, Sheikh Abdullah had been interned from 1965 to 1968. This had been ordered by Nehru's successor, Lal Bahadur Shastri, and was continued by Nehru's daughter, Indira Gandhi. The Sheikh's party, the Plebiscite Front, was also banned in 1971. This had allegedly been done to prevent him and the Plebiscite Front from taking part in the elections in Kashmir. The Sheikh was exiled from Kashmir during 1971–72 for 18 months, and it was during this time that war between India and Pakistan broke out in the winter of 1971.

When I got to Srinagar in 1988, both Omar and Safia were away, studying at Lawrence School, Sanawar. Our daughter had finished class X while we were still in Bhopal, and we were having some difficulty in finding a good school for her in Srinagar. That problem resolved itself when we got her admission in Sanawar, where my wife, Paran, went to school, in the same year when Omar was the head boy. Founder's Day was in October, and as it neared, Farooq called me.

'Aren't you going to your daughter's school for Founder's Day?' he asked.

I laughed. 'Sir, to do that I have to take leave!'

In his inimitable way, Farooq said, '*Chhodo na, mere saath aao.* [Let it be. Come with me.] Tell Delhi that you're watching the chief minister. Come with me in my chopper.'

My first recollections of father and son was that Omar was a very good son and Farooq was a very good father. It was a good relationship. Farooq was very proud of his son. Behind every young boy who believes in himself is a father who believed in him first. As I see it, Farooq is part of a transitional generation. He is the son of the Sher-e-Kashmir and the father of the hope of Kashmir. For the Kashmiri across several generations, the Sheikh is a father figure. Farooq figures more in a fraternal sense. He has always been conscious of keeping his father's legacy going. But in the early 1990s, the thought of Omar's entry into politics had not yet entered anyone's head, and Farooq was busy keeping track of the other dynamics that were at play.

Khalida's husband, Gul Mohammad Shah,[2] was out in the cold, so to speak. It was the Begum, Farooq and Khalida's mother, who decided that the two families should patch up.

Father and Son

She didn't approve of what Gul had done to her son, but she could hardly go against her own daughter either. As I observed her, it was a difficult tightrope to walk, but she did it remarkably well. When Farooq became chief minister, his mother ran a kitchen cabinet, literally and metaphorically, though by 1988 it was not as powerful as it had once been. Farooq was an indulgent son, but the Begum made sure not to meddle in everyday affairs. Nor did she speak while her son was speaking. Slowly, relations between the two families began to improve. Khalida visited regularly, and her son, Muzaffar Shah, whom everyone called 'Muzy', often came along. By 1988, Muzy had drawn close to Farooq. There was never a sentence which wasn't prefaced by 'Mamu this' or 'Mamu that'. Farooq himself had grown very fond of the boy – fond enough for Muzy to begin expecting some kind of political reward. After all, Omar was away at school while Muzy was around.

For years, Omar was away, out of the Valley. When he came back from Sanawar, he spoke Kashmiri only haltingly. Then it was time for college, for which he enrolled at Sydenham College in Mumbai. Omar lived then at the residence of his father's political chum, Sharad Pawar. From here, he would enter the corporate world, working for the Oberois for about five years or so. It was in this job that he met his wife, Payal.

In the old days, there were whispers in the family about Farooq's philandering, and as Omar grew up and spent more time at home, he would also laugh and join in these jokes about his father. None of these jokes tickled Farooq, I noticed.

The Chief Minister and the Spy

If there was any souring of relationship between father and son, it was after Omar married Payal. If there was anything that sharpened Omar's taste for politics, it was the sight and sound of his father back in the chief minister's chair in 1996, a chief minister on his own terms. In all of this, he was egged on by Payal. In her mind, it seemed to me, she wanted to be the chief minister's wife – the earlier, the better.

Doctor Sahib and his wife dropped in one evening in the summer of 1994 at our home in Kidwai Nagar to inform us about his son's engagement to Payal and the impending nuptials. Farooq asked me if it was all right for Omar to marry a non-Kashmiri Hindu girl. My wife, Paran, was present but she didn't comment. I, however, took the liberty of asking, 'What is the problem, sir? You're broad-minded enough to accept whatever Omar wants.'

In a peculiar way, it seemed as though Farooq was seeking our approval but there was obviously no question of our disapproving the match. Payal was a strong-willed woman and didn't fit in easily with the Abdullah family. My wife and I couldn't help think that Payal could not have found better or more understanding in-laws.

But that is another story, of course.

Then, in the general elections of 1998, the personal dynamics between Farooq and Khalida's families came into play yet again. As I've said, Muzaffar had been expecting some kind of political concession to come from his close ties with Farooq. In fact, he had begun to eye a seat in Parliament. When it became known that Omar would be contesting in the 1998 elections (Kashmir chose three representatives to the Lok Sabha, from Srinagar, Anantnag and Baramulla), Khalida's family felt short-changed again. For them, it was the early 1980s all over again, when Gul Shah had lost to Farooq in the race for the Sheikh's successor. This time, it was Muzy losing to Omar.

The sad part is that Muzy has drifted away from Farooq, yet when the PAGD was formed in 2019, Muzy had a key role to play. He was with Farooq, and when the district development elections were held in 2020, Muzy worked very hard. Farooq noticed this and told me, '*Usko mubarak de dena, bahut kaam kiya hai usne.*' (Congratulate him. He's worked very hard.)

Such are the ways of families.

As the years have passed, father and son have shared a fantastic relationship on the surface. But their politics has been quite different, in their method and process, if not in their ideology. Farooq has always been the quintessential Kashmiri politician, seen everywhere all the time. He has what the Kashmiris called *lachak* – the flexibility and charm that is important to conducting politics. He is 100 per cent Indian and more than 100 per cent Kashmiri.

Omar, on the other hand, presents a picture of contrasts: 100 per cent Indian, but only 50 per cent Kashmiri, and 50 per cent still the head boy of Sanawar. Apart from his youth and freshness, he's straighter, much more open than anyone else in Kashmir. In addition, he's correct and honest, a trait that has not always gone down well in his state. He has never been quite at ease with the Kashmiri *lachak*. In Kashmir, people still say that Omar is too much of an Englishman. We have seen Omar grow up, and as a young lad, admired him in the family. He was particularly fond of my wife and referred to her as 'Paran Aunty'.

The man that Omar has become is smart, articulate and well-spoken. After the years he worked in corporate life, he would have made a good CEO, but by the early 2000s, as I say, his appetite for politics had been whetted.

Omar was keen to become chief minister. Before the elections of 2002, Omar went around citing Sheikh Sahib's example while campaigning and bypassing his father altogether. From what he said, it sounded as if Farooq was bad news, and Dadaji (Sheikh Sahib) was everything. This, I don't think, paid him any dividends. Omar seemed to have forgotten that if it hadn't been for his father, he would not have become chief minister. Ultimately, his repeated reference to Sheikh Sahib while ignoring his own father did not go down well in Kashmir. Rubbishing Farooq was counterproductive.

Farooq, as I said, was always everywhere – among the people, sitting with them on the floor, and eating lunch off a traditional *trami* (platter). It was the same in the run-up to the parliamentary and assembly elections in Kashmir in 2024, with Farooq working very hard to ensure his party's success. Omar may be the hope of Kashmir, but Farooq is the face of the NC in ways that only the Kashmiri's heart can recognize. His brand of canvassing, and the ways in which he can reach the voter, is unique. And he uses no social media –

Father and Son

unlike Omar – to do so. Farooq's charm lies in his personal touch.

In the ways of Nehruvian politics, Farooq is perennially out there, among his people, listening to what they tell him. In the three decades that I have watched him, I have seen him develop into a much-loved popular face, capable of being both charismatic and disarming. Once, in 1997, Farooq asked me to accompany him on a trip out into the Kashmiri countryside, to Doda, to attend a District Development Council meeting. Now these were years when, as I have said before, our chemistry was at its best, but I was still taken aback.

'*Sir, main wahan kya karunga?*' I asked. (Sir, what will I do there?)

'*Arrey chalo na*,' Farooq said casually. '*Doda jayenge.*' (Why don't you come? We will go to Doda.)

So he swept me off to Doda. Once the meeting was over, Farooq said, '*Chalo, ab mujhe sheher bhi jaana hai.*' (Let's go, now I have to visit the city too.)

So we went to the city as well. By this time, it was around lunchtime. Suddenly, Farooq left my side and walked off, quite randomly, into a nearby house.

I was alarmed, and not a little unsure of what to do next. This was obviously a house known to Farooq, perhaps belonging to one of his party people, but I could hardly enter as well. So I remained standing awkwardly outside. After about five minutes, someone came to summon me inside. I went in, uncertain about what to expect. I found Farooq seated on the floor, surrounded by the family, eating lunch with them companionably.

'What are you doing, standing outside?' demanded Farooq. 'Are you ashamed of sitting on the floor?'

'No, sir,' I said sheepishly.

'Then come and join us! Eat.'

As a story, I think there's no better example to illustrate just how easy Farooq is among the Kashmiri people.

With Omar, on the other hand, there is a correctness, a punctiliousness of attitude that cannot be replaced. In the ways of the younger generation, he prefers to use social media in order to reach out, perhaps to a wider audience. But that's the thing about Kashmir and the Kashmiri people. You cannot reach out to Kashmiris only via the smartphone, iPad or Twitter.

Omar has depended too much on security, which has never gone down well in Kashmir. You don't need to be a genius to know that unemployment and development cannot be dealt with through the security paradigm. That said, of course, both Delhi and Islamabad prefer Omar to Farooq – but the Kashmiri knows better. And this isn't just my opinion. In 2002, when Omar lost his family's traditional bastion in Ganderbal, just out of Srinagar, my colleague at the IB, K.M. Singh, gloomily told me that the NC had lost because it had projected Omar as the next chief minister. If it had projected Farooq, K.M. observed, then it would not have lost power.

Omar himself was sanguine. 'I believe to go straight into office in 2002 would not have been, in hindsight, the most appropriate thing. I was able to learn a lot more about the state. In terms of personal growth, there is nothing like an election loss to teach you a whole lot of lessons which you don't learn from winning. It taught me humility. I was perhaps a little cavalier in terms of some public pronouncements which, as I said, the period of opposition helped temper and set right. And then I guess the biggest lesson is that all your contact with people is direct and on the ground. You don't have advantages of state planes and helicopters to buzz from place to place. There is no better way to learn about the geography of your state than to criss-cross it by driving across, which is what I did. It taught me the lay of the land, the way people think.'[3]

If that was what he took away from it all, then it was similar to what I was told when I met Mufti Mohammad Sayeed in 2014. In fact, during the course of our conversation, Mufti made two remarks that are very telling about both father and son. 'Farooq has a feel for Kashmir,' he said, before adding, 'Omar is over-dependent on security and is far too insular for Kashmir. Here he's called "tweet CM".'

Even in 2002, it was clear that nobody believed that Omar could lose. But he did, because he was out of touch with the ground reality. That has been his problem throughout his political career.

Why, you might wonder.

Well, as I see it, the thing is that Omar has always had a peculiar kind of hang-up about his father, one that was evident especially in the 1990s. When he began to enter the political limelight more and more in the 2000s, he began to express his doubts: he felt Farooq was gullible, that Farooq was misled by bad advisors, and that he, Omar, was going to do things his own way when he became chief minister. There was, in fact, a time when it seemed as though he *would* do things his own way.

In 2008, Omar was the great hope of the youth of Kashmir. But unfortunately his dependence on the security paradigm, and his lack of political confidence meant that he was unable to match his father. After the 2008 elections, Omar Abdullah became chief minister in Jammu and Kashmir on a wave of hope. The Kashmiris liked what they saw and heard of this fresh-faced young man, with his honesty and plain talk. Omar had also made a huge impact in Kashmir and in Delhi with a statement he made in Parliament during the July 2008 debate on the Indo-US nuclear deal, when he declared that it had been a mistake not to resign from the NDA after the 2002 riots in Gujarat, and that Kashmiris would never let any harm come to the pilgrims going to Amarnath. He had also visited Pakistan at the invitation of General Pervez Musharraf in 2006, the first mainstream Kashmiri politician to do so. Musharraf had been very impressed with Omar. From his point of view, Omar was a smart, upfront Kashmiri who spoke well and appeared honest, quite the opposite of the Hurriyat guys who said one thing, did another and meant something totally different.

Given all of this, the Kashmiris were willing to give Farooq's son a chance. The objective of this chapter isn't to analyse Omar's tenure as chief minister. We all know how that turned out, but the gist of what I am trying to say is that both father and son have always had very different ways of doing things. As I have often said before, Farooq finds it important to stay on the right side of Delhi. In order to do this, he keeps his cards close to his chest, even as he keeps his political doors open to all options. In that sense, he is a politician's politician. He worked quite well with the intelligence and security apparatus, because he knew he had to. But when it came to managing the affairs of his state, he did it in his own way. His primary objective has been to keep the Kashmiris engaged and Pakistan too, to the extent possible. His conviction is that nothing else will give the Kashmiri respite. That is the difference between him and Omar – Farooq is willing to go along with you so long as it suits him and Kashmir, and Delhi is not unreasonable.

I can give you an example. In a conversation he had with Brajesh Mishra at our place over dinner in 2002, Brajesh got him to agree to both the participation of separatists in the election and for elections to be held under Governor's Rule, given that he would be made vice-president of India. But the moment he found Delhi backtracking from its word, he was quite blatant about backtracking from his. When asked about the possibility of elections under Governor's Rule, Farooq said, 'What Governor's Rule? I'm good enough. There's no need for Governor's Rule.' That was when he had realized that Delhi was trying to fool him.

Omar, on the other hand, has a more blinkered view of doing things, an approach that is dependent heavily on a model based on security. Why does this become important for Omar? To keep Delhi happy is the obvious answer. At this point of time, Kashmir is willing to forgive Farooq for much more than it is Omar, who still remains under scrutiny. The whole business of a security paradigm first arose in 2008, during Omar's chief ministership, and among others, Mufti Sahib used to say that Omar has remained too dependent on security. If you look back, Farooq never allowed that impression of him to gain currency. Omar is far more open and straighter than his father, which can be somewhat of a disadvantage. Omar himself has said on more than one occasion that the chief ministership of Jammu and Kashmir is the most difficult job in the country.

When Afzal Guru was hanged in February 2013 for his involvement in the December 2001 attack on Parliament, Omar was chief minister. He was extremely annoyed, asking what the rush was to hang Guru. After all, there were 12 other convicts who had been waiting for far longer on death row. But he really had no choice: Delhi believed that, in return for its support, it could ram anything it liked down his throat. The consequences were obvious. Guru immediately became a martyr in Kashmir, not because he was a fugitive freedom fighter like Maqbool Bhat, but because he came to represent the victimization that Kashmiris felt.

Farooq's pride in his son, of course, has always clearly shone through. He has never been one for interfering in the ways of his son, and even less for the way his son handled the reins of power. He watched Omar's first chief ministership from afar, and believed that it was the summer of 2010 that saw his son cutting his wisdom teeth on the bone of power. In 2012, *India Today* interviewed both of them – the father at a hearty 75 years old, and the 42-year-old son, then chief minister for three years. Even in the profile, the two men couldn't seem more different. Farooq was far more gregarious and outgoing, Omar said in the interview, and 'likely to go stir crazy if you ever place him in a room with a book and music'.[4] The son praised his father for letting him run Jammu and Kashmir his way, not 'backseat driving' as in some other cases, while also – in a curious case of history repeating itself – insisting that he was not his father: 'I cannot mould myself on what he is.'[5]

Farooq is aware of the fact that Omar, then and now, would be looking at a very different Kashmir than the one he had known in his youth. The kind of crises that Omar faced in 2008 onwards were baptism by fire. 'The worst phase Omar had was in 2010 when 117-odd young people died … He was at breaking point when that happened. It was only courage and friends. Thank God he overcame that. That taught him and made him what he is today.'[6] Farooq knows better than anyone else that there comes a time in everyone's life which is an undoubted turning point. In his view, 2010 was the year that changed Omar forever. 'The summer of 2010 made a lot of change to his understanding of politics, of the way things have to be done. He became a better person. A much better person.'[7]

Farooq has been clear-eyed about his son. In April 2006, a 'sex scandal' broke out when the police discovered two video CDs showing Kashmiri women being sexually exploited. The investigations led to the unearthing of a massive prostitution racket initially said to involve two ministers of the then Congress–PDP government, a deputy inspector-general of the Border Security Force, ten senior police officers, an Indian Administrative Service (IAS) officer and many businessmen. Police said forty-three women, including a minor, were in the ring run with the patronage of influential men. In the months that followed, the entire Valley saw violent protests with mainstream and separatist groups joining hands. Following allegations by PDP's Muzaffar Hussain Baig in the Assembly in 2009, an emotional Omar offered to resign as chief minister until his name was cleared of all charges.[8]

Farooq was furious with Omar and went charging up to Srinagar to tell him that resignation was out of the question. Chief ministers don't resign over petty provocations.

In its clarification, the CBI said that the Jammu and Kashmir chief minister's name did not figure in the case and added that no member of the Abdullah family was involved in the scandal.[9]

Over the years, Farooq has often felt that he has been too soft on his son. I can never recall a time when Farooq has been harsh on Omar. In fact, Mollie has been the disciplinarian that Omar needed. 'I was too soft. My wife brought him up. That's where he gets his discipline with time and money. Lawrence School, Sanawar, made him stand on his feet.'[10]

Omar's choice to join politics took Farooq aback, though perhaps it shouldn't have, given the kind of family he was from. When Omar told his father that he wanted to join politics, Mollie was the first person Farooq called. 'I rang her up saying, "Moll, what do we do?" She said, "If he wants to, let him try." I said, "Good luck."'[11] Omar, listening to this, laughed it off. 'I don't think my father was surprised. It is the defence mechanism he has with my mother when things are not going as good as he wishes them to be.' But the son acknowledges the same trust deficit that his father has seen over the years. If anything, since he is now in charge of a post-abrogation Kashmir, he is fully aware that the Kashmiri is not to be blamed for that trust deficit. 'Almost every institution that they could count on failed them, whether it is the courts, the police, the government, civil society or the political leadership.'[12]

Today, are father and son on the same page politically? Ask anyone in Delhi and people will tell you that they are not. Their public statements sometimes reveal that. Every now and then, Omar takes a dig at the Congress, since the assembly elections in which the Congress collapsed in Jammu in 2024. In January 2025, for instance, he said, 'If the INDIA alliance was only about fighting the parliamentary elections, then it should be wound up.' To which Farooq promptly retorted, 'The INDIA alliance is a permanent one!'

If they appear not to be on the same page, I cannot tell you the reason for it – except that Doctor Sahib has always kept his doors politically open to everybody. On the other hand, Omar is somewhat more rigid, a bit like the Vajpayee–Advani relationship, where Advani could never challenge Vajpayee. I can never imagine Omar challenging his father, nor can I imagine him being as hands-on as Farooq. Take, for example, the formation of the Congress–NC alliance during the assembly elections in Jammu and Kashmir in September 2024. As talks for the alliance panned out, Congress president Rahul Gandhi came to Kashmir several times, as did Mallikarjun Kharge, K.C. Venugopal and Salman Khurshid. On each occasion, they met and talked with Farooq. But Omar was nowhere to be seen.

Where, a voter might wonder, is Omar?

Perception does matter in Kashmiri politics, after all. As does adjustment and compromise. His father is skilled at navigating politics with an ease that is foreign to Omar. When Farooq was getting myriad political constituents together after the abrogation of Article 370, I remember asking him how he intended to accommodate Mehbooba Mufti's PDP.

'It isn't about accommodation now,' he told me. 'It's about togetherness.'

In that sense, Mufti Sahib was right in his assessment of Farooq: he really does have a feel for Kashmir. A huge amount of empathy has grown in the mind of the Kashmiri for Farooq. Whatever Delhi might think of him, the bigness of Farooq has really emerged after the abrogation in particular.

Vijay Dhar told me the same thing after the assembly elections of 2024: Omar, despite his father's faith in him, has

Father and Son

a tough time ahead of him. I remember meeting eminent educationist Vijay Dhar at the launch of Sushilkumar Shinde's book in September 2024, when I inquired what he thought would happen in Kashmir. I asked if Omar would be chief minister. He said, 'No, not at all. This would be a very difficult period. No one other than Farooq could manage it.'

Now, Omar has two tall, strapping wonderful lads of his own, who, despite having trained to become lawyers, are always at his side. They both have shown immense interest in politics and have spent considerable time in Srinagar with their father. Indeed, in the assembly elections of September 2024, they canvassed for Omar, who was standing from both Ganderbal and Budgam. Will the patterns of father and son be repeated in Omar's case?

'I sincerely hope I am the last of the Abdullahs to head the National Conference and that the party moves on and chooses someone from within its ranks.' Omar mused, nearly a decade ago. 'Should my children join politics, I hope it is when I have left and they can chart their own course.'[13]

What happens now, in the face of not just parliamentary elections but an assembly election that has, in the winter of 2024, seen Omar's return to power? Will Farooq continue to be a sage to his son? Will Omar be able to carve his own legacy, just as his father has?

Only time will tell.

8

Abrogation and Its Aftermath

In April 2019, a handful of months before the abrogation of Article 370, PDP leader and former chief minister of Jammu and Kashmir, Mehbooba Mufti, warned that the ruling BJP would be 'playing with fire' if it attempted to do away with the state's special status. In a tweet that same month, Mufti quoted a famous couplet by the Urdu poet Allama Iqbal which reads:

Na samjho gay tou mit jaouge aye Hindustan walo
Tumhari dastaan tak bhi na hogi dastaano main.

(O you people of Hindustan, if you don't understand, you will perish, your story will be erased from history.)[1]

Her protest was along the same lines as Omar Abdullah, who quoted Faiz:

Dil na-umeed tou nahi,
Nakaam hi tou hai,
Lambi hai gham ki shaam,
Magar shaam hi tou hai.

(My heart is helpless,
But that doesn't mean it is
hopeless,
The evening of sorrow is long,
But it is just an evening.)[2]

What of his father? Well, since April 2019, Farooq had warned of an impending political crisis in Kashmir. 'If it [India] does not pay heed to the wishes of the people, the consequences are grave,' he said. 'We will fight for the rights of people …'[3]

Farooq was, as always, being a consummate politician. Nobody could choreograph an election better than he, with elan and charm, yet forcefulness. Farooq, in all the many years that I have known him, has never issued an ultimatum or laid down the law for Delhi. In 1990, shortly before I left Kashmir, he told me quite clearly that he was not his father.

Farooq was not the Sheikh.

He was in politics to work *with* Delhi, not against it. Because of what the Sher-e-Kashmir suffered, Delhi has always remained in Farooq's consciousness, no matter who was in power. Like his father, he saw a commonality with the Congress, but other than in Rajiv Gandhi's time, he invariably felt let down. Deve Gowda remained his favourite prime minister. Sadly, those whom he cared for let him down the most. Who would blame him, then, even if he joined the BJP, knowing fully well that Kashmir would never forgive him, as it has never forgiven the Muftis?

If Farooq preferred the Congress, it was because of its secular DNA. Perhaps he saw something of himself in it as Sheikh Sahib did, which kept Kashmir with India. The Sheikh's aura helped maintain Kashmiri ego. Farooq has Allah's canopy over him, and God knows he still has much to do. For him, the abrogation of Article 370 was a political problem and it needed to be dealt with as such. He knew it was on the BJP's manifesto. That it would come quite like this, I am not sure he expected. In the days leading to the abrogation itself, both Farooq and Omar met with Prime Minister Narendra Modi. What transpired during the meeting, nobody will ever know. Farooq has certainly never mentioned it. But on 5 August 2019, the Centre abrogated Article 370 of the Constitution. The decision led to the reorganization of the state of Jammu and Kashmir into two Union territories and denuded it of its special privileges.

The state was readied for a backlash. Section 144 was declared, preventing the gathering of people in public places. Schools, offices and educational institutions were closed. On 4 August, satellite phones were distributed in central, north and

The Chief Minister and the Spy

south Kashmir among the security forces. The government ordered a total communication blackout, shutting down cable TV, landlines, cellphones and the internet. Doctors and district administrators were advised to remain on standby. The Abdullahs and the Muftis were put under house arrest on 4 August, even as a large number of Indian army troops were moved into the Valley.

At 11.30 p.m. on the night of 4 August, as he awaited the Centre's announcement the next morning, Omar tweeted, 'There [is] no way of knowing if this is true, but if it is, then I will see all of you on the other side of whatever is in store. Allah save us.' In yet another tweet, that night, he wrote, 'To the people of Kashmir: we don't know what is in store for us, but I am a firm believer that whatever Almighty Allah has planned, it is always for the better. We may not see it now, but we must never doubt his ways. Good luck to everyone. Stay safe, and above all, please stay calm.'

The political and popular reaction in the state was visceral. Omar called the Government of India's move on Article 370 'a total betrayal of the trust that the people of Jammu and Kashmir had reposed in India, when the state acceded to it in 1947'. Asgar Ali Karbalai, the former chief executive councillor of Kargil's Hill Development Council, said that the people of Kargil considered the division of the state on any grounds – religious, linguistic or regional – to be undemocratic.

On 16 September, New Delhi detained Farooq and slapped him with the Public Safety Act, a stringent law under which he could be in jail without trial for six months, extendable up to two years. Other top leaders detained included Omar and Mehbooba Mufti. For me, Farooq's arrest stood out almost starkly in comparison to everyone else. Not just on humanitarian grounds, but because it highlighted just how grimly determined Delhi was to stamp its authority on the Valley. There was no better symbol of that than jailing Farooq.

There were some Kashmiri youngsters who were quite happy to see him detained and said, *'Aur bolo "Bharat Mata Ki Jai!"'* (So much for shouting 'Bharat Mata Ki Jai!') This was based on a video which ultimately turned out to be fake. At the same time, my friend, General Asad Durrani from Pakistan, also said, 'Good for him! He deserves to be kept locked up for a long time!'

Ironically, a couple of weeks later, when the paperback version of the book I co-authored with Gen. Durrani – *The Spy Chronicles* – appeared, where, in his foreword, Doctor Sahib had been highly complimentary of the General, Durrani promptly sent me a message, 'Express my gratitude and convey my regards to Doctor Sahib!'

The abrogation of Article 370 – which has since been upheld by a Supreme Court verdict in 2023 – gained widespread criticism from Kashmiri and other political leaders. Former home minister P.C. Chidambaram called it an 'unconstitutional coup'. He also addressed Parliament on the subject of Farooq's house arrest in 2019, arguing that it was a monumental blunder, since there was no one in modern India more devoted to the cause of a united India than Farooq

Abdullah. Opinions on the subject appeared in mainstream national dailies as well. An editorial in *The Indian Express* on 17 September 2019 argued that the detention of Farooq under the Public Safety Act 'beggars belief'. There was no need to detain a man 'who was the face of moderate politics in Kashmir, apart from being the standard bearer for India on the Kashmir issue'.[4]

The then chief minister of Punjab, Amarinder Singh, a Congress leader, also termed the revocation of Article 370 as 'totally unconstitutional' and said 'this will set a bad precedent as it would mean that the Centre could reorganise any state in the country by simply imposing President's rule'.[5]

Then Congress president Rahul Gandhi criticized the central government for arresting Kashmiri leaders and called the detentions 'unconstitutional & undemocratic'.[6]

Farooq was terribly hurt. Just as the BJP had never hidden its intentions towards Kashmir as far as Article 370 was concerned, so, too, had Farooq been extremely open about his willingness to work with Delhi. Maybe, he said, the NC could even have had the proposal passed in the legislative assembly in Jammu and Kashmir. 'We would have helped,' he told me when I met him in 2020. 'Why were we not taken into confidence?'

If that sounds like a contradiction to the quote with which I opened this chapter, let me tell you – Farooq is a contradiction himself! To my mind, this remark in 2020 just highlighted his great practicality under the most appalling political and popular pressure. But it also revealed – at least to me – how deeply he was hurt by Delhi's arbitrary actions. I genuinely felt that in all of 2019, Farooq's house arrest was the saddest story in Kashmir. Here was a man who had been chief minister thrice, who had been a union minister, and who was promised at one stage the vice-presidentship of India, and who might well have been the president of India today if luck had favoured him. God knew why he had been detained. He was not well. He was getting on in age. He was in his mid-80s. He had had a kidney transplant. And his heart was not in the best condition. He was also diabetic. In fact, he had multiple problems, except that he is a gutsy guy. So to me, it made no sense. I could only hope, in those long months, that he was all right.

If there was anything that had shattered Farooq at that moment – and God knows he has been through a lot in the course of his political career – it was this house arrest. When he spoke to me about the abrogation later, he was forthright, '*Kar lo agar karna hai,*' he said, somewhat bitterly. '*Par yeh arrest kyu karna tha?*' (Do it if you must, but why arrest us?)

In December 2019, I had gone for the military literature festival in Chandigarh organized by Captain Amarinder Singh. I was part of a panel discussion on Kashmir. Other members included the analyst Manoj Joshi, BJP secretary Ram Madhav, Congress MP Manish Tiwari and myself. During the session, Ram Madhav was asked a direct question on the issue of Kashmir's statehood. He replied, 'We have already made a commitment. Statehood will be restored soon.'

It's never been restored, as readers will know.

But Madhav did tell me that day, '*Sirf aapka dost band nahin hai, humara dost bhi band hai,*' in reference to Sajad Lone. (It is not just your friend who's locked up, ours is also suffering from the same plight.)

Since then, I have written and spoken about and against abrogation. My point was always – why rip away the fig leaf of dignity that the Kashmiris possess? Other than that, my concern has always been Farooq's health. When communications in the Valley were shut down, I was very worried. I called him as soon as the lockdown on communications lifted.

'*Kaise ho aap, sir?*' (How are you, sir?)

'*Main bilkul theek hun,*' he replied. 'I'm perfectly fine. Don't worry about me.'

'Suppose I was to come to Srinagar for a day or so, just to see you,' I suggested.

'*Woh toh poochhna padega,*' he said, meaning he would need to ask the requisite authorities.

I called my colleague in the state thereafter. 'I wanted to come and see Doctor Sahib and enquire about his health,' I told him.

That, he answered, would require Delhi's permission. 'If you want, I can ask Delhi.'

I told my colleague that he was very kind to suggest that, but since I was already in Delhi, it would make more sense if I asked Delhi if I could go.

I can't, obviously, go into everything, but that, in a nutshell, is the background to the story. And so it was that a call came in early 2020, six months into a constitutional and political event that had made headlines across the country.

'*Aap Doctor Sahib se milenge?*' (Would you like to meet Doctor Sahib?)

'I've always wanted to meet Doctor Sahib,' was my immediate reply.

That's how I landed in Srinagar on 12 February 2020.

Ultimately, as everyone knows, Farooq was released on 13 March, a few days before India went into lockdown against the worldwide COVID-19 pandemic. On 15 March, the journalist Karan Thapar interviewed me for The Wire, and told me, 'Obviously you're responsible for Farooq's release.'

'No,' I said. 'I didn't do it.'

Be that as it may, it is ironic that when Delhi remembers Farooq, even today, it also remembers me. Farooq knew that a call would come to me, at some point. He was nobody's fool. 'They will need you again,' he told me, shortly before the abrogation. 'Keep your doors open.'

'My doors, sir, are always open,' I said laughingly. 'But who is coming through that door, I can't say!'

And sure enough, Delhi did call me again in the winter of 2020.

Despite the brevity of the conversation with the voice at the other end of the line, I could tell that Delhi was thinking of releasing Farooq from detention. They wanted someone to gauge his mood upon release, but at the same time, the obvious concern was that Farooq should not talk publicly either about the abrogation or about Pakistan. For that, it was imperative that the person who *did* go to see Farooq be someone who knew him well. It should also be a person who knew him well enough that these words would not have to be directly spoken. It would have to be done in such a way that Farooq and Delhi were on the same page, without any writing on the page, so to speak. My brief, then was simple: to suss out Farooq's mood in 'accepting the new reality of Jammu and Kashmir, after the nullification of Article 370'.[7]

The morning of 12 February 2020 was cold and grey. We landed in Srinagar to a temperature of 5 degrees centigrade. The roads were wet and snow could be seen in the shaded areas of the city. The Abdullah house on Gupkar Road looked desolate. The main gate was barred, with a couple of bored security men sitting in front of a rod heater. I had been escorted by the SP in charge of Doctor Sahib's security. I walked up the stairs to the house and rang the bell.

The door was opened by Safia, who jumped back with a startled 'Uff!' as if she'd seen a ghost.

'Sorry for surprising you,' I smiled. 'I hope it's not an unpleasant surprise!'

Recovering quickly, Safia smiled back. 'Friends are always welcome,' she said, ushering me inside. On the way up to Farooq's study, I met some women from Khalida's family coming down the stairs. Adversity had clearly brought the family closer together.

I took off my shoes as I entered, the age-old practice in the Abdullah household. I met Mollie outside Doctor Sahib's study. She half-smiled and said hello to me as she entered the study along with me to ask Farooq what soup he would like for lunch.

'I hope you don't mind soup for lunch,' she told me apologetically. 'That's all we have. So, mushroom or asparagus?'

Farooq opted for mushroom, and so did I, and Mollie withdrew, in her typically self-effacing manner. She left behind a quiet atmosphere. Farooq was sitting by himself in his study, a bank of telephones on one side of him and an open Quran on the other. That moment stands out clearly in my mind. After all, this was the first time I was seeing Farooq after his detention. I noticed that he didn't let the phone ring more than once before answering it and was eager to talk to whoever was calling. That's what loneliness does to a person.

Still, he appeared happy to see me.

'It's nice to see you,' he said. 'You've come on an auspicious day. It happens to be the day of my actual birthday.'

After soup and fruit, a delicious chocolate cake – baked by Safia – was brought in. Doctor Sahib's diet was being strictly controlled by Mollie, but it was a quintessential English meal in an equally quintessential Kashmiri household. I found myself thinking idly that it was the first time that I had ever eaten a vegetarian meal in the Abdullah household. After the meal was over, it was inevitable that our conversation should turn to politics – though I really didn't want it to.

'*Main aaya hun toh samajh lo ki Dilli baat karna chahti hai,*' I told him. (Now that I've come, you may take it that Delhi wants to talk to you.)

'*Haan,*' he said. '*Main samajh gaya.*' (Yes, I understand that.)

The Chief Minister and the Spy

Neither of us knew what lay ahead, but I had been briefed on what to tell him: he was not to speak to the media, nor was he to mention the abrogation or anything about Pakistan. I knew that I really didn't have to spell it out for someone as seasoned as Farooq. But when I did mention it briefly, he shrugged, '*Media se baat nahi karunga. Jo bhi bolunga, Parliament mein bolunga.* [No, I won't speak to the media. Whatever I say, I will say in Parliament.] The matter is sub judice now. Let the court decide. I have confidence in the courts.'

That was about the extent of any political conversation we had. I respect Farooq's intelligence and I knew that he would not need to be instructed per se. He was far too well-versed in Delhi's ways. So I changed the subject, taking the conversation into more mundane channels, such as his health. Farooq was pleasant. When I enquired after his health, he said, 'I'm fine, you can see for yourself. The only thing I miss is golf.' But I knew it was more than just a desire to play golf that was plaguing the great man. He didn't look well – he seemed tired, haggard and certainly not his sartorial, confident self. He was attired in a simple kurta pyjama with a cream-coloured jacket and chappals. Without his glasses, his eyes looked tired.

I didn't want to talk politics with him and so I avoided the subject altogether. Yet, as if to demonstrate his determination, Farooq said, 'We have this one fight, and we are all in this together.'

I didn't want to labour that particular point, so I merely said, 'Yes, but you need to look and think ahead.'

'Yes, of course, I am,' agreed Farooq. 'But we are Indians first and last. That's the way my father was and that's how we have been brought up and that's how we have brought up our children. The only thing is that it is difficult to explain to our grandchildren what Delhi has been doing in the last six months. If abrogation had to happen, then why did it happen like this?'

In the course of that two-hour conversation with him, he excused himself twice to pray. Still, the time I spent with him passed in both of us reminiscing about the old days – about Rubaiya's kidnapping and the hijacking of IC-814, and the many adversities that both of us had seen together in Kashmir.

I found him reflective and introspective – that previous edge of imperious urgency had gone. It was not the most exhilarating two hours I had spent with him, but eventually, my time was up and I had to go. Normally, Doctor Sahib does not permit anyone the luxury of spending two hours with him, but like I said, loneliness does strange things to a person.

Somehow, I mused, that period of house arrest seemed to have impacted him more deeply than I had expected. Later, much later – when the period of his silence was up – Farooq spoke publicly about the humiliation of that enforced period of detainment. It was the same note of bitterness that one has heard in his voice through the years when it comes to speaking about Delhi. 'I never thought I would be repaid in this fashion,' he told *The Hindu*. 'I

The Chief Minister and the Spy

always thought they [Delhi] would increase our degree of autonomy. We never revolted against India. My people died, my Ministers and workers died holding the tricolour. Did they realise this before [what] they did [on] August 5 [2019]? Who was here in 1996? Was the BJP here or any party? I was alone.'[8] He was despondent and blunt, speaking in the emotional hyperbole that he sometimes resorted to under strain, 'I was treated like a criminal. That I am a thief and the three families have looted the place. That I am a terrorist. I wonder whether I would have been better off as a terrorist …'[9]

For him, that period of house arrest has been one of the most difficult that he has undergone in his life. 'My daughter [Safia] came to see me but she was not allowed. She collapsed at the door. We had to get doctors to treat her for some days. That was the most tragic. I had to bear this all.'

It was a terrible time that Farooq survived, he insisted, because of the Quran. I know that he got his faith from his mother. The Sheikh had never been a religious man, finding his faith in his politics rather than in the Quran. It had been the old Begum who had been religious, with her deep belief in the power of Allah. Now, her son was turning to Allah in the same way. That grey February day, I had seen a Farooq in pain, in such despondency that he had turned to his faith as never before. 'I survived because of the Quran. I recited it every day. And God spoke. That gave me strength and courage. That is what gave my mother strength,' he told Peerzada Ashiq of *The Hindu* in August.[10] Here was Kashmir's tallest leader, forced to endure humiliation for nothing that he had said or done. Yet Farooq maintained that even under these gruelling circumstances, he had not lost hope. 'I am an optimist. That is not what Islam is. Islam taught me to be strong. There is far greater power than this worldly power.'[11]

It was a change in tenor and tone from the fire and drama that he had brought to public statements before. Gone was the belligerence and the thundering. Here was a quiet man who spoke with dignity. Farooq's optimism, given how bad things had become post the abrogation, was a trait I admired from afar. The pandemic and the abrogation had changed much in him, as much as it had in all of us – and yet, Farooq still found new ways to hope.

The Hindu termed the post-abrogation era in Kashmir a 'new chapter of alienation', which is an apt way to put it. Farooq was quietly blunt, 'I blame the great Prime Minister of India for the new chapter of alienation. Who else? Every decision is taken at his level. There is no other man. We [Omar and he] met the Prime Minister and discussed many things on August 3 [2019] and I pointed out the unprecedented troop movement, by road and by air … He was so nice that even sugar could not melt in one's mouth. He made the Home Minister announce it. So that he is above it.'[12]

Farooq was never above speaking the truth, even if that truth stung. In his intrinsic honesty, he is certainly one of the last of India's great politicians. They do not do politics like that any longer. That honesty has been yet another binder between him and me. Farooq and I are both men who like to state things as they are, though of course, my job requires that I do it with a certain amount of tact. He, on the other hand, has both shocked and sometimes exasperated Delhi with his refusal to be anything but straight-talking. This man of 2020, though, was a different one from the man I have seen over the years.

Under usual circumstances, Farooq rarely persists with serious or heavy topics for a long time, freckling his conversations with fun and frolic. Like Faiz, who once famously wrote, '*Aur bhi dukh hain zamaane mein mohabbat ke siva*' (There are other sorrows in life apart from love), Farooq believed that there was more to life than politics. This was the only life he had, after all – and it had taught him that laughter was a better way out of sorrow than shedding tears.

Better, he felt, to live life to the hilt – rather than not live at all.

All this seemed a thing of the past in 2020, when I met a sombre Farooq, tired with the incarceration, despairing of what had been done to his state, seeking a way out for himself, his family – and for Kashmir most of all.

This is not to say that Farooq was never a religious or spiritual man, but he had never, in the time that I have known him, sought solace in it to this extent. In July 2020, I witnessed yet another astonishing example of how deeply Farooq has begun to seek refuge in faith. He was in Delhi, staying at his Tilak Marg residence. His wife was going to England, and he had come to see her off. It was his first trip out of the Valley since his release from house arrest. While he was staying in Delhi for a while, he wanted to be among friends. I was asked to have lunch with him.

Usually, our lunches have been private, one-on-one affairs, but this time, there were a few others there. The conversation was full of history and old memories, much of which had to do with Sheikh Sahib. While talking to his friends, I noted that Farooq was referring to Sheikh Sahib as 'Papa'. It was a touching insight into how deeply Farooq was now immersed in his family and friends. We all sat down to an elaborate *wazwan*, but as lunch finished, Farooq rose and said grace. He thanked the Lord not only for what we had eaten, but prayed for the people of India and for Kashmir. After everyone had left, I stayed behind to chat with him for a little bit longer. I was a little concerned, I must confess, because I recognized very few of the people who had come for lunch.

'Are you sure there were no moles?' I asked.

Farooq shook his head. 'No, no,' he said. 'They are friends.'

To my mind, this moment pointed to a time when Farooq looked to friends rather than family for succour. There are times in one's life when friends are your chosen family – when they can provide you with the warmth and support that family sometimes cannot. Farooq has always been a family man, and he loves his family more than anything in this world, but after the abrogation, his spirit was seeking friendship.

It also showed me the many ways in which Farooq has changed since the abrogation, as a man and as a politician. In fact, each meeting has only served to drive home the fact, to me, that if you don't understand Farooq, you will never understand Kashmir. He would never openly jeopardize Kashmir's chances by going against Delhi's orders. When it comes to politics, Farooq puts his emotions aside in favour of practicality. Contrast this with his daughter, whom I met when I went to Srinagar in February 2020. She and her aunt, Farooq's sister Suraiya, had been detained in Srinagar during the protests against the abrogation. She was plainly agitated. 'All this doesn't make us feel like we belong to India,' she told me.

Yet, paradoxically, broken though he might have been, the events following the abrogation had only made him doubly determined to fight for the rights of his state. In 2019, for example, it was Farooq who was the main player in bringing political parties together in the form of the PAGD, an electoral alliance between the several regional political parties in the state of Jammu and Kashmir, with the aim of restoring special status along with Article 35A of the state. Farooq is its president. The evolution of the PAGD had a remarkable impact on Farooq. My old friend Sajad Lone told me – and this was back when he was still a member of the PAGD – that in his new avatar, Farooq was a man possessed, determined to fight for the dignity of Kashmir. I feel this, too. As he told me in the aftermath of the 2020 District Development Council elections, 'Accommodation doesn't matter to me anymore. We must accommodate, but what matters is togetherness.'

Listening to him, I was reminded of the great historian Arnold Toynbee, who once said, 'What we mean by greatness of any degree in a human being is the power in some measure and in some field to move other human beings.'

Every time I have met him since February 2020, I could not but be moved by Farooq. When I met him in his beautiful garden in Gupkar Road in June 2022, he was engrossed in understanding an interpretation of the Quran.

When the issue of the Prophet came up, he reminded me that there was no God but God, and the Prophet was his messenger.[13] This is what he told his party men even as he wept at a convention at Khanyar the previous day, even as he insisted that faith, unity and honesty were paramount in a country such as ours. For Farooq, these three qualities (or their lack thereof) have been the beating heart of India's history and politics. He's often wondered where India would be without them, and that's a thought we both share, having seen the things we have seen in the course of our respective careers and lives. In that context, I think that between 2022 and 2024, Farooq found these three qualities embodied in Rahul Gandhi.

As cynical as he has seemed about the Congress, Farooq – along with the rest of the nation – sat up and took notice when the Congress announced that Rahul would be walking across 3,570 kilometres, beginning at Kanyakumari on 7 September 2022. The yatra would end at Srinagar and cover 12 states in 150 days. It was a massive undertaking, and in all fairness, it electrified the country. In the course of his *padyatra*, Rahul met and walked not only with politicians, but with farmers, fisherfolk, marginalized communities and common citizens. It was the first time in years that India had seen a politician – and one so young at that – truly connecting with the people. The yatra recast Rahul as a new mass leader. He even declared that he had killed the old Rahul Gandhi and emerged as a new person!

The older generation – myself and Farooq included – has seen something like this before. After all, India has a storied history of long walks and rallies by political leaders in support of social, political and economic causes. But to see it happening in these times, particularly given the political context of it, was another feeling, another experience altogether. It enlivened the idea of India and gave Kashmiris hope in an apparently hopeless situation. As the NC MP and the foremost Shia leader in Kashmir, Aga Ruhullah Mehdi was to say to me at the dawn of the New Year in 2025, 'The idea of India flows from Kashmir.'

Farooq, who walked with Rahul during the yatra, was impressed. Here, he felt, was a young leader capable of taking the country forward in the best sense of the word. He telephoned me shortly after. I remember it was around five o'clock in the evening, and I was sitting and having my evening tea. He sounded energized, 'You know, I walked with this boy today. When the walk ended and he hugged me, I've not felt so emotional in a long time.' It's a rare human being who can make Farooq Abdullah emotional.

But then, Farooq has always had a bit of a soft spot for Rahul. When Rahul's yatra entered Kashmir in the cold of January 2023, he was there, along with the people of Kashmir, to watch this young leader establish his presence. After passing through the nine-kilometre-long Banihal tunnel, Rahul continued his padyatra in the Kashmir Valley amid sub-zero temperatures. It was the first major political activity in the region since the abrogation of Jammu and Kashmir's special status in 2019, and thousands of people welcomed Rahul at the march's conclusion. Rahul seemed to recognize that this, after all, was the home of his ancestors, for during this final stage of the yatra, he highlighted his Kashmiri 'roots'.

Moved by the sheer scale of the yatra and by Rahul's honesty, Farooq travelled 350 kilometres from Srinagar to Lakhanpur to meet him. Speaking there, he compared Rahul's journey from Kanyakumari to Kashmir to the one undertaken by the Vedic scholar Shankaracharya in the eighth century.

That part of the march was, to me, a sight unlike anything I had seen in modern times. It was raining and sleeting heavily that day. Most flights into the state had been cancelled and the roads were slick with moisture and snow. Nothing seemed to curb the people's enthusiasm. Rahul united the entire political and popular spectrum of Kashmir, and, indeed, of India. Omar walked with him, in the Banihal area of Ramban district; Mehbooba, along with her mother and her daughter Iltija, walked from Awantipora's Chersoo village. Priyanka Gandhi Vadra also joined her brother on the final leg of the yatra in Kashmir.

On 29 January, Rahul Gandhi took a 30-minute break from the foot march in Sonawar to visit the Jammu and Kashmir

Pradesh Congress Committee headquarters at Maulana Azad Road before proceeding to Srinagar's clock tower, also known as the Ghanta Ghar. The Indian flag was unfurled, and Rahul gave a press conference, where he emphasized the importance of statehood for Jammu and Kashmir and the restoration of democratic processes. Opposition leaders also joined him as he marked the end of the Bharat Jodo Yatra. The event was attended by leaders from the Dravida Munnetra Kazhagam, NC, PDP, Communist Party of India, Revolutionary Socialist Party and Indian Union Muslim League. Like I said, it was a fascinating moment – for all of us, I'm sure.

In 2020, Farooq had quietly told me, 'Our family has always been with India. We will remain with India. That's how I brought up my own children. That's what I taught them. But now, today, my grandchildren ask me – is this the India you want us to be with?' In fact, one of his children also said that she no longer felt Indian but only Kashmiri.

It reminded me of another question that he had flung at journalists, before being locked into his house in Srinagar in 2019, 'How do you think one would feel when your body is being carved, the body that stood together in all odds, fought every evil unitedly ... They divided religions, will they divide hearts too?' He demanded, 'I thought my India was for all, everyone who believes in secular unity.'[14]

That question echoed in my mind some four years later, as India went into its 18th Lok Sabha elections. The country was facing a momentous crossroads. Would the ruling BJP return for a historic third term? And if so, would the newly constituted INDIA alliance – of which the NC was a part – be a real opposition? The elections of 1996 had been a milestone in their own right, bringing democracy back to a Valley wracked by the ravages of militancy. Could the general elections of 2024 be yet another milestone for Kashmir and for India?

It was as though new life had been breathed into Indian politics. I spoke to Farooq in the months leading up to the elections. He was optimistic, different from the quiet *susti*, the lethargy, that I had found in him in 2020.

'India is changing,' he told me. 'The people are changing. You will see.'

It was a reminder, to me, of Farooq's deep-seated patriotism. He is, at heart, a nationalist – who believes with all his extremely large heart in the power of the people to do the right thing. In June 2024, the results proved Farooq right. The BJP had not managed to scrape together a majority, coming in at 240 seats, some 32 seats below a majority in Parliament. A coalition government was back, but just how its term would shape up remains to be seen.

9

The Importance of Being Farooq Abdullah

From 18 September 2024, spread across three phases, Jammu and Kashmir voted in its first assembly elections in a decade. Chief Election Commissioner Rajiv Kumar waxed lyrical on the subject, quite literally: '*Lambi kataron mein chhupi hai badalte surat-e-haal yani jamhooriyat ki kahani. Roshan ummeedein ab khud karengi gawah apni taqdeer-e-bayani. Jamhooriyat ke jashn mein aapki shirkat duniya dekhegi napak iraadon ke shikasht ki kahani,*' he intoned. (These long lines tell the story of changing times and rekindled hopes; your participation in the festival of democracy signals the defeat of those with nefarious intentions.)[1]

Although three Lok Sabha elections, in 2014, 2019 and 2024, were held in Jammu and Kashmir, June 2014 was the last time that Vidhan Sabha elections were held. Apart from the timing, the 2024 elections were significant because they would follow the delimitation process. This involved redrawing the boundaries of parliamentary and assembly constituencies based on population data from the most recent census (2011) to ensure equal representation. Completed in May 2022, this process would increase the total number of seats in the assembly to 114, with 24 seats reserved for Pakistan-administered Kashmir and Gilgit Baltistan. The remaining 90 seats would be contested, with 43 in the southern Jammu region and 47 in Kashmir to the north.

Omar welcomed the announcement, saying his party was ready for the elections. '*Der aaye durust aaye.* [Better late than never.] The National Conference was ready for this day.' There was a lot of talk, after the announcement of the poll dates, about democracy winning the day. Union Home Minister Amit Shah said, 'The assembly election will further strengthen the roots of democracy, opening the door to a new period of development for the region.'

Watching this, I didn't know about democracy – but what I *did* agree with was the fact that these elections were going to be even bigger than those of 1996. Taking place as they were a mere handful of months after the Lok Sabha elections, the NC – and the Abdullahs – had a lot to prove.

The results of the general elections had seen the rise and success of what are known as BJP's B-teams (or C-teams, depending on who we're talking about!) in the Valley. Omar had lost in Baramulla to Engineer Rashid, an independent candidate backed by the Awami Ittehad Party (and jailed since 2019, in a terror-funding case).

The Importance of Being Farooq Abdullah

The assembly elections, then, pointed to the need for the Abdullahs to unite with the Congress, to pull together against adverse circumstances. More importantly, Farooq needed to step up to the plate, with his customary aplomb. Since 2020, and particularly in the aftermath of the Lok Sabha elections, Doctor Sahib had been quieter, more *sust*, as we Punjabis call it. He wasn't his usual ebullient, dynamic self, and he kept to himself in a way he never had before, at least not since I had known him.

As someone who has seen Farooq rise above every kitchen sink that life has flung at him, I must confess that this time, I was worried. I had no doubts about Farooq's abilities as a politician, but this time, it would take a harder pull. In the run-up to the assembly elections, Doctor Sahib proved yet again that he was far from being beaten. In an interview, given to veteran journalist Neerja Chowdhury of *The Indian Express*, Farooq insisted that it was going to be difficult to fool the people of Kashmir a second time around. 'We have tried to tell them the truth …' he said. 'They [the people] know they [a reference to Engineer Rashid] were released to divide our votes. But they won't be able to divide our votes. *Ya hum bewakoof hain, ya woh bewakoof hain* [Either we are fools, or they are] … A man charged with receiving Pakistani money, also calling for a plebiscite and a free J&K, how has he suddenly become a friend of the BJP?' It was a rhetorical question, of course – but it was a defiant one. Farooq was not going to give up without a fight, but more importantly, as far as I was concerned, he had hope.

The Chief Minister and the Spy

To my mind, he has never lost that hope. It is what has kept him going for so many turbulent decades of Kashmiri politics. Doctor Sahib's forming of the PAGD with the other political parties of Jammu and Kashmir in 2020 was a masterstroke in the aftermath of the abrogation of Article 370. The first PAGD meeting, at Mehbooba Mufti's home, was attended by Mehbooba herself, Mehboob Beg, Farooq, the Awami NC's Muzaffar Shah, Jammu and Kashmir People's Movement's Javaid Mustafa and CPI-M leader M.Y. Tarigami. The statements that came from the PAGD members underlined Farooq's credo of unity and his understanding of the historical baggage that the Valley carried. 'We have faced everything together and want to assure the people of Jammu, Kashmir and Ladakh that we will always raise their voices, whether in Parliament or elsewhere. Do not misunderstand us. We shall be on the side of people, who are suffering,' said Tarigami. Farooq himself quoted his father and said, 'Like him, I will stay in fire and douse the flames. We will fight in Parliament and raise issues … Our doors are never shut. If and when called [by the Centre], we will go.'

This call for understanding has been constant since the abrogation of Article 370. I have written in numerous articles that, despite the hue and cry around its abrogation, Article 370 was a mere fig leaf over Kashmiri dignity. It had been abolished in all but name since 1975, when Sheikh Abdullah and Indira Gandhi signed an accord, under which the Sheikh agreed to accept the position of chief minister under the Indian Constitution, effectively dropping the demand for a plebiscite. Article 370 gave legal and constitutional validity to the accession and sought to define the state's special status within the Indian Union. This essentially was the political safeguard that the Kashmiri Muslim sought for the protection of Kashmiriyat and his identity. For all other purposes Kashmir had become a part of India.

Problems arose subsequently when Kashmiris began to perceive that India was reneging on preserving their special status and defending their unique identity. At a fundamental level, Kashmiri movements since then have not focused as much on leaving India as on defending their spiritual and political identity: Kashmiriyat. Delhi's constant stonewalling and backtracking has led to a change in Kashmiriyat on the ground – and of that I think there can be no doubt, irrespective of whom you speak to in Kashmir. I have still held on to hope. If you had asked me, in 2016, like Nandita Haksar did at the Tata Literature Live Festival, whether Kashmiriyat was over, I would have argued with you – as I did with her. I kept asking her, 'How can Kashmiriyat be over?'

But the truth of it is that 2016 was the beginning of the end of Kashmir as we knew it. It was the year Burhan Wani was killed by security forces. Wani's death sparked massive protests across the Valley, in what became the worst span of unrest in the region since 2010. Huge crowds turned out to attend Wani's funeral as his body, wrapped in the flag of Pakistan, was buried next to his brother Khalid, in Tral. Militants present at the funeral offered Wani a three-volley salute. The unrest across the state was immense, with separatist leaders calling for a statewide shutdown and police and security forces repeatedly attacked by mobs. Stone-pelting was reported across the Valley, with Kashmiri Pandits fleeing again. The internet was shut down and the national highway was closed off. Thousands – civilians and military personnel alike – were injured and nearly a hundred people lost their lives. D.S. Hooda of the Northern Command appealed for peace. 'What can the army possibly do?' he said in a statement on 16 June 2016. 'We are helpless when entire villages come out in support of militancy and against us.'

Force, when applied, will always lead to increased separatism and radicalism. That is a fact of life and it has been proven in insurgencies across India, time and again, from the Naxals to the situation in the Northeast. Why, then, go to the abrasive length of abrogating Article 370 legally? Farooq has often plaintively asked me this question too. More than anything, his awareness of just how badly this can damage the state has been painful for him. Indeed, the abrogation was a sad day for Jammu and Kashmir. One gets the feeling that it was totally uncalled for. It was a bad move, because Article 370 was a hollow provision. There was no need to have touched it, for it prevented nothing. Small wonder, then, that Kashmiriyat as it once used to be in the old days stands in danger of extinction today. Over the years, it has been clad in all kinds of hues of nationalism, brushing aside any question of its evolution and original historical context. To my mind, however, Kashmiriyat is beyond a concrete definition. The

The Importance of Being Farooq Abdullah

best way that I can think of describing it is 'togetherness', or 'unity'. Farooq is the last of the Kashmiri leaders to espouse this trait. He not only emphasizes it but he also embodies it. As long as he is alive, so too is Kashmiriyat.

But there is no denying that he is a worried man – and has been since 2019. Abrogation is one thing. Bifurcation of the state is worse, because now you're going back from what you were trying to do in 2014. At least, that was the impression when the BJP and the PDP came together. Then, there was just that glimmer of hope that maybe now Jammu and Srinagar would come closer together. Mufti Sahib overestimated himself and underestimated Narendra Modi. Indeed, bifurcation, in my opinion, would have a much worse impact. In 2008, the polarization between Jammu and Kashmir began with the Amarnath land agitation. With the bifurcation, the seeds were sown for communalism to flourish further. Don't forget that Jammu is not just Hindu, it has a substantial Muslim and Sikh population as well. To dismiss it as just a Hindu-majority region would be wrong. This is precisely where the NC – and Farooq – will come in. Time and again, articles and opinion pieces claiming that the NC is over have been written. But if there is a party that has real historical roots in Kashmir, and that unites it, it is the NC. If there is a family with whom Kashmir has an instant association, it is the Abdullahs.

But you see, that has always been a problem in the state: the disability in recognizing the importance of Farooq. As I have come to know him, I have observed that he understands

Pakistan, he understands Kashmir, he understands India and he understands human beings. The abrogation of 370, in Farooq's eyes, marked a shift in the way politics is being conducted in India. It also highlighted for him the abysmal state of regional leadership in the state. Leadership in the state has been a perennial failure: the separatists were useless; the so-called mainstream has also not been the best. The Centre took advantage of this as well as of the weakness of the Congress party and the so-called Opposition in 2019.

In 2019, I gave an interview to *The Print*, to Jyoti Malhotra, in which I asked the question: What has stopped Rahul and Priyanka from going to Kashmir when they have a loose kind of alliance with the NC? After all, if that alliance had been a serious one, even then, the Congress would have found a strong foothold in the state. In 2019, I went so far as to say that the Congress had abandoned Jammu and Kashmir. Three years later, when Rahul Gandhi began walking across the length and breadth of India in 2022, Farooq was not just fascinated, but genuinely inspired. Here again, I found something to admire in the great man. Time and again, he had been let down by the Congress. Over the years, from Indira to Rahul, the Congress had taken him as lightly as anyone else. But Farooq never lost hope for some kind of alliance, for some kind of bridge to be built between Delhi and Srinagar. In his eyes, the hope for a better India, and a better Delhi that recognizes and gives Kashmir its true worth, is what keeps him going.

The Importance of Being Farooq Abdullah

Rahul is decades younger than the Sher-e-Kashmir's son, and he still has lessons to learn – as we have seen in the results of the assembly elections in Haryana and Jammu in 2024. There is no real need for a man of the stature and season of Farooq Abdullah to take heart from Rahul. Yet, for Farooq, he represents dignity and hope for the kind of India that Farooq still believes in. In the INDIA alliance, he sees a face that is completely different to those of the BJP and the RSS. 'He [Rahul] has shown the courage to fight them in Parliament ...' he told Neerja Chowdhury in October 2024. 'He wants to build an India where there is no hatred, where we live in honour and dignity.'

Farooq viewed Rahul's September 2024 visit to the Valley as a salutary reality check for those who branded Kashmiri leaders as separatists. 'It is the need of the hour. We want to take everyone along for the development of Jammu and Kashmir ... He [Rahul] is a big voice for our nation. It is a slap on the face of those who accused us of being Pakistanis or Khalistanis ...'[2]

If that meant casting the lot of the NC with the Congress, then so be it. That has always been Farooq's way of doing politics: never closing the doors on dialogue or fruitful alliances. In the course of time, the Kashmiri leadership, from Mehbooba Mufti to Mohammed Yousuf Tarigami to Muzaffar Shah and others, began to realize the heights to which Doctor Sahib has soared; even those who disliked him acknowledged that he was the tallest leader in Kashmir. Mehbooba has told me more than once that Doctor Sahib

The Chief Minister and the Spy

was their leader. The credit for the NC's success in the assembly and even the parliamentary elections goes to Farooq Abdullah. These were elections where plenty was at stake, and where Farooq's importance shone brightly.

Farooq has always sought to be on Delhi's right side, but not on Delhi's terms. He always looked for a level playing field and, in the end, did it his way, which Delhi could never comprehend. For instance, after his release from detention in March 2020, Delhi expected him to come and meet the prime minister. But he took his time on the excuse that he needed cataract surgeries in both his eyes. He came to Delhi only in July 2020. That is the difference between Farooq and Omar. When Omar says he wants a good relationship with Delhi, he goes out of his way to please Delhi. Farooq does what he thinks will go down best with his people.

In the 2024 assembly elections, the BJP didn't want the NC to cross 30 seats, thus giving it enough room to reach out to the party and offer to make the kind of alliance it had made with Mufti Sahib, which would have made Farooq uncomfortable. In fact, as I recall, many people at the time believed that if push came to shove, the NC *would* ally with the BJP. Indeed, the BJP did try to reach out to Farooq in the run-up to the assembly elections, to try and speak with him behind the scenes.

Do you remember a time when the RSS supported Indira Gandhi, when she was on her winning streak as prime minister of this country? It was the same logic: to be on the winning side is the endgame in politics, anywhere in the world, after all. Somehow, though, Delhi has almost always missed the bus with Farooq.

In the winter of 2014, when Farooq had gone for his kidney transplant, I was holidaying in Goa, when I got a call from IB headquarters in Delhi, 'Do you have Doctor Sahib's London telephone number?'

'I do,' I replied. 'But I hardly have it here on the beach! *Baat kya hai? Ab aap phone karna chah rahe ho*, but it's too late now.' (What is the matter? If you want to call him now, it's too late.)

'*Nahi, nahi,* we just wanted to enquire about his health.'

'Well, even there you're too late.'

It was another indicator of how tall a leader Doctor Sahib is. It was an indicator, as well, of how, try as Delhi might to dismiss him, it can never ignore Farooq. He is the face not just of his party but of the Valley in modern India. He is aware of the history he carries and the politics he needs to enforce. I think every Kashmiri leader – beginning with Farooq himself – will agree with me when I say that, for this sensitive state, it is difficult to govern without relations with the Centre being as amiable as circumstances allow. As Farooq himself told Neerja Chowdhury caustically, 'We are slaves of Delhi.'

The Farooq I have known has never been afraid to take a swing at Delhi when he sees the need to do it and the opportunity to do it. One example of this – and a fiery one at that! – was during the hijacking of Indian Airlines flight IC-814. Everyone knows the story of that ill-fated aircraft, brought back to the forefront of national memory by the Netflix web series on the hijacking.

Briefly, on 24 December 1999, five members of the Harkat-ul-Mujahideen hijacked Indian Airlines Flight IC-814, an Airbus A300, while it was en route from Kathmandu to Delhi. The plane was flown to Amritsar, Lahore, Dubai and eventually Kandahar, in Afghanistan, where the hijackers demanded the release of militants jailed in India. The hijack lasted seven days and ended on 31 December 1999 when the Indian government released three prisoners to the Taliban in exchange for passengers and crew.

The release of those men was not an easy decision. Once Ajit Doval – then an excellent negotiator and IB man – and the other negotiators had whittled the hijackers' demands down to three terrorists, Masood Azhar, Omar Sheikh and Mushtaq Zargar, the Indian government had to take a call. I was not in the IB in 1999, having joined as chief of the R&AW. But I remember it being a time of intense pressure. The media added to the cauldron-like atmosphere, flashing visuals of protesting families and crying relatives outside 7 Race Course Road (Lok Kalyan Marg).

India's hands were tied. Once the plane took off from Amritsar, we lost any advantage we might previously have possessed. Reluctantly, the green light was given to release the three terrorists – until it was suddenly realized that this

The Importance of Being Farooq Abdullah

could hardly happen without Farooq's agreement. It was a measure of how much Delhi has relied on the unlikely friendship between the chief minister and the spy that I was picked to do the dirty work in this case.

Brajesh Mishra asked me to go to Jammu without wasting any time. The foreign minister, Jaswant Singh, called Farooq and formally let him know that the R&AW chief was being sent to him. When I rang him, Farooq seemed to shrug over the telephone, 'You might as well come and stay with me.'

It wasn't a promising start, but then I hadn't expected anything about this to be pleasant. As the R&AW aircraft landed in Jammu, the sun was setting on 30 December 1999. It was the month of Ramzan. I went straight to Farooq's residence, where I found him sitting at his dining table by himself.

'I know why you've come,' he said curtly. 'Just let me go and say my prayers.'

I sat and waited for him.

After his prayers he came out and had his juice.

Then it began.

Wheeling on me, he said angrily, 'You again? *Tumne Mufti ki beti ke liye kiya tha, phir wohi kar rahe ho.*' (You again? You did this once before, for Mufti's daughter – and now you're back again.)

He wasn't wrong. During both Rubaiya's kidnapping and this case, he was the chief minister of Jammu and Kashmir, and in both cases, I was the one representing Delhi – and asking him to do things that he did not want to do. Most people would be wary of raising their voice with the R&AW chief, but Farooq, as I've told you, never gave a damn about who he was talking to. For three hours, I sat there quietly as he shouted at me. I knew, instinctively, that he was not shouting at *me* – but at Delhi, via me. Farooq was always one for theatre, and if this was a chance to give some shit back to Delhi, he wouldn't miss it for the world.

'You were there during Rubaiya's kidnapping,' he snapped. 'How could you come back again?'

'Sir, I was solidly with you that time, but this time I'm with the Government of India,' I said soothingly. 'At that time, I was pleading along with you. This time, I'm pleading *with* you.'

This only served to infuriate him further. 'I said then that whatever you are doing is wrong, and I'm saying it again,' he shouted. 'I don't agree with it.'

When I look back at it, it was as though Farooq was experiencing waves of anger. He would calm down and then he would start all over again. The theme never varied: how weak Delhi was; what a big mistake this was; they were all buffoons. In any other circumstance, it would have been frankly awe-inspiring, because Farooq's rage never flagged, nor did his eloquence.

When I could get a word in edgewise, I seized the chance, 'Sir, there is no other option; this has to be done.'

Farooq didn't seem to be listening.

He flung around to his telephone and rang up Jaswant Singh, '*Aap jo bhi kar rahe hain, galat kar rahe hain.*' (Whatever you're doing, you're doing the wrong thing.)

He stormed and banged the phone down. He called others up in Delhi. He kept banging the phone down.

Then, tiring a little, he finally sat down and looked at me. 'Those two bloody Pakistanis or whatever they are, I don't give a damn. Let them go to hell.' He was referring to Masood Azhar and Omar Sheikh. 'But I will not let this Kashmiri fellow [Zargar] go, he's a killer. He will not be released.'

That could not be.

'Sir,' I said remonstratively. 'This will not happen without Zargar.'

'I don't care if it happens or not!' Farooq raged. Then he pulled out his own trump card, 'Fine, I'm going to the governor and giving him my resignation.'

But here, he had reckoned without my knowledge of his personality. I had known that, at some point in this conversation, he would say this.

'Sir, if you're going to the governor, then at least take me along.'

At ten o'clock that night, we went to see Governor Girish Chandra 'Gary' Saxena. Gary was a former R&AW chief himself, so I wasn't worried. He knew how to handle Farooq and a touchy situation.

The chief minister entered and spoke without preamble, 'These fellows want these terrorists released and I've told the

R&AW chief I won't be a party to it,' Farooq told him. 'I would rather resign, and that's what I have come to do.'

'Doctor Sahib, come, sit down, relax,' Gary said soothingly. 'You're a fighter, you don't give in so easily.'

Out came a bottle of Black Label whisky. As he poured it, Gary again invited Farooq to sit down. 'These bloody fellows don't know what they're doing,' the chief minister ranted, though he did sit down. 'They're making a huge mistake.'

'Maybe,' Gary agreed, 'but at this point, there is no other option. We have to go along with it.'

I kept quiet. I had no desire to be shouted at again. Anyway, to cut a long story short, Gary was able to calm Farooq down, and between the both of us, we got him to agree to Delhi's demands.

The next morning, I decided that before leaving for Delhi, I wanted to make up for those three hours of shouting. There were things I needed done: transfers and other favours for friends in Kashmir, the kind that normally would have got stuck in a forest of red tape. Farooq, I felt, owed me one. So, as we sat for breakfast, I said lightly, 'Sir, I need a few things done from the state government.'

I knew that Farooq, after he has lost his temper or been unreasonable or imperious, is usually charm itself. I was not wrong in this case. Whatever I asked him for, he agreed to without a word: 'Done. Done. Done.'

Just like that.

He never mentioned it to me again, but as an incident, it was a good example of not just how much Farooq could play to a gallery, but how much he was beholden to Delhi's orders even when he didn't want to be. It was also an example, in retrospect, of how much Delhi relied on me to meet its own ends when it came to Farooq. The universal perception seemed to be that here was a man who could get Farooq to listen to him, and to ensure that Farooq did what Delhi wanted him to do. I admit that was my brief, but in reality, it was not difficult to make Farooq see reason. Once you understood the basic principles and the basic heart of the man, you could understand where he stood on his personal political and ideological spectrum. In itself, that was a great help in doing my own work in Kashmir.

That, you see, was the key to getting to know Farooq Abdullah. You had to understand his history, his legacy and his personality – and you had to understand how closely woven it all was with the state that he loved so much. You also had to understand that he took great pride in all of this – and to ask him to spurn it, to betray it, or to compromise it in any way, would be unthinkable. Once you knew and factored all this in, it became easier to navigate for your own ends. Without that understanding, without the flexibility to be occasionally as spontaneous as he himself was, you couldn't get anywhere fast with him.

When it came to our friendship, it was never purely personal, nor was it wholly political. For instance, in 1999, though I was working as the chief of the R&AW and though India and Pakistan were, at the time, embroiled in the war in Kargil, Farooq still invited me for his daughter Safia's wedding. I went off in July 1999 and attended the happy occasion, though I did make a detour to take stock of the ongoing fighting over the Himalayas. Occasions like this often brought home to me how unusual our friendship was – it continued to evolve against some extremely larger-than-life political contexts. You might think that the context of it caused a strain on both of us, but on the contrary, it merely strengthened the bond between us.

Through all of this, Delhi has been the inevitable backdrop. That is why I think that the recent NC–Congress victory in the assembly elections of 2024 is a test for Delhi. Both Prime Minister Narendra Modi and Home Minister Amit Shah travelled across Jammu and Kashmir to campaign for the BJP in September 2024. They were confronted by a rising popular rejection of the ruling party's 'Naya Kashmir' narrative and by the NC's insistence on restoration of statehood. In my opinion, the sooner statehood is restored, the better it will be for Delhi's credibility. That is what every Kashmiri craves desperately. I think Kashmiris have gradually come round to accepting the status quo. All they need Delhi to talk about – and that is a term I repeatedly use – is not even autonomy, it is accommodation. The Kashmiri expects that if he is treated as part of the country, he should be treated like the rest of India. Why is he treated differently? That is the issue or that was the issue. As I said in an interview to the *Hindu* in 2019, 'Ultimately we are going to get nothing. So let's have peace with honour, dignity, justice.'[3] Those were the things that Delhi needed to talk about.

The Importance of Being Farooq Abdullah

For these reasons, the NC's alliance with the BJP was never going to happen. It comes back to a rejection of the politics of hatred and an awareness of the ruling party's methods to retain power, which Farooq has been very open about in recent times. 'We are a Muslim-majority state which joined India,' he told *The Indian Express* in October 2024. 'They [the BJP] want to completely remove that. They want to change the demographic position of the state.'[4]

That is about as literal as Doctor Sahib has ever been, and it is clear that he was speaking against a backdrop of rising turbulence in the state post-2019. When I met him at a mutual friend's daughter's wedding in Delhi in 2024, I asked him directly what the impact of the abrogation had been on the people of Kashmir in the assembly elections. 'It has been huge,' he said frankly. 'There is hatred for Delhi and the BJP in Kashmir.'

Even for Farooq, this honesty was something else.

Now we have to see what will happen. But I anticipate that on the question of statehood there would be some protests, here, there and in courts, etc. If Delhi were to look at Kashmir a little more sympathetically, this would be a good way out. You've removed Ladakh and made it into a Union territory, which is fine. You thought that was the best way to deal with the state. If that be so, Jammu and Kashmir could remain a state.

But here again, the ground is delicate. Article 370 is gone. It will not come back.

The Chief Minister and the Spy

The restoration of statehood? That is a whole different ball game. In fact, I would go so far as to say that for the relationship between state and Centre to come back to normalcy, statehood *must* be restored.

You see, that is why governing Kashmir is like manoeuvring a peculiarly sensitive chessboard. You must know how to play Delhi's game as well as your own, while keeping the doors open for dialogue. Farooq has, for years, been the real bridge between Srinagar and Delhi. It is no surprise that every major political party – from the PDP to the Congress to the BJP – would reach out to the NC, to keep that bridge open. When he was asked, in the weeks before polling in 2024, whether he was ruling out any parties or independent candidates, Farooq said, 'Let's see. Nothing is ruled out in politics, except [that] we are not going with the BJP.'

As far as even the independents were concerned, he shrugged, '*Koi parvaah nahi*. [We don't care about that.] If they have the same values as we have, I am sure the Congress and we won't deny them entry. We want a strong government, an inclusive government.'

That was his bottom line: an inclusive state government that works cooperatively with Delhi.

Nobody has the political instinct or the imagination to choreograph an election in Kashmir better than Farooq. After a decade since elections were last held, and five years since the abrogation of Article 370, the fact that these elections were held without violence or a single bullet being fired is a monumental achievement. In the months before

The Importance of Being Farooq Abdullah

the parliamentary elections of 2024, Farooq was sure that change was in the air and that the BJP would not return with the kind of majority it had had in 2019. He was also sure that the NC would win all three seats in the Valley. He displayed his instincts to perfection by putting up a Shia and a Gujjar along with Omar Abdullah as the three candidates from the Valley, hoping that all three would win. So when Omar lost in Baramulla, it was a setback to both father and son. But the efforts they both made thereafter only added to their determination not to fail in the assembly elections. Amazingly, this time, not only the Shias and the Gujjars, but the Jamaat-e-Islami also appeared to have supported the NC in its resounding victory.

Everyone's logic at the time was that the Jamaat would be on the PDP's side – but a look at the results proved the opposite. The PDP was all but wiped out. This is not to say that Mehbooba and her daughter do not have a role to play in the future. They most certainly do. But in these elections, given the feelings on the ground, there was no way the Jamaat would have cast its lot with the PDP. So it was that Omar's determination and hard work finally laid to rest the ghost of north Kashmir. Engineer Rashid, out of jail, fizzled away from the Kashmiri mind.

Ironically, a couple of years ago, sitting with Farooq and Shafi Sahib (senior NC leader Mohammad Shafi Uri) in his garden in Srinagar, I enquired which way the Jamaat would go in the event of an assembly election. Shafi Sahib was of the view that the Jamaat, which had been close to Mufti

Mohammad Sayeed, would always vote for the PDP. When I said, 'Why not the National Conference?' Farooq looked at Shafi and said, '*Batao?*' (Tell us?) Shafi had no answer, but I think Doctor Sahib understood what I was trying to say. Though always a nationalist and secular leader of Kashmir, Farooq has also been able to tweak his imagination to the old times when the NC was still the Muslim Conference (before 1939) and has used it to the party's benefit.

Interestingly, despite doubters around him, Doctor Sahib was always emphatic that the assembly elections had to be held, and would be held, in September 2024. As voting began, and the Congress campaign appeared to be weakening in Jammu, it became clear that the mandate was so emphatic that any such tie-up even in the future would require time. It only underlines the point that the BJP needs to realize how and why they disappointed Farooq and wasted four years. In this lament, I am somewhat of a stuck record, for I have lost count of how many times I have pointed to Delhi's lack of understanding and its inability to read the writing on the wall.

The lack of the Centre's capability in understanding a simple task has often left me astounded. After all, what has Delhi wanted since 1947? To mainstream Kashmir and to eliminate the Pakistani element.

Now, as far as I can see, the Pakistani element is indeed largely gone, in the sense that Islamabad does not matter so much anymore. The Kashmiri does not care any longer about Pakistan, particularly after the terror attacks of 9/11. The turning point, as far as I could see, was when US President George W. Bush read Pakistan's President Pervez Musharraf the riot act and demanded that he join the global war on terror. Musharraf's meek acquiescence at the time incensed the Kashmiris.

If this fellow could so easily turn his back on them, they wondered, what was the point of throwing in their lot with Pakistan? I'd say they had a point!

So why could Delhi not build on this opportunity? Kashmir has several interesting and suitable elements, all waiting to be used as Delhi desires. There is the Mirwaiz himself, and there are the separatists – and these are just the characters beyond the towering figure of Farooq himself. So what Delhi has essentially done is waste this entire cast of characters for the hundredth time in history. It would have been wise to go to Farooq and begin doing business, at least with him, directly. He was, after all, more than willing.

Instead, what Delhi did was to put up proxies, alas all pygmies who faded into insignificance before the big man as time went by. In the 2024 assembly elections, all but Sajad Lone were decimated. As a strategy by Delhi – and I don't want to mince my words – it was senseless. Nobody could have hoped to match the stature and leadership of Farooq Abdullah. Farooq's politics is of both the head and the heart. If he joined the INDIA alliance, it was because the BJP left him with no option, and after walking with Rahul Gandhi in the Bharat Jodo Yatra, his heart took him towards the Congress. This ultimately resulted in the NC–Congress alliance in Jammu and Kashmir. But who knows what may have happened if the NC had not got 42 seats in the assembly elections? A few days before the results were announced, the BJP, in the hope of a 30-30 verdict between them and the NC, was still searching for Farooq Abdullah.

Doctor Sahib told me recently that at his deathbed, Sheikh Sahib had told him to always stay with the Congress, for its secular DNA and for its idea of India. These are ideas that Farooq represents to me today as well. The last of many dying arts and qualities, but importantly, the true Nehruvian art of politics. Here is a man who is utterly committed to the cause of secularism, of faith and humanity. He can sing bhajans at Hindu religious functions as much as he reads and interprets the Quran. He can let go of his inhibitions at wedding parties and dance to Bollywood tunes. Farooq's oratory has often shocked and angered his supporters and critics alike, but only at the cost of their finding out that he hadn't been serious after all. Over the years, Farooq has perfected the art of honing his political and public personality, by simply acknowledging and working with his inconsistencies and flaws, a quality that people love and hate simultaneously.

Time and again, in recent years, he has called openly for a better understanding of each other, for a more civil political discourse, for a more evolved understanding of the aspirations of the people of Kashmir. Farooq has not mellowed with age. If anything, he has ripened into a man who sees far beyond the political skirmishes that most parties engage in in the state. The years have taught him to understand the heart of

The Importance of Being Farooq Abdullah

his state much better than anyone else ever could. He may be nearly ninety years old, but I don't think you can ignore Farooq Abdullah even now.

In the coming years, it would be a huge mistake for the NC to ignore the Congress, which is the only bulwark, if required, against the BJP in Jammu. The Congress, of course, needs to pull its socks up and figure out what went wrong in Jammu. The redoubtable Tarigami, MLA five times out of five, has said that this (the verdict of the 2024 assembly elections) is a victory for Kashmir. Indeed it is, but it is also a huge victory for Omar Abdullah and Doctor Sahib, the sultan of politics.

From where I stand, this is also the Kashmiri's victory. The Kashmiris *wanted* to come out and vote in these elections. They wanted a way to make their voices heard, to make their opinions known. They chose to do it via the ballot, as generations of citizens have done in this astonishing democracy of ours. In many ways, I think this was also the victory of Kashmiriyat, of Farooq's ultimate goal of unity in the face of crushing odds, of a reassurance to the Kashmiri that they will always be a majority, at least in the Valley.

On the unseasonably warm evening of 16 October 2024, I got a call from Farooq. 'The swearing-in ceremony is tomorrow,' he said with his typical briskness. 'When are you coming?'

'Sir,' I protested, laughing. 'How can I come at such short notice?'

'Nonsense! What is it? Tickets? *Hum bhej denge.*' (I'll send them.)

When I demurred yet again, he dismissed me with a flourish, 'I'll see you tomorrow. When you reach here, go straight to the Taj.'

And so, Paran and I took the flight to Srinagar and went off to the Taj where everyone was staying. There was Akhilesh Yadav with his army of red caps, the communist leader Prakash Karat, D. Raja, Kanimozhi and Supriya Sule. The young Gandhis arrived the next morning, along with K.C. Venugopal and Mallikarjun Kharge. As I settled down in my seat in Raj Bhavan, I could see Farooq's hand behind keeping the INDIA alliance alive in Kashmir. The hall was packed.

Mehbooba was present too, which I was pleased to see. The event went off smoothly – a 'new beginning' as Omar's sister, Safia, posted on X (formerly Twitter). More than the great political tamasha it was clearly meant to be, it was a huge family showing of support as well. The elections had been Farooq's show, but this ceremony was Omar's. It was, in many ways, a befitting answer to the BJP's constant harping on the need to do away with 'dynasty politics'. This was the people's answer, not the Abdullahs themselves. 'This question of family raj should be put behind us,' Farooq told Rajdeep Sardesai. 'It's a democracy, so it's people's raj. They are the ones who elect you or not.'

The Importance of Being Farooq Abdullah

That much was on display at the swearing-in ceremony.

Still, though I was expecting a lot of Omar's friends and guests from Delhi and elsewhere, I was surprised to see that everyone who was there was present because of Farooq and their respect for him. Once again, he towered over everyone. Mollie had arrived from England, and Omar's sisters were in attendance too. The only dark spot, I'd say, was that Farooq's sister, Khalida, was not present.

Watching Omar, I could see that he was flushed with a new, bright confidence. He was a changed man that day, and there was a moment of pure emotion as he signed his name to the order that made him chief minister of Jammu and Kashmir. 'My hand is shaking!' he whispered over the microphone – as he signed, and glancing at Doctor Sahib, I caught a gleam of tears in his eyes.

It was now time for the son to shine.

Still, whether it is the confidence of the verdict, or Doctor Sahib's own inner feeling, the transition of power between father and son has been incredibly smooth. I see a closer bond between the two now. As Omar moves ahead in his chief ministership, he will need his father's sage advice and wisdom.

In his interview to Rajdeep Sardesai, Farooq said honestly that this was an emotional moment, and a proud one for him as a father. This should put to rest all stories about differences between the two. Doctor Sahib has, however, warned Omar that he is inheriting a crown of thorns, which Omar needs to bear in mind as Doctor Sahib steps back. 'The responsibilities are far greater than the victory,' he told Rajdeep. As always, he has hit the nail on the head. Demands for statehood aside, there is the question of Jammu and its possible alienation from the Valley and from the politics of the NC. 'Jammu is one eye and Kashmir is the other eye,' Farooq has insisted. 'Both eyes have to function for the state to progress.'

The road ahead for Kashmir is not a smooth one. Bridges will have to be built, not just between Srinagar and Delhi, but between Srinagar and Jammu. Farooq might insist that these are not new challenges, but one cannot ignore the fact that Omar will have to navigate them carefully now. Farooq is not the kind of man, or father, who interferes with his son's handling of a certain situation. In his mind, Omar is ready for power, and while he will always be on hand to give advice should his son need it, he is equally clear that this will be Omar's journey.

Still, Farooq has continued to speak about Kashmir – for he is still the biggest voice in the state. In September 2024, he countered the BJP's claims about improvement in the security situation in the Union territory after the abrogation, saying tourists 'come like prisoners and go like prisoners'. Speaking at Aaj Tak's 'Panchayat' event in September 2024, on the banks of Srinagar's iconic Dal Lake, Farooq cited the massive security deployment during the Amarnath Yatra to hit out at the Centre's claim that normalcy had returned to Jammu and Kashmir. 'There never used to be so many forces during [the] Amarnath Yatra ... They [tourists] come like prisoners and are taken away like prisoners in caged buses.'

He also refuted any claims to Kashmiri independence. 'It is not easy to be independent. On one side, there is Pakistan, a nuclear power, and on the other, there is China, another nuclear power. How is it possible? Where is your economy as you are dependent on everything? Those who are doing this are living abroad and do not know the ground situation. They have wrong thinking because we are part of India and will remain so.'[5]

There is nobody better qualified than Farooq to speak for Kashmir. With over four decades of experience, nobody understands the political landscape of Jammu and Kashmir like he does, at least within the NC. I'm reminded of what the eminent intellectual Agha Ashraf Ali once told me. Initially, he thought I was a spook and was reserved – but one day, I asked him, 'Please tell me about the Sheikh.'

'The Sheikh had a heart of gold, but not much in his top storey,' said Agha Ashraf. 'He could not understand Pandit Nehru's compulsions, because of what was happening in north India after Partition. Farooq, on the other hand, understands everything. He may pretend not to, but I have never found him wanting in political intelligence. In fact, sometimes I think he's the smartest of the Abdullahs.'

Before he died, Agha Ashraf told me, 'Nobody could stand up to Modi except Farooq. But eventually, Omar is the future of Kashmir.'

Turning this over in my head, I couldn't help but agree with the old man. The Sheikh lived through different times, a time that was more assured than today. Often, he would say,

'I'm with India because of two people: Gandhi and Nehru.' He had that support, whereas his son had none. Farooq has lived through much more difficult times all alone, except for the days of Indira Gandhi – and even she betrayed him in the end.

Given the kind of history and politics that he has seen and been in the midst of, I think Doctor Sahib has a greater role to play on a national stage now. The INDIA alliance – after the death of CPI-M stalwart Sitaram Yechury and its recent disastrous performances in Haryana and Maharashtra – needs constant attention and navigation too. I've often wondered whether Farooq would make it to the seat in Rashtrapati Bhavan, but given the mess that the INDIA alliance is currently in, Farooq is a great candidate to be its leader. It is clear to me that his time on the political stage is far from over. It is equally clear that the true importance of Farooq Abdullah is that he can never be ignored or underestimated.

He *is* Kashmir.

10

The Lion in Winter

Who knows how, where and when this world will end? Only a fool would say. However, the Prophet (Isaiah 65; 17:25) offers hope of a transformative vision, symbolizing the removal of hostility and fear between all creatures, where the wolf and the lamb could coexist peacefully. That's what Farooq has always hoped for and dreamt of. As was said of the Bollywood actor Mahmood, and what the Nobel laureate Bob Dylan says in one of his better-known albums, Doctor Sahib is a man of many moods and contradictions. He often quotes this beloved Urdu couplet, '*Zindagi zindadili ka naam hai, murda-dil khaak jiya karte hain.*' (You should never lose heart, otherwise what life is worth living?)

In Delhi at the launch of *Covert* in May 2024, Doctor Sahib spoke to a full house in the India International Centre and poured his heart out. He was confident that the parliamentary elections would go well, and he was in his element that night. It reminded me of a couplet by Ghalib:

The Chief Minister and the Spy

Ghalib, chhuti sharaab par ab bhi kabhi kabhi,
Peeta hu roz-e-abr o shab-e-mahtaab mein.

(Ghalib, I've quit drinking, yet still, I sigh,
I drink on cloudy days and moonlit nights.)

It must have been a full-moon night.

'Where will this go? When will we think let's sit down and talk? The minute I suggest this, it's *Farooq Abdullah Pakistan ki baat karta hai. Toh kiski baat karu? Mar toh hum rahe hain. Uss ethnic cleansing se kya tumne samjha ki Kashmir tumhara ban jayega?*' (The minute I suggest this, they say that Farooq Abdullah only talks of Pakistan. Then of what else should I speak? We are the ones who are dying. If you conduct ethnic cleansing in the state, do you think Kashmir will become yours?)

I'm going to give you his words in full, because I think that there is nothing greater than Farooq's eloquence when it is unleashed:

'*Arrey yaar, Muslimon ki haalat dekhiye jo aapke mulk mein hain. Kitne hai bade-bade daftar mein? Kitne aapke high commissioner ya ambassador hain? Bais crore Muslims hain – kya aapne kabhi socha ki woh bhi Hindustani hain, aapke tarah hain? Zinda rehna chahte hain? Nafrat se koi zinda nahi rehta. Hum Kashmiri Pakistan jaa sakte the, Pakistan humare border pe tha, Kashmir aur Srinagar ke sirhat ke kinaare pahunch gaye the – kyun nahi gaye phir? Main aapko imandaari se kehta hu – agar Pakistan ne woh humla na kiya hota toh Maharaja Hari Singh Kashmir ko independent banane wale the. Woh unki sabse badi tamanna thi. Hindustan–Cheen–vagairah ka centre Kashmir bane.*

The Lion in Winter

[Friends, have you seen the condition of the Muslims in your land? How many are there in big or prominent offices? How many are high commissioners or ambassadors? There are 22 crore Muslims in this country. Have you ever thought that they too are Hindustani, just like you? That they want to stay alive? Nobody will stay alive through hatred. We Kashmiris could have gone to Pakistan. Pakistan was once upon our borders. Why didn't we go then? I want to tell you honestly that if Pakistan had not attacked, then Maharaja Hari Singh wanted to stand independent. That was his biggest dream: that Kashmir should be at the centre of Hindustan and China.]

'*Ab aaj kya ho raha hai? Kya kabhi aap sochte hain? Hum logon pe ungli uthti hai. Humein batate hain ki hum Hindustani nahi hain. Kab aap samjhenge ki hum Hindustani hain? Haan humein Pakistan se mohabbat hai. Isme koi shaq nahi hai. Woh humare padosi hain. Agar ek din Allah karey – jab bhi road khul jaye – agar woh aayein, aur mutually baat-cheet karke insaniyat se reh sakte hain, toh hum rehne denge. Iska yeh matlab nahi hai ki hum Pakistani ban jayenge. Sawal hi nahi hai iss baat ki. Par Allah ke vaaste, watan ko bachaane ki koshish kijiye. Watan ka kasoor kya hai. Itne crore insaan, yahan aur wahan –* how long are we going to live in this hatred for each other?

[Today, what do you think is happening? Have any of you ever thought of it? People point fingers at us. They say that we are not Indians. When will all of you understand that we are Indians. Yes, we love Pakistan. There is no doubt about that. After all, they are our neighbours. If one day, should Allah will it, the road between our two countries should open, and if dialogue is restored, then we will leave it as such.

This does not mean that we will become Pakistani. There is no question of that. But for the love of Allah, try to save your motherland. That is your duty towards your motherland – how long are we going to live in this hatred for each other?]

'This is the question. I was a doctor in England, and in our medical register, they brought a patient who kept saying that he wanted to jump into the Thames. The doctor and the psychiatrist had to sign a form to admit him into the hospital. That professor of psychiatry talked to him for two hours, even as the man insisted that he wanted to jump into the river. I was sitting there and I said to myself, God Almighty, if the fellow wants to jump, what the hell are we doing here? Let's sign the form and admit him.

'*Humari haalat wohi hai. Woh bhi chhalaang marna chahte hain samundar mein aur hum bhi chalaang maarna chahte hain.*

[That is our condition as well. They want to jump into the ocean and so do we.]

'*Main kabhi kabhi apne aap se sochta hu, yaar kya woh din aayega, jab main Lahore jaa paunga, Lahore ki galliyon mein ghoomunga, main unka fashion, ghazal, mujra dekhu? Apni gaadi mein Peshawar kab jaunga? Woh din aayega?*

[Sometimes I think to myself – when will that day come when I too can go to Lahore? When will I be able to wander the streets of Lahore, wear their fashions, listen to their ghazals and mujras? When will I be able to drive off to Peshawar? When will that day come when there is peace between our two countries?]

'I am now two years less than ninety. I don't know how God has given me strength. We want peace. How do we achieve it? I think we need leaders in both countries, like Charles de Gaulle when he walked out of Algeria. I have never forgotten that he said enough is enough – many of the French protested it, they saw it as a loss of power, but he insisted on saying it, on doing it. He lost the elections soon after, but today, I praise him. He is the kind of leader we need, who has the courage to say, "Enough!" I hope that happens soon. To the Indians and Pakistanis in you, I say, for God's sake, let's mend our fences, let's forget our animosity. It's been 75 years. *Bahut ho gaya. Ab Allah ke vaaste, humein maaf karo. Hum Kashmiriyon ko maaf karo. Hum Kashmiri barbaad ho rahe hain. Na wahan humari izzat hai, na yahan humari izzat. Kahan pahunchaya aap logon ne humein?* [It's enough. Now for the love of God, forgive us all. Forgive us Kashmiris. We are getting destroyed. We have no respect no matter where we are. Where have you all left us?]

'I'm going to stand by what I say and what I stand for. I'm part of this nation and I will remain part of this nation. But I will not remain part of a divided nation, where Hindus and Muslims are divided. I'll fight it to the last breath I have. How does it matter what religion you hold? Let's be human beings. Let's start understanding each other.

'Why take a state and make it a Union territory, after 5 August 2019? When we met the prime minister, I had just recovered from COVID. I said I wasn't able to come, but they said you have to come. When they asked me to speak, these are the words I used: I said, you don't trust us, we don't trust you. Straight. In the end, what he said was: yes, *dil ki doori aur Dilli ki doori bahut hai. Iss doori ko door karna hai. Par kaise karein?* [There is a great distance between our hearts and Delhi. How do we remove that distance?]'

In Srinagar a week later, Farooq was a different man, overwhelmed by the deafening silence of the Valley. At dinner at Dilshad's on 29 May 2024, he hardly spoke, prompting those present to observe to me, 'Your friend appears preoccupied and not himself.'

Indeed, he was not.

When he finally had the time to see me a couple of days later on 31 May, he sat meditatively in his beautiful garden in 40 Gupkar Road. That morning, his disinterestedness or wise passivity – call it what you will – was inexplicable and indescribable. His isolation and loneliness appeared absolute, as deep as the soul of man could go. Had he learnt somehow of Omar's impending defeat in Baramulla in the general elections? Had he had some kind of premonition that his calculations would be upset? I have no answer.

Farooq called out to his sister Suraiya and also to Safia, since both live on either side of him. He needed proxies to do the talking at emotional moments, as in the past, like when I visited him when he was under detention in February 2020. Then it was Safia who stood in for his silence, and now it was Suraiya who came out of her bath, with her hair still wet in a towel, to amuse me. All the while, Farooq was calling out to the bulbul hopping around in the garden.

'*Aaja bulbul, aaja!*' he called, while feeding it strawberries. (Come bulbul, come!)

'Does it recognize you?' I asked jokingly.

'Of course not,' he responded with customary crispness.

The Lion in Winter

Yet the bulbul was attracted to him, as is the rest of Kashmir. No one can contain his largeness of being. You cannot play upon him because he is cleverer than anyone else. As a young Kashmiri admirer told me, *yeh baap ka bhi baap hai*. (He is the king of all kings.) He would always win at the odds. The irony is that Farooq has thought not too much, but too well. He is impossible to outwit. As NC MP Aga Syed Ruhullah Mehdi recently told journalist Karan Thapar, it is Farooq who is 'more Kashmiri nationalist' and more suited to lead what he called the 'resilience' of the Kashmiri people.

Come what may, nothing ever prevented Farooq from being himself.

When I got up to leave two hours later, knowing that it was time for his Friday namaz, he said, 'Sit down, I still have ten minutes.'

I never felt like an intruder, even though he didn't talk to me. Dilshad has already spoken of the purity of his soul. My friend, Ashok Bhan, the eminent Kashmiri Pandit lawyer, once said to me that Doctor Sahib's ultimate wish was to be buried as chief minister next to the Sher-e-Kashmir. That dream died with Omar's victory. It was the summer of the Lok Sabha elections and they were important ones for Kashmir. The NC was fighting as part of the INDIA alliance, but it was not an easily won alliance. Knowing Farooq, I never thought it would be. He was already in a belligerent mood. He had been since the beginning of the year. In January 2024, the Enforcement Directorate issued a summons to Farooq. He had been charge-sheeted in 2022 on allegations of financial irregularities within the Jammu

& Kashmir Cricket Association, including alleged diversion of funds to personal bank accounts and unexplained cash withdrawals. He was taken in for questioning for over six hours. I was really worried that day, and as soon as I heard that he had been released, I rang him up.

'Are you all right?'

'Yes, yes,' he said, sounding tired but unbeaten. 'They won't break me.'

It was the old Farooq talking – the young boy who had been trained to never give up and to keep moving forward in the face of a crisis, the young man who had grown up in the shadow of trouble. Defeat is not in Farooq's DNA.

On the other hand, he kept the Congress guessing right to the end. In January 2024 itself, Farooq alarmed the INDIA bloc by stating firmly that the NC would go solo in Jammu and Kashmir during the Lok Sabha elections. 'I want to make one thing clear: that the National Conference will fight on its own. There's no second thought about that.'

It was a typical Farooq statement: he wanted to show that he was in the driver's seat, to show that Kashmir would not do anyone's bidding. Of course, later, the two parties would join hands to fight the assembly elections, but it made one thing clear again: you can never take Farooq Abdullah for granted.

Yet his mind has been in turmoil since the abrogation of 2019. Presently he appears to be torn between his love for Kashmir and his son. It reminds me of a story of when Sheikh Sahib went to Pakistan in 1964, to meet President Ayub Khan, at Nehru's bidding, to find a way forward for Kashmir. At the time, the Sheikh took Farooq with him. But

The Lion in Winter

the Sheikh had barely met Ayub when Panditji passed away, forcing the Sheikh to rush back to attend his friend's funeral. Farooq, on the other hand, stayed back. It was his last visit to Pakistan. He told me, '*Maine socha ki thoda Pakistan ghoomte hain.*' (I thought I might as well explore Pakistan now.)

It was during this visit that Farooq met the poet Faiz in Karachi. He was staying at the government guest house there. Faiz had married an Englishwoman, Alys, and Sheikh Sahib had married the two of them in a *nikah* ceremony in Srinagar. It was why he wanted to meet the Sheikh. Faiz came reluctantly to meet Farooq, because he was so anti-government and against the current dictatorship of Pakistan. He told Farooq, 'I actually wanted to meet your father.'

Farooq recalled, 'I told him that my father had to go back because of Panditji's death.'

'Well, now sadly, after Nehru, we will never have a solution for Kashmir.' Significantly, Lord Mountbatten had said something similar to Nehru when he was in Delhi as a special guest for Republic Day in 1964. He pleaded with Nehru that if Kashmir was not settled in his life, it would never be settled.

Faiz, however, continuing optimistically, added, 'But ultimately everything has to be all right, whether we are alive or not.'

'It has to be and I want to live to see it so,' Farooq replied.

Farooq is determined that the sorrows of this world will end and he will live to see it. From the way I see it, the two men were talking about the same thing: the prospects of the India–Pakistan relationship and the plight of the Kashmiri in India.

Has that come to pass?

As Aga Syed Ruhullah Mehdi told me at the beginning of 2025 in Delhi, 'Doctor Sahib is a great man, our tallest leader. Unfortunately, he is torn between his own legacy and the future of his son, between Kashmir [which he represents] and Omar Abdullah.' This has the ring of truth. Farooq had told me at least three or four times that he would be chief minister, but it was not to be. Omar's defeat in the parliamentary elections turned to victory when he was sworn in on 9 October 2024 as chief minister. It was a huge moment for him, but an even bigger one for Farooq, as he at last made way for his son. The journalist Muzaffar Raina, no admirer of Doctor Sahib, said that Farooq was a wonderful father and going up in stature all the time. As Aga Ruhullah has suggested, Doctor Sahib has conceded a generational shift, but the worry in Kashmir, as with the Aga, is how this will play out.

At Omar's swearing-in, everyone was happy, except Khalida, conspicuous by her absence. When I asked Doctor Sahib why she had not been invited, he replied briskly that the Shah family had not yet recovered from Khalida's son Muzaffar's defeat in the assembly elections.

But it was clear at the swearing-in that Farooq was looking ahead to his son's time in the sun. As the son has grown, Farooq would like to believe that by the grace of the Almighty, he has grown closer to and more protective of Omar. Since Omar became chief minister in 2024, whenever I have inquired how things are, Farooq has said that Omar is working very hard and is learning all the time. Doctor Sahib

The Lion in Winter

may be open or expressive about friends, but is a private person when it comes to family. Yet, so intense can be a father's love that in course of time, not only is he looking for something of himself in Omar, but is unconsciously glorifying him too.

As he approaches 55, there are indications that Doctor Sahib is beginning to have an impact on the young chief minister's political thought and seeing something of himself in him. Doctor Sahib can take heart from the fact that there is nothing 'fake' about his son.

Doctor Sahib was expected in Delhi in the last week of November, but when I called him a couple of days earlier, he said he had something more important to do. He was accompanying Omar on umrah to Medina and Mecca. More recently, he appears to have rushed back from Dubai, cutting short his golfing holiday, to be with Omar when the party's senior MP from Srinagar, Aga Syed Ruhullah Mehdi, appeared to be challenging the young chief minister's writ. Nobody has ever dared challenge Farooq. Omar has a long way to go in politics. But it's difficult to visualize the NC without Doctor Sahib's guiding hand. Would the party remain intact, split, become more radical – who knows? The Kashmir story, or riddle, is not over yet – nor can it be wished away. But what is frightening is the prospect of the growth of Pakistan and the ISI in the absence of Farooq in the Valley. Pakistan has never been comfortable with the Abdullah family since Sheikh Sahib turned down Jinnah's approach to him to join Pakistan. Omar may be half acceptable, but Doctor Sahib is not. Islamabad finds him more difficult to handle than Delhi does. A popular Pakistani High Commissioner in Delhi

The Chief Minister and the Spy

told me that Pakistan had reservations about Doctor Sahib because he was 'unmanageable'.

When I once mentioned to Doctor Sahib that the Pakistanis were afraid of him, he characteristically replied, '*Yehi toh musibat hai. Dilli aur Islamabad dono yehi kehte hain. Lekin humse baat koi nahin karta hai.*' (This is the problem. Both Delhi and Islamabad react similarly, but neither side engages with me.)

Over the years, I've watched Farooq from both close quarters and afar. Even when I left Kashmir and came to New Delhi to join the IB headquarters, it was both a professional mandate and a personal privilege to watch him. I suppose that is the root of this unlikely friendship that it is both professionally ordered and personally enjoyed, at least by me – I know better than to speak for the man himself! Ours is an association forged by Delhi as much as it has been forged by Kashmir. Shakespeare once wrote that adversity makes for strange bedfellows. I'd paraphrase that and say that it makes for strange friendships.

When I came to Srinagar all those years ago, I told you that I felt intimidated, even a little uncertain. It was as hard then, as it is now, to know quite where you stood with Farooq. But over the years, both he and Mollie have opened their homes to Paran and me. Doctor Sahib has always been mercurial and temperamental, but he has never been unreasonable. Speak to him with reason and logic, and he has always listened. He has never ignored Delhi's wishes, even though sometimes, as in 1999 and 2002, he has been furious. He has always known that between Delhi and Srinagar, there must never be a gulf. That is why I keep repeating ad nauseum that there is nobody quite like Farooq in either modern India or in Kashmir. More and more people are beginning to understand Farooq's qualities of head and heart, but for which this story would be meaningless.

The abrogation changed everything for him, in ways that perhaps neither he nor I could have foreseen. Yet even Harinder Baweja, the journalist who has watched him since 1989, has noted that he has changed, 'I have been a witness to his changing mood swings. He can go from deathly silence to bluster. He can swing from song and dance to introspection. Whatever his moods, what has stood out has been his deep passion for India.' I would agree with that. I have never seen Farooq defeated, as I said, but the abrogation and bifurcation of the state has left its mark. He has become more introspective, more contemplative, quieter. Turning to his faith has provided him with great mental and emotional succour, but Farooq has not lost his fire. As Allama Iqbal says, 'Faith is the highest passion in a human being.'

Farooq's rhetoric about Kashmir has always been passionate. The one thing that I have never seen him compromise on has been peace in the Valley and the maintenance of the Kashmiri identity. In fact, if anything, he has become even more vehement in the aftermath of the abrogation of Article 370. As early as 1984, when he was dismissed by Indira Gandhi, he raged publicly about the Centre's attempt to erode

Kashmir's Muslim identity. He has continued to emphasize the need to maintain Kashmiri identity over the years. It may seem, to those who have watched him as closely as I have, as though he has deliberately banked the impulsive fires that have been his trademark over the years. In truth, his is one of the last voices fighting for Kashmiriyat in this day and age.

The lion in winter is no less dangerous despite his deliberation now. When Baweja met him after the abrogation, however, she saw a different Farooq, 'The nullification of Article 370 changed him deeply. He felt betrayed and told me that he was now seeking refuge in the Quran.' Farooq told Baweja that he was deeply upset that Narendra Modi's BJP had drawn the Hindu–Muslim fault line. 'The man who had always stood by India like a rock, the man who was passionate about the idea of India was nursing a deep injury.' He told Baweja much the same thing that he told the audience at the IIC in May 2024, 'The Pakistanis have always hated me, now the Indians think I am a separatist and my own people think I am a stooge of Delhi.'

This, Baweja told me, was a man at war within himself.

Farooq has always been intensely passionate, in his politics as much as he has been in his life. It was a situation like this that would prompt his children and grandchildren to ask of him whether this was the India that they should stand by.

Over the years, Farooq has changed. Perhaps that change is inevitable – not all of us are the men or women we once used to be. But in Farooq, time has wrought a certain steadiness, a mellowness to his fiery edges and a practicality that sometimes wins over his instinctive impetuosity. In 2015, two hardliner Hurriyat Conference leaders, part of a delegation sent by Syed Ali Geelani, met with Pakistan High Commissioner Abdul Basit in Delhi, to tell him that Islamabad should maintain 'consistency and firmness' over its Kashmir policy. They insisted that Pakistan should play an 'active role in highlighting the human rights violations' in Jammu and Kashmir at all international fora. The matter was a sensational media controversy in India, but it was not really so controversial, given the fact that – as Asad Durrani himself once told me – Pakistan had given the separatists this political platform from which to negotiate.

Throughout that controversy, I remember that Farooq remained unruffled. In that unflappable reaction, I noticed a palpable shift from the hot-headed young man I had worked with in Srinagar in the 1980s and 1990s. Back then, Farooq's line used to be: these bloody Pakistanis need to be taught a lesson. It was an aggressive reaction. But then, as the old saying goes, much water has flowed down the Jhelum. A lot has changed between India and Pakistan since then. Vajpayee's bus went to Lahore – and though attempts at keeping the peace have often been shattered by militancy and terrorist attacks, Farooq's line of thinking through it all has also slowly shifted. Now, he feels it is important for India and Pakistan to be at peace because it is, at the end, the Kashmiri on the ground who suffers as a result of violence. In this belief, he has put his finger squarely on the pulse of the modern Kashmiri, who is characterized by a curious mix of aggrieved oppression and defiance.

I've noticed, through my long years of association with the state, that even though you might discriminate against them or give them their due, the Kashmiri is not easily cowed. Instead, they have learned, over the years, to be purely devious. It is, for them, the key to survival. They will not trust you easily, and they will trust each other not at all. As Brajesh Mishra often used to say, 'The only thing straight in Kashmir is the poplar tree!'

In my memoir, I wrote on the changing sense of Kashmiriyat on the ground in the state, so I won't go too much into that. After all, it's a separate subject in itself. But specifically in relation to Farooq, I can think of no one else who defines it more comprehensively than he does. You see, to put it simply, Kashmiriyat has no real definition in Merriam Webster's Dictionary. You won't find it in any textbook either. It's always been elusive: the spirit of Kashmir. Today, the term is widely accepted in the discourse on Kashmir, signifying a sociocultural and secular Kashmiri identity. Over the years, it has been clad in all kinds of hues of nationalism, brushing aside any question of its evolution and original historical context. I find that it's easier to define Kashmiriyat in the people who walk its land: in old Agha Ashraf Ali, for instance, the father of the great poet Agha Shahid Ali – and indeed, in Farooq himself.

Over the years, I have watched Farooq as Kashmir and he have dreamt of stability. In and out of power, he has never stopping batting for India's cause in Kashmir, a stand he stuck to despite its unpopularity in the state. My work with him in the

1990s only highlighted his awareness that Delhi desperately needed a well-known Kashmiri leader to stand by its cause. His presence in the political arena in the Valley brought with it not just his influence, but his father's legacy. You might doubt the Sheikh, as B.K. Nehru writes in his memoir, *Nice Guys Finish Second*,[1] but Farooq is as straight as anyone might want him to. Farooq never forgets his friends. After B.K. Nehru died in 2001, Farooq continued to visit Kasauli, where Nehru's wife Fori lived, even after she had gone blind.

By turns, he has been pragmatic and passionate. I saw his pragmatism during the kidnapping of Rubaiya Sayeed, when he cooperated fully with Delhi to arrange her release. He and I had both known that his hands were tied.

Two parallel games were playing out in Delhi: one was for the release of Mufti's daughter, and the other was the chance to get rid of the incompetent, no-good chief minister. Farooq recognized the games as clearly as he recognized the practicality of working with Delhi in that moment. To me, these are respectable qualities. Here is a man who is fully aware of the games being played around him and who can yet find time to play a round of golf before work in the morning.

I have seen his despair too. But despair has never kept him down for long. Like the great poet Ghalib, Farooq also believed, '*Guzar jayega yeh bhi daur Ghalib, zara itmenaan toh rakh, khushi hi na reh saki, toh gham ki kya aukaat hai.*' (This too shall pass, you just need to believe, if happiness could not survive, what chance does despair have?)

With Delhi, when as a minister in the United Progressive Alliance-II government, he went on record in an interview to journalist Saeed Naqvi and said outright, 'Delhi doesn't trust us.' Imagine, a minister of the Union saying that – in Delhi! His stand on Delhi has, in fact, been his greatest source of sorrow over the years.

In a democracy, it was always the people who would decide what was right for them and what was wrong. All through the three decades that I have known him, Farooq has placed his faith in the voters, while also being ready to fight on every front. 'A soldier has to work on many fronts,' he once said. 'When I find this front ready, you will not find me lacking. I shall be with my Patton tank, in the front.'[2]

It was this indomitable quality of his that I grew to admire over my days in Kashmir. In fact, now that I look back, I think the reason he and I got along so well was that strange unconventionality that we both possess. That formed the solid foundation to getting to know each other. Our friendship, as with any other relationship, has seen its ebbs and flows. There was a time, when, in London, the writer and former head of the BBC, Andrew Whitehead, came over after a conference panel on which both Farooq and I had been discussing Kashmir. 'You two are like peas in a pod!' he exclaimed. I've never forgotten it. It's a great compliment when I think about it. Those were the days when our friendship was at its zenith and, in Farooq's eyes, I could do no wrong. I'll be the first to admit that things changed – subtly but definitely – when I became head of the R&AW in 1999. It's not easy to navigate a friendship when you're also heading a position of national and international security. My time in the R&AW was the time when our relationship was

The Lion in Winter

at its most formal, because I was devoting more and more of my time to discussing Kashmir with the separatists.

Then, of course, there was Delhi's betrayal during the 2002 elections. There was a time when I went to Brajesh Mishra, in 2003, and I said to him, 'Why don't you relieve me?'

'Why? What's happened?'

'Nothing. I've done everything now,' I replied. What I didn't say was there had been sufficient behind-the-scenes drama (that I cannot go into for obvious reasons) that had changed my mind.

'What's the rush?' Brajesh asked. 'If you're so hell-bent on leaving, let's wait until after the [general] elections [of 2004] are over.'

Despite difficulties like these, the balance of our friendship sustained, though of necessity, there was a distance born of formality.

Now, as I write this book in the dusk of 2024 and the dawn of 2025, I must admit that the chief minister and the spy remain somewhat ironically linked: when Delhi thinks of Farooq, it inevitably thinks of me. In all the years that I have known Farooq, he remains two steps ahead of every intelligence game – the ISI, for one, could never get hold of him. I myself struggled to remain close to the man.

This trait of his personality has underscored both personal and political ties. As far as Delhi has been concerned, ever since Farooq entered the scene, Delhi has never sought to know him, nor has it ever had the patience to put in that effort. Instead, it has sought to own him all at once, which is not possible.

The Chief Minister and the Spy

More than once, Farooq has shown himself to be willing to do whatever Delhi wants him to (within reason, of course). Time and again, he has insisted that he is not his father, and that he wants to do things differently. But that chance has never been given to him. Instead, opportunities to build bridges have gone by the wayside.

Over the years, I have watched Farooq grow to dominate the political landscape of the Valley. The old Sher-e-Kashmir was before my time, and he passed away in 1982, but even during his father's last days, Farooq was already becoming much larger than life. The stories about him were and are multitudinous and that's not surprising, for he possesses an indubitable charisma that makes it hard for even his strongest critic to ignore him. In one of my conversations with her, Barkha Dutt has memorably called him one of India's last *zinda-dil* politicians. I think that's a fabulous way to put it. Farooq has lived life on a grand scale. He has never been afraid to take life (and love, if you believe everything you hear!) by the horns.

Yet Farooq is a man of simple pleasures. Henry Kissinger once said that after a dinner of Peking duck, he would agree to anything. In the same way, Doctor Sahib loves food more than anything else. If he has a weakness other than golf, it is good food. He has a terribly sweet tooth. In the summer, in his lawn in Srinagar, you can find him often gorging on strawberries and cream as he could well do in the middle of a golf game, sharing more cream than strawberries with friends. The food in the Abdullah household in Srinagar is always mouth-watering, cooked by Farooq's khansamah,

The Lion in Winter

Ghulam Ahmad Parra, sometimes referred to as 'Ahmad' but most lovingly as 'Ama'. At our home, despite being diabetic, he can never resist the kulfi–falooda or the halwa. There is nobody more affable, more charming, and nobody readier to help than he. He used to love a good drink until his kidney replacement. Now he doesn't drink because, as he says forthrightly, 'I cannot afford to.' He loves a game of golf, chatting with friends, and can dance with Ranveer Singh as brilliantly as he can talk to heads of state. To President Musharraf, whom he met at a state dinner, Farooq was at his best. He introduced himself with unmatchable aplomb: '*Log humein Farooq Abdullah kehte hain.*' (They call me Farooq Abdullah.)

He loves his family, almost as much as he loves the storied state he is from. Farooq is now closing in on ninety years old, and as time has passed, the push and pull between politics and his personal life as the patriarch of a big, colourful family has only grown. I suppose that is natural. Over a period of time, there emerges the conflict of knowing and pretending not to know.

Politics is in Farooq's blood. Kashmir has obsessed his heart and mind as much as it did with his father, and even in his recent interview to Neerja Chowdhury, he insisted that he would never leave politics until the day he died.[3] That's the literal truth, I know.

Farooq can never fully step away from politics. But with the abrogation of Article 370 and with Omar's election to the chief minister's chair post the assembly elections, he is almost automatically slowing down. There is a quieter side to him now,

The Chief Minister and the Spy

a deeper and more spiritual side, a paternal, gentle side that is proud of his son's achievements. For Farooq, keeping politics and family apart was easier when he was younger. I remember talking to him about Khalida and Gul Mohammad Shah. 'We're fine,' he told me then. 'That's politics, but this is family.' That was the distinction for him. He used to leave politics outside the door when he came home – a trait that didn't quite come so easily to the rest of his family. When Farooq was at home, he was the loving patriarch, the head of his family, who loved his golfing, his sisters, his children and his wife. To his friends, he always has been the caring Doctor Sahib.

As with the great Charles de Gaulle, whom Farooq has always admired, the theatre will not end as long as he is alive, leaving people to wonder if he is the play or the playwright. 'I saw a man who was emotionally torn,' Harinder Baweja told me, 'but his heart will always beat for India. That is who Farooq Abdullah is, under the bluster and the madness for golf.'

He who comes must, of course, go. After a while, remembrance also slowly fades, but what remains is greatness. The great man's saga will not end in a whimper, because Farooq is not an ordinary man. Delhi cannot afford to give up on Farooq because without the singer, the song of Kashmir is not complete.

Acknowledgements

First and foremost, my gratitude to Dr Farooq Abdullah, who permitted me to write this book that has always been on my mind.

I must also hugely thank my first and ultimate guru, M.K. Narayanan, at whose side, if not feet, I got the first whiff of the mysteries of intelligence, for writing the foreword to this book, which provides the icing on the cake.

A big thank you to the Abdullahs for admitting me into the family, which has facilitated this book. A special thank you to Khalidaji for sharing her views despite being in and out of the family. What attracted me to her beautiful home was her charm and her delightful English tea. And to Suraiya, for providing me with notes and books not available in any library and unwittingly letting me into the riddle of Baba Pyare Lal Bedi, and for also tolerating long conversations with me.

Acknowledgements

Thanks also to my dear friend and former vice-president of India, Hamid Ansari, for not just inspiring but pushing me to write this book. As he simply put it, 'You must do it.'

My thanks to Narayani Basu for helping me arrange and make sense of this book, and to Kanishka Gupta for being an agent par excellence. Thanks also to Swati Chopra for being my favourite editor, always patient and understanding, and Chiki Sarkar for pulling me to Juggernaut Books and for her enthusiasm at every step.

My friend and colleague Hormis Tharakan helped me find and understand, with the help of a priest, the interpretation of Prophet Isaiah's prophecy, which I have quoted in the book.

Last but not the least, I am grateful for the support of my family, my wife, Paran, in particular, who, because of her personal relationship with the Abdullah family, has never been more enthusiastic about me writing a book.

Notes

1. Getting to Know the Chief Minister

1. Praveen Donthi, 'How Mufti Mohammad Sayeed Shaped the 1987 Elections in Kashmir', *Caravan*, 23 March 2016. Available at: https://caravanmagazine.in/vantage/mufti-mohammad-sayeed-shaped-1987-kashmir-elections.
2. Ibid.
3. Sushim Mukul, 'When Guns Got to the Kashmir Valley after Rigged Polls of 1987', *India Today*, 19 April 2024. Available at: https://www.indiatoday.in/history-of-it/story/jammu-and-kashmir-1987-assembly-election-pm-modi-lok-sabha-jknc-farooq-abdullah-terrorism-militancy-valley-jklf-2525956-2024-04-19.
4. Harinder Baweja, 'The Only Thing We Want Is the Autonomy that Kashmir Had Must Be Restored, Says Farooq Abdullah', 14 February 1994, *India Today*. Available at: https://www.indiatoday.in/magazine/interview/story/19940215-the-only-thing-we-want-is-the-autonomy-that-kashmir-had-must-be-restored-says-farooq-abdullah-808812-1994-02-14.
5. Aditya Sinha, *Farooq Abdullah: Kashmir's Prodigal Son* (UBS Publishers' Distributors Ltd, 1996), p. 173.
6. Sinha, *Kashmir's Prodigal Son*.
7. Barbara Crossette, 'Abducted Woman Freed in Kashmir', *The New York Times*, 14 December 1989. Available at: https://www.nytimes.com/1989/12/14/world/abducted-woman-freed-in-kashmir.html.

8. A.S. Dulat, *A Life in the Shadows* (Delhi: HarperCollins India, 2023).
9. Sinha, *Kashmir's Prodigal Son*, p. 205.
10. Sinha, *Kashmir's Prodigal Son*, p. 197–99.
11. Ibid.
12. Sinha, *Kashmir's Prodigal Son*, p. 204.
13. Victoria Schofield, *Kashmir in Conflict* (IB Taurus & Co., 2003), p. 148.
14. Jagmohan, *My Frozen Turbulence in Kashmir*, (Delhi: South Asia Books, 1992).
15. Chitralekha Zutshi, *Sheikh Abdullah: The Caged Lion of Kashmir* (Delhi: 4th Estate, 2023), p. 388.
16. Sinha, *Kashmir's Prodigal Son*, p. 228.

2. The Making of Farooq Abdullah

1. Ashwini Bhatnagar and R.C. Ganjoo, *Farooq of Kashmir* (Delhi: Fingerprint! Publishing, 2023), p. 27.
2. Sinha, *Kashmir's Prodigal Son*, p. 174.
3. Ibid., p. 230.

3. 1984: The Coup

1. Farooq Abdullah with Sati Sahni, *My Dismissal.* (Delhi: Vikas, 1985).
2. All quotes here are from 'Sheikh Mohamad Abdullah Passes On His Legacy to His Son, Farooq Abdullah', by Suman Dubey, *India Today*, 15 September 1982. Available at: https://www.indiatoday.in/magazine/cover-story/story/19820915-sheikh-mohammad-abdullah-passes-on-his-legacy-to-son-farooq-abdullah-772196-2013-08-27.
3. Sinha, *Kashmir's Prodigal Son*, p. 168.
4. Ibid., p. 169.
5. Ibid., p. 170.

Notes

4. Conversations and Confidences

1. A.S. Dulat with Aditya Sinha, *Kashmir: The Vajpayee Years* (Delhi: HarperCollins India, 2015).
2. Tania Anand, Nirupama Subramaniam and Javed Ansari, 'Hazratbal Siege Turns Kashmir into International Issue, Pushes Tide in Pakistan's Favour', *India Today*, 15 November 1993. Available at: https://www.indiatoday.in/magazine/cover-story/story/19931115-hazratbal-siege-turns-kashmir-into-international-issue-pushes-tide-in-pakistan-favour-811821-1993-11-14.
3. S. Narendra, *India's Tipping Point: The View from 7 Race Course Road* (New Delhi: Bloomsbury, 2023), p. 155.
4. Harinder Baweja, 'The Only Thing We Want Is the Autonomy that Kashmir Had Must Be Restored, Says Farooq Abdullah', *India Today*, 14 February 1994. Available at: https://www.indiatoday.in/magazine/interview/story/19940215-the-only-thing-we-want-is-the-autonomy-that-kashmir-had-must-be-restored-says-farooq-abdullah-808812-1994-02-14.
5. Ibid.
6. Ibid.
7. Ibid.
8. Ibid.
9. Ibid.
10. Agha Shahid Ali, *The Country Without a Post Office* (New Delhi: Penguin, 2013).
11. 'Over to Geneva', *Kashmir Life*, 25 September 2016. Available at: https://kashmirlife.net/over-to-geneva-118716/.
12. Shekhar Gupta, 'India Shows the World It Means Business on Kashmir Issue at Geneva Meet', *India Today*, 31 March 1994. Available at: https://www.indiatoday.in/magazine/cover-story/story/19940331-india-shows-the-world-it-means-business-on-kashmir-issue-at-geneva-meet-808937-1994-03-30.
13. Ibid.
14. 'Over to Geneva', *Kashmir Life*, 25 September 2016. Available at: https://kashmirlife.net/over-to-geneva-118716/.
15. Baweja, 'The Only Thing We Want'.

16. Ibid.
17. Ibid.
18. Ibid.
19. Ibid.
20. Ibid.
21. Ibid
22. Ibid.
23. Ibid.
24. Harinder Baweja, 'Unlike Hurriyat, I Am Not Pro-Pakistan', *India Today*, 30 November 1995. Available at: https://www.indiatoday.in/magazine/cover-story/story/19951130-and-unlike-the-hurriyat-i-am-not-pro-pakistan-farooq-abdullah-807997-1995-11-29.
25. Syed Junaid Hashmi, 'Dr Farooq Abdullah's Political Evolution', *Straight Line Magazine*, 12 December 2023. Available at: http://straightlinemag.com/dr-farooq-abdullahs-political-evolution-from-boycotts-to-participation-in-elections.
26. Inderjit Badhwar, 'Spurning of PV Narasimha Rao Re-election Package Turns into Another Example of His Sham', *India Today*, 29 November 1995. Available at: https://www.indiatoday.in/magazine/cover-story/story/19951130-spurning-of-p-v-narasimha-rao-p re-election-package-turns-into-another-example-of-his-sham-808040-1995-11-29.
27. K.V. Krishna Rao, 'Elections at Last', in *In the Service of the Nation: Reminiscences* (New Delhi: Penguin Books India, 2001).
28. Peerzada Ashiq, 'People Governing Delhi Believe in No Constitution: Farooq Abdullah', *The Hindu*, 25 August 2020. Available at: https://www.thehindu.com/news/national/people-governing-delhi-believe-in-no-constitution-says-farooq-abdullah/article32432501.ece.

5. 1996: A Pivotal Election

1. Sugata Srinivasaraju, *Furrows in a Field: The Unexplored Life of H.D. Deve Gowda* (Gurgaon: Penguin Vintage, 2021), p. 387
2. Harinder Baweja, 'Critical Challenges', *India Today*, 29 June 1996. Available at: https://www.indiatoday.in/magazine/cover-story/story/19960630-critical-challenges-753538-1996-06-29.

Notes

3. Srinivasaraju, *Furrows in a Field*, p. 297.
4. Ibid., p. 299.
5. Ajith Pillai and Masood Hussain, 'A Peace Offering At Last', *Outlook*, 19 June 1996. Available at: https://www.outlookindia.com/national/a-peace-offering-at-last-news-201573.
6. Harinder Baweja, 'I Am Not Scared of the Gun', *India Today*, 30 August 1996. Available at: https://www.indiatoday.in/magazine/interview/story/19960831-i-am-not-scared-of-the-gun-farooq-abdullah-833826-1996-08-30.
7. Harinder Baweja, 'PM Deve Gowda Sets Tone for Revival of the Political Process in War-Weary Kashmir Valley', *India Today*, 31 July 1996. Available at: https://www.indiatoday.in/magazine/nation/story/19960731-pm-deve-gowda-sets-tone-for-revival-of-political-process-in-war-weary-kashmir-valley-833653-1996-07-31.
8. Baweja, 'I Am Not Scared of the Gun'.
9. Srinivasaraju, *Furrows in a Field*, p. 300.
10. Ibid., p. 304.
11. Parliament Debates, 2 August 1996.
12. Srinivasaraju, *Furrows in a Field*, p. 306.
13. Ibid.
14. Pillai and Hussain, 'A Peace Offering At Last'.
15. Srinivasaraju, *Furrows in a Field*, p. 310.
16. Baweja, 'I Am Not Scared of the Gun'.
17. Ramesh Vinayak and Inderjit Badhwar, 'UF Believes in Strengthening the Nation First and the Party Later: Farooq Abdullah', *India Today*, 30 October 1996. Available at: https://www.indiatoday.in/magazine/interview/story/19961031-uf-believes-in-strengthening-the-nation-first-and-the-party-later-farooq-abdullah-834000-1996-10-30.
18. Kenneth J. Cooper, 'Kashmir's Peace Hopes Put to a Vote', *Washington Post*, 7 September 1996. Available at: https://www.washingtonpost.com/archive/politics/1996/09/07/kashmirs-peace-hopes-put-to-a-vote/66e2da16-3cb5-4bf3-ab8f-3cb00b8250e8.
19. Srinivasaraju, *Furrows in a Field*, p. 310.

20. Pillai and Hussain, 'A Peace Offering At Last'.
21. Srinivasaraju, *Furrows in a Field*, p. 310.
22. NDTV, 'Farooq Abdullah Meets Former PM Deve Gowda in Bengaluru', 7 June 2023. Available at: https://www.ndtv.com/india-news/farooq-abdullah-meets-former-pm-deve-gowda-in-bengaluru-4101951.

6. Power Plays and Betrayal

1. 'Interview – J&K Chief Minister Dr Farooq Abdullah: "Musharraf's Speech Has Made No Impact on Militancy"', MEA Media Centre, 5 February 2002. Available at: https://www.mea.gov.in/interviews.htm?dtl/4523/Interview++JK+Chief+Minister+Dr+Farooq+Abdullah+Musharrafs+speech+has+made+no+impact+on+militancyhttps://www.mea.gov.in/interviews.htm?dtl/4523/Interview++JK+Chief+Minister+Dr+Farooq+Abdullah+Musharrafs+speech+has+made+no+impact+on+militancy.
2. Harinder Baweja, 'We Will Show Our Neighbours that Elections in J&K Will Be Held: Farooq Abdullah', *India Today*, 8 September 2002. Available at: https://www.indiatoday.in/magazine/interview/story/20020909-we-will-show-our-neighbours-that-elections-in-j-k-will-be-held-farooq-abdullah-796355-2002-09-08.
3. Ibid.
4. Ramesh Vinayak, 'Abdullah Raj Ends in Jammu and Kashmir, Spells Opportunity for Mufti Mohammed Sayeed, PDP', *India Today*, 21 October 2002. Available at: https://www.indiatoday.in/magazine/cover-story/story/20021021-abdullah-raj-ends-in-jammu-and-kashmir-spells-opportunity-for-mufti-mohammed-sayeed-794060-2002-10-20.

7. Father and Son

1. Richard Nixon, 'Proclamation 4127—Father's Day | the American Presidency Project', The American Presidency Project, 1 May 1972. Available at: https://www.presidency.ucsb.edu/documents/proclamation-4127-fathers-day.

Notes

2. Ghulam Mohammad Shah was also known as Gul Mohammad Shah and G.M. Shah.
3. Priya Sahgal and Kaveree Bamzai, 'The Summer of 2010 Made Omar a Leader, Says Farooq Abdullah', 29 November 1999, *India Today*. Available at: https://www.indiatoday.in/magazine/cover-story/story/20121224-the-summer-of-2010-made-omar-a-leader-says-farooq-abdullah-761051-1999-11-29.
4. Ibid.
5. Ibid.
6. Ibid.
7. Ibid.
8. 'CBI Gives Omar a Clean Chit in Sex Scandal', *India Today*, 28 July 2009. Available at: https://www.indiatoday.in/headlines-today-top-stories/story/cbi-gives-omar-a-clean-chit-in-sex-scandal-53035-2009-07-27.
9. Ibid.
10. Ibid.
11. Ibid.
12. Ibid.
13. Ibid.

8. Abrogation and Its Aftermath

1. Mehbooba Mufti, quoted in *The Print*, PTI press release, 'Not Just J&K, South Asia Will Burn if Article 370 Is Abrogated', 8 April 2019. Available at: https://theprint.in/politics/not-just-jk-south-asia-will-burn-if-article-370-is-removed-warns-mehbooba-mufti/218815.
2. Omar Abdullah, quoted in *Livemint*, 'How Mehbooba Mufti, Omar Abdullah Reacted to Article 370 Verdict', 11 December 2023. Available at: https://www.livemint.com/politics/news/jammu-and-kashmir-article-370-abrogation-supreme-court-omar-abdullah-ghulam-nabi-azad-mehbooba-mufti-narendra-modi-11702285528993.html.
3. Ibid.

4. 'Public? Safety?', *The Indian Express*, 17 September 2019. Available at: https://indianexpress.com/article/opinion/editorials/farooq-abdullah-psa-detained-jammu-kashmir-6000960.
5. 'Indian Punjab's CM Slams Revocation of Article 370 as Totally Unconstitutional', *Dawn*, 5 August 2019. Available at: https://www.dawn.com/news/1498246.
6. 'Arresting Leaders Will Allow Terrorists to Fill Gap: Rahul Gandhi', *India Today*, 5 August 2019. Available at: https://www.indiatoday.in/india/story/rahul-gandhi-on-mehbooba-mufti-omar-abdullah-arrest-1577863-2019-08-06.
7. Harinder Baweja, 'Ex-RAW Chief Flew to J-K to Gauge Farooq Abdullah's Mood on Article 370 Repeal', *Hindustan Times*, 27 February 2020. Available at: https://www.hindustantimes.com/india-news/raw-ex-chief-tried-to-gauge-farooq-abdullah-s-mood-on-new-order-in-j-k/story-WbhlwlOF2vM4cALCQMLOrJ.html.
8. Peerzada Ashiq, 'People Governing Delhi Believe in No Constitution', *The Hindu*, 25 August 2020. Available at: https://www.thehindu.com/news/national/people-governing-delhi-believe-in-no-constitution-says-farooq-abdullah/article32432501.ece.
9. Ibid.
10. Ibid.
11. Ibid.
12. Ibid.
13. Isaiah 65:17-25.
14. Harinder Baweja, 'Not Fair to See Farooq as Enemy of the State', *Hindustan Times*, 17 September 2019. Available at: https://www.hindustantimes.com/india-news/raw-ex-chief-tried-to-gauge-farooq-abdullah-s-mood-on-new-order-in-j-k/story-WbhlwlOF2vM4cALCQMLOrJ.html.

9. The Importance of Being Farooq Abdullah

1. Quoted from Sushim Mukul, 'What Jamooriyat Ka Jashn After 10-Year Pause Means for Jammu and Kashmir', *India Today*, 17

Notes

   August 2024. Available at: https://www.indiatoday.in/india/story/jammu-and-kashmir-assembly-election-2024-significance-delimitation-article-370-importance-jk-polls-2583347-2024-08-17.
2. 'Alliance with Congress Need of the Hour: Farooq Abdullah', *Deccan Herald*, 4 September 2024. Available at: https://www.deccanherald.com/india/jammu-and-kashmir/alliance-with-congress-need-of-the-hour-farooq-abdullah-3176306.
3. Vidya Subrahmaniam, 'Saddest Story in Kashmir Is Farooq, Who Was Once Promised the Vice-Presidentship: A.S. Dulat', The Hindu Centre for Politics and Public Policy, 27 August 2019. Available at: https://www.thehinducentre.com/the-arena/current-issues/article29259964.ece.
4. Neerja Chowdhury, '"Not Easy for Congress to Say We'll Back Art 370... Why Not First Look at What We Can Do, on Progress, Jobs?": Farooq Abdullah', 1 October 2024, *The Indian Express*. Available at: https://indianexpress.com/article/political-pulse/congress-article-370-progress-jobs-farooq-abdullah-interview-9597144/.
5. 'Those Dreaming of J&K's Independence Unaware of Ground Realities: Farooq Abdullah', *The Hindu*, 16 November 2024. Available at: https://www.thehindu.com/news/national/jammu-and-kashmir/those-dreaming-of-jks-independence-unaware-of-ground-realities-farooq-abdullah/article68876137.ece.

10. The Lion in Winter

1. B.K. Nehru, *Nice Guys Finish Second* (New Delhi: Penguin Viking, 1997).
2. Baweja, 'The Only Thing We Want'.
3. Chowdhury, '"Not Easy for Congress To Say We'll Back Art 370... Why Not First Look At What We Can Do, on Progress, Jobs?": Farooq Abdullah', 1 October 2024, *The Indian Express*. Available at: https://indianexpress.com/article/political-pulse/congress-article-370-progress-jobs-farooq-abdullah-interview-9597144/.